‘Having worked with Christian Aid for more than thirty years, I commend *Justice Song*. The book not only chronicles the organisation’s history but also explores the evolving meaning of development and the changing nature of Christian engagement with global justice. It traces the shift from charity to partnership, from aid to advocacy, reflecting broader changes in theology, politics and practice. *Justice Song* serves as an inspiring reminder that faith, when united with justice, can transform both communities and the global structures that shape their lives.’
Robert Beckford, Professor of Climate and Social Justice, University of Winchester

‘As a door-to-door collector, a partner (in Haiti) and a director (with Michael Taylor) – from pulpits, in lecture halls and from the red benches (in the House of Lords) – it seems as if Christian Aid has become part of my DNA. This book arrives at a kairos moment in the world we’re living in – there was never a greater need for its message.’
Leslie Griffiths, Lord Griffiths of Burry Port

‘Christian Aid has transformed lives and given hope to so many in some of the most daunting parts of the world. As this book clearly shows, we should all be so proud of their commitment and achievements in the fight against international poverty.’
Andrew Mitchell, former UK Secretary of State for International Development

‘My first introduction to Christian Aid was collecting for them during Christian Aid Week. Many years later, I had a Christian Aid poster on my wall declaring that they believed in life before death. I have been a long-term fan of their work and, having a family member work for them also, am delighted to endorse the publication of this very fine book by Michael Taylor. This is an ideal book for all those wanting to know the back story of the admirable work undertaken by Christian Aid.’
Anthony G. Reddie, Professor of Black Theology, University of Oxford

'*Justice Song* is a story that needed to be told, not least as a reminder of the extraordinary impact that is created when committed people work together for a better world. Michael Taylor weaves together an account of how, from its foundation in the aftermath of the Second World War, Christian Aid has tried – and usually succeeded – in being a champion of peace, justice and human rights, challenging those in authority to use their power for the common good.'
Mary Robinson, former President of Ireland, and UN High Commissioner for Human Rights

'There are many words one might use to describe the story of Christian Aid, which Michael Taylor's book tells with admirable freshness and energy, but the one I would choose is partnership – an organisation that is sufficiently humble and theological to want to work with rather than for or instead of others. It's an approach and a story we would do well to listen to today.'
Nick Spencer, Senior Fellow, Theos

'Christian Aid was born into a world where people had woken up afresh to the scale of suffering and disruption around them and were eager to discover what they could do to honour the dignity of their fellow human beings facing displacement, poverty and prejudice.

Eighty years on, Christian Aid is not out of business, and the urgency is even greater. No one could be better qualified than Michael Taylor to tell this story. In this welcome book, he gives a lucid, lively account of both the thinking and the action that have shaped Christian Aid's identity – and tells us unmistakably why the imperatives are still there for all of us.'
Rowan Williams, former Archbishop of Canterbury

Michael Taylor is Emeritus Professor of Social Theology, University of Birmingham, and was Director of Christian Aid from 1985 to 1997.

JUSTICE SONG

The Story OF Christian Aid

MICHAEL TAYLOR

Foreword by Gordon Brown

First published in Great Britain in 2025

SPCK Publishing
Part of the SPCK Group, Studio 101, The Record Hall, 16–16A Baldwin's Gardens, London EC1N 7RJ
spckpublishing.co.uk

Text copyright © Michael Taylor 2025
This edition copyright © Society for Promoting Christian Knowledge 2025

Michael Taylor has asserted his right under the Copyright, Designs and Patents Act, 1988, to be identified as Author of this work.

All rights reserved. No part of this book may be reproduced or transmitted in any form or by any means, electronic or mechanical, including photocopying, recording, or by any information storage and retrieval system, without permission in writing from the publisher.

SPCK Publishing does not necessarily endorse the individual views contained in its publications.

The author and publisher have made every effort to ensure that the external website addresses included in this book are correct and up to date at the time of going to press. The author and publisher are not responsible for the content, quality or continuing accessibility of the sites.

Scripture quotations are taken from the New Revised Standard Version of the Bible, copyright © 1989 by the Division of Christian Education of the National Council of the Churches of Christ in the USA. Used by permission. All rights reserved.

Every effort has been made to seek permission to use copyright material reproduced in this book. The publisher apologizes for those cases where permission might not have been sought and, if notified, will formally seek permission at the earliest opportunity.

EU GPSR Authorised Representative
LOGOS EUROPE, 9 rue Nicolas Poussin, 17000, La Rochelle, France
Email: Contact@logoseurope.eu

British Library Cataloguing-in-Publication Data
A catalogue record for this book is available from the British Library

ISBN 978-0-281-09198-0
eBook ISBN 978-0-281-09199-7

1 3 5 7 9 10 8 6 4 2

Typeset by Fakenham Prepress Solutions, Fakenham, Norfolk NR21 8NL
First printed in Great Britain by Clays Ltd

eBook by Fakenham Prepress Solutions, Fakenham, Norfolk NR21 8NL

Produced on paper from sustainable sources

To a host of angels

Contents

List of plates xi
Foreword by Gordon Brown xv
List of acronyms xix
Introduction xxv

1 How it all began 1
When I needed a neighbour 19
2 Afghanistan 21
South Africa's national anthem 32
3 On the campaign trail 33
4 Brazil 49
Momento novo – *'A new moment'* 55
5 Christian identity, faith and theology ... we believe in life before death 56
6 Burma/Myanmar 71
Common ground 78
7 Christian Aid Week ... the little red envelope 79
8 Haiti 90
9 Partnership ... you'll never walk alone 101
Welcome to the Feast 112
10 India 113
11 Learning to care 126
12 Palestine 141
Sent by the Lord 151
13 The Big Issue 152
14 The Philippines 163
15 Sierra Leone 169

16 Pie charts and all that 181
17 Sudan and South Sudan 194
18 Untold stories 203
Magnificat 209
19 Hope and realism 210

Appendix 217
Timeline 219
Notes 224
Subject index 238

Plates

1. Janet Lacey CBE, director of the British Council of Churches Inter-Church Aid and Refugee Department, renamed Christian Aid in 1964: Hay Wrightson © National Portrait Gallery
2. Disasters Emergency Committee (DEC) emergency appeal poster for Rwanda, 1994: © DEC
3. Hungarian refugees in front of the World Council of Churches refugee truck in Austria, January 1957: © WCC
4. Yana, 71, takes part in a psychological support session with Heritage Ukraine, a partner of Christian Aid in 2024: © Christian Aid
5. Boats pushed ashore by the force of the tsunami that struck Southern Asia on Boxing Day, 2004: Tim Hetherington © IWM (DC 124693)
6. Timothy Goggs, who died clearing landmines in Afghanistan in 1992: © Alamy
7. Gul Shah, a 70-year-old widow, making more than $200 by selling cocoons spun by silkworms in Afghanistan: Sarah Malian, 2011 © Christian Aid
8. 70,000 people form a human chain around Birmingham city centre to raise the issue of debt justice during the 1998 G8 summit held in the city: © Debt Justice
9. In November 2023, Christian Aid, alongside other UK-based NGOs, delivered a series of campaign actions calling for a ceasefire in Israel and the Occupied Palestinian Territories, including this projection onto the Houses of Parliament: © Christian Aid
10. An aerial view of flooding triggered by a dam collapse near Brumadinho, Brazil, in 2019, killing 270 people and unleashing tons of toxic waste into the rivers: © Bruno Correia/Nitro via AP Stock Photo – Alamy

11 Undated portrait of Brazilian ecologist Chico Mendes, assassinated in his house in Xapuri, near the Amazon forest, in 1988: © Antonio Scorza/AFP via Getty

12 Lesley Williams abseils down St Mary Magdalen Church in central Oxford, March 2016, raising £600 for Christian Aid: © Christian Aid

13 Christian Aid Week poster subverting the traditional Christian belief in life after death, 1985: © Christian Aid

14 The Edinburgh annual Book Sale in 2019 (going back to 1973), the UK's biggest fundraising event for Christian Aid Week: © Christian Aid

15 Hundreds of supporters complete the Forth Bridge crossing in 1980, a fundraising initiative for Christian Aid Week: © Christian Aid

16 The 'Tree of Life', constructed from decommissioned weapons by Mozambique artists Cristóvão (Kester) Canhavato, Hilario Nhatugeuja, Adelino Mate and Fiel dos Santos, in 2005 at the end of a 16-year war: © Shutterstock

17 Christian Aid's partner, Ekta Parishad, organises around 100,000 landless people to march from Gwalior to Delhi to demand a fairer share of land and resources (2012): © Simon Williams

18 Bezwada Wilson of Safai Karmarchari Andolan (SKA), a leading Dalit rights activist and long-time Christian Aid partner, addresses supporters in London in 2025: © Christian Aid

19 Cholo Ngaramata prepares a meal for her family in Ethiopia, captured on camera by a member of her community as part of the Picture Power project (2024): © Christian Aid

20 In the aftermath of the 2015 earthquake in Nepal, Christian Aid sent the 'Truth Truck' to affected communities to receive feedback on the process of aid distribution: © Robin Prime, Christian Aid

21 Judi Dench filming *In the Field of the Shepherd*, a Christian Aid film, for the BBC in 1968: © Christian Aid

22 75-year-old Sabha, displaced from eastern Khan Younis to western Khan Younis in 2024, during the conflict in Gaza: © Christian Aid

23 Mother and daughter in the flooded street outside their house in the Khilgaon area of Dhaka, Bangladesh in 1998: © Mike Goldwater

24 The first commercial woman beekeeper in Honduras, Juanita Victoria Marquez, 42, with her husband Jose Alonzo Ramira Rosales, 43, extracting honey from their traditional hive in 2016: © Christian Aid

25 Messah Brewah cares for one of the metal savings boxes in the village of Bumbeh Pejeh, Pujahun district of Sierra Leone, in 2019: © Christian Aid

26 Three female puppets: Elineide from Brazil, Feroza from Bangladesh, and Jaylan from Syria, each representing real women who have been forced to flee their homes due to violence, war, earthquakes or floods, brought to life at Greenbelt by Cecil Green Arts Bradford, 2016: © John Sargent/jackharrybill

27 The Twic Olympics, an annual sporting event in Twic County, South Sudan, helping to reconcile communities that were divided by years of conflict and civil war, 2008: Tom Pilston

28 Supporters carry placards of Christian Aid's posters from across the years at the 80th anniversary service at Westminster Abbey, June 2025: © Christian Aid

Foreword
by Gordon Brown

All who read this inspiring and timely book will have their own experience of Christian Aid and its unique combination of idealism and pragmatism that has shaped its first eighty years of service in support of the world's poorest.

From my earliest years Christian Aid enthused me, motivated me and changed my life as for so many others.

Christian Aid Week (CAW) ranks high among my childhood memories. It was introduced to me by my mother. Every year in May she enlisted me and my two brothers to deliver little red envelopes to each house in the streets near where we stayed and then return to collect donations from dozens of friends and neighbours.

Christian Aid was a central part of home and church life, connecting the local to the global, linking the person next door to the person in another country we would never meet but with whom we felt empathy. For all who supported Christian Aid it seemed the most practical way of living out the parable of the good Samaritan and the injunction 'to never walk by on the other side' – a message needing to be heard ever more urgently in a world scarred by war, disease, droughts, floods, fires and poverty, and beggar-thy-neighbour politics.

In fact, the work my mother asked us to do for Christian Aid inspired my older brother to set up a local charity. I was his assistant when he published his own newspaper and ran a charity shop that raised money for Africa.

No one ever forgets their formative childhood experiences, and when I became Chancellor, I was happy to endorse the Christian Aid campaign for debt relief and the cancellation of Third World debts. Indeed, I could have done no other. One day during our preparations for the G7 meeting that Nelson Mandela attended in London, a Treasury official handed me a petition from Christian Aid calling for action. It was signed by my mother. She had written asking me to endorse the campaign but, prudent as she always was, she added, 'No need for a reply, you can save money on stamps.' This was 2005, when the world wrote off what eventually added up to around $200 billion of unpayable debt and doubled aid for Africa.

I was always grateful when Christian Aid representatives attended our regular sessions at No. 11 Downing Street with international aid organisations and informed our thinking about development. In subsequent years I've had many opportunities to connect with Christian Aid, some of them recounted in these pages. One memorable occasion was a visit to India where I saw at first hand the work being done in local neighbourhoods in support of the Dalit community. So impressed was I by the idealism and aspirations of the young Dalit teenagers I met, only wanting the chance of a job, but also so alarmed by the poverty and hardship I saw, that I pressed India's richest company owner, Ratan Tata, to give them opportunities for skills training and apprenticeships.

Three things have always stood out for me in these encounters.

First, Christian Aid has always managed to combine practical work to relieve human suffering – from its first refugee response in 1945 – with a willingness to ask the difficult questions about why that need exists and so address the underlying causes of poverty. You can have idealism without action, which leads nowhere, but you can also have action without idealism, which takes you to a dead end. It is the combination of idealism and action that makes the difference, and that is what Christian Aid has demonstrated. I saw it at first hand in the organisation's mobilisation of many thousands of members of the British public in support of a new deal for Africa at the Birmingham G7, and as part of the Make Poverty History campaign in 2005. But it did not end there. Christian Aid sponsored and supported many of the successful projects that followed. It is by combining the vision of a better world with practical action to achieve it that Christian Aid has made its name over eighty years of service.

Second, Christian Aid has brought faith to the centre of international development and humanitarian work without ever wanting to be patronising or paternalistic. Many observers say that religion helps people cope with the difficult events, including suffering, that befall us all. Religion also creates a sense of community as people come together and find what they have in common. Even agnostics and atheists recognise that faith also inspires people to do what they might never have done otherwise and motivates people in a way that can help change the world for the better. Without ever being complacent about what has been achieved and what still needs to be done, the record of the last eighty years demonstrates how people, inspired by faith, have found purpose in their lives and made a difference.

Third, Christian Aid has been an ecumenical organisation that has not only helped to harness the huge potential of churches and faith groups in Britain and around the world but has also helped build bridges between different Christian traditions and people of different faiths and beliefs. It has never lost sight of the common goal we can all share: to build a more just and equal world in which every person's dignity is upheld. In other words, Christian Aid has not only brought people closer together but shown, through partnership, how we can achieve far more by working as one than anything we can achieve on our own.

I have always been struck by Christian Aid's determination to promote partnerships with others, from its central role in founding the Fairtrade movement, to the Disasters Emergency Committee (DEC) and VSO. These shared initiatives and networks, now including shared engagement with environmental groups on climate change, mean that so many people who are not officially part of Christian Aid are now part of the history of Christian Aid.

Michael Taylor has done a remarkable job of drawing together the diverse strands of Christian Aid's story into a compelling whole. At the same time, as he reminds us, the next chapter is still being written in a world where – for all the progress made – millions of people's lives remain scarred by poverty and inequality, and where millions of people, motivated by their faith, will continue to confront injustice. We cannot ever be at ease when millions are ill at ease, be comfortable when so many live in such discomfort, or ever be content when there is so much discontent. But we can spread the message that we are, to paraphrase the words of the late Jonathan Sacks, richer when we care for the poor, more secure when we help the insecure, and all of us stronger when the strong help the weak. That is the never-ending story of Christian Aid. We see inequality and want to diminish it. We see poverty and want to eradicate it. We see squalor, pollution and all kinds of injustice and want to put an end to it.

Acronyms

AACC	All Africa Council of Churches
ACT	Action of Churches Together
APP	Action Plan for Peace (Sudan and South Sudan)
APRODEV	Association of Protestant Development Agencies in Europe
BAN	Budget Advocacy Network (Sierra Leone)
BCC	British Council of Churches
BOAG	British Overseas Aid Group
CAFOD	Catholic Agency for Overseas Development
CAP	Church Action on Poverty
CAPHIL	Christian Aid Philippines
CAPL	Change Alliance (India)
CASA	Churches Auxiliary for Social Action (India)
CAW	Christian Aid Week
CCM	Christian Council of Mozambique
CDC	Community Development Committee (Afghanistan)
CFTA	The Culture and Free Thought Association (Palestine)
CHED	Commission Haïtienne des Églises pour le Développement
CICARWS	Commission on Inter-Church Aid, Refugee and World Service (WCC)
CII	Confederation of Indian Industry
CIIR	Catholic Institute for International Relations
CLIMA	Climate Monitoring Action Project (Nicaragua)
CLIO	Cadre de Liaison Inter-Organisations (Haiti)
CMS	Church Mission Society
CNI	Church of North India
CONIC	National Council of Christian Churches of Brazil

COP	Conference of the Parties
CPI-SP	Comissão Pró-Índio (Brazil)
CSI	Church of South India
CSO	Civil Society Organisation
CTBI	Churches Together in Britain and Ireland
DCA	DanChurchAid
DDCI	Debt Development Coalition Ireland
DEC	Disasters Emergency Committee
DFID	Department for International Development
DICARWS	Division of Inter-Church Aid and Service to Refugees (WCC)
DP	Displaced Person
DR	Dominican Republic
DRC	Democratic Republic of Congo
DRRNet	Disaster Risk Reduction Network
ECLOF	Ecumenical Loan Fund
ECPAT	Every Child Protected Against Trafficking
ECRP	Enhancing Community Resilience Programme
ENCISS	Enhancing the Interaction between Citizens and the State in Sierra Leone
EPA	Economic Partnership Agreement
ERD	Ecumenical Relief Desk
EZE	Evangelische Zentralstelle für Entwicklungshilfe
FCDO	Foreign, Commonwealth and Development Office
FCRA	Foreign Contribution (Regulation) Act (India)
FGM	Female Genital Mutilation
FRELIMO	Mozambique Liberation Front
GARR	Groupe d`Appui aux Rapatriés et Réfugiés (Haiti)
GATT	General Agreement on Tariffs and Trade
GBV	Gender-based Violence
GEP	Gender Equality Programme
GK	Gonoshasthaya Kendra (Bangladesh)
GPS	Global Positioning System

H2H	House-to-House Collection
HIPC	Highly Indebted Poor Countries
HR	Human Resources
IAM	International Afghan Mission
IBT	International Broadcasting Trust
ICARS	Inter-Church Aid and Refugee Service (BCC)
ICCO	Dutch Interchurch Coordination Committee on Development Aid
ICRC	International Committee of the Red Cross
IMF	International Monetary Fund
INESC	Institute for Socio-Economic Studies (Brazil)
IOCC	International Orthodox Christian Charity
ITL	In Their Lifetime
J2000	Jubilee 2000
KORAL	Konbit pou Ranfòse Aksyon Lakay (Haiti)
KWIGN	Kailahun Women in Governance Network (Sierra Leone)
L2G	Local to Global Initiative
L2GP	Local to Global Protection
LMIC	Lower and Middle Income Countries
MAB	Movement of People Affected by Dams
MECC	Middle East Council of Churches
MGNREGA	Mahatma Gandhi National Rural Employment Government Act
MISSEH	Mission Sociale des Églises Haïtiennes
MIT	Massachusetts Institute of Technology
MPH	Make Poverty History
MST	Landless Workers' Movement (India)
NACDOR	National Confederation of Dalit Organisations
NCCI	National Council of Churches in India
NCCK	National Council of Churches Kenya
NCCP	National Council of Churches Philippines
NCCSL	National Christian Council of Sri Lanka

NCHR	National Committee of Human Rights (Haiti)
NETHIPS	Network of HIV Positives in Sierra Leone
NGO	Non-Governmental Organisation
NLD	National League for Democracy (Myanmar)
NSCC	New Sudan Council of Churches
OCDIH	Organismo Cristiano de Desarrollo Integral de Honduras
ODA	Overseas Development Administration (UK)
OPEC	Organization of the Petroleum Exporting Countries
OSIL	Operation Save Innocent Lives
PACJA	Pan African Climate Justice Alliance
PACS	Poorest Areas Civil Society (India)
PARC	Palestine Agricultural Relief Association
PCHR	Palestine Centre for Human Rights
PCR	Programme to Combat Racism
PHIA	Partnering Hope into Action (India)
PICOT	Partners Initiative for Conflict Transformation (Sierra Leone)
PLO	Palestine Liberation Organisation
PMRS	Palestine Medical Relief Society
PPA	Partnership Programme Arrangement
PVCA	Participatory Vulnerability and Capacity Assessments
RAADA	Rehabilitation Association and Agricultural Development for Afghanistan
RENAMO	Mozambique Liberation Front
REST	Relief Society of Tigray
RPF	Rwanda Patriotic Front
RRAA	Rural Rehabilitation Association for Afghanistan
RUHSA	Rural Unit for Health and Social Affairs (India)
SABI	Strengthening Accountability and Building Inclusion (Sierra Leone)
SACC	South African Council of Churches
SAFER	Shared Aid Fund for Emergency Response

SAP	Structural Adjustment Policy
SCIAF	Scottish Catholic International Aid Fund
SCLR	Survivor- and Community-led Response
SEND	Social Enterprise Development (Sierra Leone)
SFO	Sempreviva Feminist Organisation (Brazil)
SKA	Safai Karmachari Andolan (India)
SMS	Short Message Service
SOAS	School for Oriental and African Studies
SODEPAX	Joint Committee on Society, Development and Peace (WCC)
SOMO	Centre for Research on International Corporations (Netherlands)
SOPPEXCCA	Society for Small Producers for Coffee Export
SPLA	Sudan People's Liberation Army
SPLM	Sudan People's Liberation Movement
SSCC	South Sudan Council of Churches
SSOM	Operation Mercy (Sudan and South Sudan)
SUPRAID	Sudan Production Aid
TNC	Transnational Company
TPLF	Tigray People's Liberation Front
TZAC	Zionist Advocacy Center
UCT	Unconditional Cash Transfer
UN	United Nations
UNFCCC	United Nations Framework Convention on Climate Change
UNHCR	United Nations High Commissioner for Refugees
UPA	Urban Poor Association (Philippines)
VHA	Voluntary Health Organisation (India)
VSLA	Village Savings and Loans Association
VSO	Voluntary Service Overseas
WAC	Women`s Affairs Center (Palestine)
WB	World Bank
WCC	World Council of Churches

WDM	World Development Movement
WEEL	Women`s Economic Empowerment and Leadership (Sierra Leone)
WFP	World Food Programme
WHO	World Health Organisation
WTO	World Trade Organisation
YEU	Yakkum Emergency Unit (Indonesia)
ZELA	Zimbabwe Environmental Law Association

Introduction

In Nathan Hill's sprawling prize-winning novel *Wellness*,[1] Jack and Evelyn have returned to the American prairies where they were born and brought up. She, a photographer, is taking 'tight shots of the grass' and then of 'the broad, windswept landscape', and comments to Jack about what she calls a paradox: 'What was monolithic from afar was infinitely varied and complicated once you get up close.'

At a superficial glance, much the same could be said of Christian Aid: 'monolithic' not so much in size as in the way it has stuck to its last over eighty years, responding to the needs of poor and desperate people by providing humanitarian aid, supporting longer-term development projects, and tackling the underlying causes of their distress. That was clear at the start when refugees were cared for after the Second World War, thousands displaced from their homelands resettled, and the work of peacebuilding was resumed; and it is still true in countries like South Sudan and Myanmar, to name but two, where the wounds of war are dressed, fields are replanted and the endless search for justice continues.

So what more is there to tell? A very great deal, 'infinitely varied and complicated once you get up close'.

Among the plethora of emergencies, projects, programmes and campaigns, I for one was confronted by a host of angels. They are not ethereal beings but down-to-earth. They come from near and far, in all colours, shapes and sizes. Many of them fly – probably far too often – but none have wings. They don't travel up and down a ladder between earth and heaven, as in Jacob's dream (Genesis 28:12), but they do travel endlessly between compassion and the poverty and injustice that puts the world to shame. They often sing as they go, despite the anger and the tears. They get called, rather unglamorously, 'supporters', 'partners', 'funders', 'staff' and 'trustees'.

Since these angels are generally self-effacing, preferring to blow other people's trumpets rather than their own, it has not always been easy to find out about them, especially in the short period of time in which this book was conceived and written, or to collect their stories between its covers where 'All Shall be Included' but for a shortage of space.[2]

Sources

One of the most fruitful sources of information has been *Christian Aid News*, published from 1969 to 2004 and edited for a number of years by Kate Phillips (who joined Christian Aid in 1977, later to become its director for communications), followed by Martin Cottingham under her watchful eye, and printed for years in Wakefield. It was determined to go beyond a so-called 'contractual' relationship with supporters, accepting their donations but, beyond that, hardly involving them in the charity's work. Instead, it gave them real insight into what Christian Aid was up to, keeping them informed about the issues of the day, internal and external, and often controversial, always respecting the intelligence of its readers and, above all, the dignity of the brave but vulnerable people who were the subject of its reports and images. It was named Charity Magazine of the Year in 2003.

In the 2020s, Jack Arthey, the longest-standing member of Christian Aid's staff, and David Muir shared the concern of many about the state of Christian Aid's archives and began to wade through the 634 boxes stored in the School of Oriental and African Studies (SOAS) and in the basement of Inter-church House in London. A great deal of work resulted in a lengthy document named 'Who do we think we are?' covering many aspects of Christian Aid's story and providing another important source of information. The document remains unfinished due to ill health, and hundreds of boxes remain unopened despite additional research during 2023–25.

An obvious place to look for information 'once you get up close' is the vast number of documents produced by Christian Aid, including annual reports, of increasing length as the years go by, strategy and policy papers, project proposals and reports, appeals, educational and worship materials, many of them still available online. Two doctoral theses were discovered among them. A lack of information about certain periods of time was quite often notable: 'gap years', as I came to think of them.

Fresh material has been created in the course of research and writing by jogging people's living memories, sometimes more than once. Fewer and fewer of them now go back to the 1940s. It was sad, for example, to just miss the opportunity to talk at length to Hugh Samson, a founder member of staff and instigator of Christian Aid Week (CAW) and *raconteur extraordinaire*, who died in 2023 just after his one-hundredth birthday.

Many of those 'interviewed' were former and present members of staff, now widely dispersed, and the board. Friends in the South provided their own perspectives, often challenging as well as heartening. Back in the UK came the memories of Christian Aid Week organisers and collectors, most of them after pounding pavements for years and thinking up endless ways to make money.

Omissions

One or two things remain to be said by way of introduction: first, about the wealth of material that came to light. Giving it some order and shape was not intended to result in a history book, though attempts have been made to give some sort of historical perspective. The writer is not a historian, lacking as he does the tools of the trade – more like a teller of tales on this occasion. Every attempt has been made to be accurate and to give a fair impression, but what has been written is inevitably selective and lacks the comprehensiveness that a full-blown history would require.

To take one glaring example: of the chapters that follow, eight are what might be called 'thematic', such as the one on campaigning; nine more tell stories about specific countries, beginning with Afghanistan – only nine, when at times Christian Aid has been at work in over sixty. The choice has nothing to do with a country's significance but with an eye on geographical spread and how far back Christian Aid's involvement went. A number of other countries, like Mozambique and South Africa, are referred to elsewhere.

Another omission is also easily spotted. Christian Aid is well known for its commitment to 'partnership', as discussed in Chapter 9. It does not go it alone, but works with others. It is non-operational with very few exceptions, born of necessity. To repeatedly refer however to 'Christian Aid and partners', or exhaustively list who they were and are, would rapidly become tedious, so the general reference to 'partners' is mostly omitted and should be taken as read on virtually every occasion Christian Aid is mentioned. It refers not to a single organisation but an extended community across large parts of the world, including churches, Non-Governmental Organisations (NGOs), local communities and their organisations, governments and the hundreds of like-minded people that come with them.

What follows tells stories about what that extended community has done and still does without comparing it with others who, for good or ill, have often done likewise.

The origins of this book lie in several informal conversations during which concern was expressed about setting the record reasonably straight before it lies forgotten or, for many of more recent generations, remains largely unknown. One such conversation was with Patrick Watt, who became CEO of Christian Aid in 2022. After consulting colleagues, he asked me to write what now follows and provided much needed support. I accepted his invitation while underlining my need for independence as an author, since I was not interested in writing a kind of hagiography – a need which has been understood and respected.

I cannot, however, be entirely objective, since I am proud to be a small part of Christian Aid's story; but I have tried not to express personal opinions (of which I have many) or give advice (despite the urge at times) or make my presence known too often, and stick to telling the stories.

Justice Song

But why call the book *Justice Song*? Partly because so many have been caught out singing as they go their different ways, voicing their pride, their faith, their defiance, their determination, their gratitude and their hopes. The songs scattered among the text are evidence of that.[3] There is, however, another reason, harder to pin down. *Justice Song* better reflects the high spirits in which many of those journeys were made. Of course the stories are about grim and costly fights for justice, against all odds and not always successful; but where there has been division of opinion there has also been camaraderie, where there has been despair there has also been encouragement, where there has been betrayal there has also been solidarity, where there has been dire poverty there has also been incalculable wealth which cannot be counted in pounds or dollars or rupees, and where there have been copious tears there have often been surprisingly wide smiles. If there is no peace without justice, maybe there is no justice that fails to burst into song.

Acknowledgements

A very large number of people, some far more than others, have been involved in the actual production of this book. Added to them are the countless numbers, including members of some of the most deprived communities on earth, together with members of Christian Aid, without whose courage, compassion and determination there would have been no stories to tell, let alone good ones. My gratitude and admiration go out to all of them; but there are too many to name and a high risk of leaving someone out, so, hoping for their understanding, I will say 'thank you' to everyone but put a name to no one. They know who they are!

Tamsin Bracher was seconded to me as a half-time research assistant in the autumn of 2023. She turned out to be a star and a pleasure to work with. Without her this book would have been far less well informed and taken rather longer to write. I owe her a special debt of gratitude.

1
How it all began

It began with a war and a woman.

After the horrors of the Second World War, with its endless capacity to kill and maim, uproot and bereave, impoverish and disillusion, came a wave of idealism determined to build not just 'a land fit for heroes' but a world fit for all humanity where such horrors would be no more. Those were the days of the Bretton Woods agreement, signed in 1944 by forty-four nations, establishing international rules for trade and managing money. It gave birth to the International Monetary Fund (IMF) and the World Bank (WB), both designed to foster a healthy and fairer world economy. They were followed in 1945 by the transformation of the League of Nations into the United Nations, designed to keep the peace. At the national level in Britain, one sign of this idealism was the Beveridge Report of 1942, a blueprint for social policy in post-war Britain, which, championed by determined politicians such as Aneurin Bevan, heralded the formation of the welfare state.

But the aftermath of those horrors remained, and compassion could not turn a blind eye. In Europe alone, 40 million people had been displaced, 11 million of them in Allied-occupied Germany. They included survivors of concentration camps and prisoners of war. They were known as Displaced Persons (DPs) and were not always welcome when they tried, or were forced, to resettle back home. Six million had been deported from Ukraine, Poland, France, Italy, Latvia, Belarus, Russia and Yugoslavia and forced to work in agriculture and industry in Germany or its occupied territories, so fuelling the war that caused their suffering. Now it was over, and they were stranded.

Working among them was a middle-aged woman characterised as 'formidable' and 'autocratic' but essentially 'deeply compassionate' and good company, who 'without being tall … confronted others as being a tower of strength' (as described by the prominent British educator Eric James). Employed at the time by the YWCA and then YMCA as education secretary, she was working on social projects that brought together soldiers from the British Army of the Rhine, now being demobbed, with young German soldiers and refugees.[1] She experienced something of the devastation and misery of post-war Europe, bad enough in the West and even worse in the East. She was also in contact with the international ecumenical movement, the nascent World Council of Churches (WCC), and church leaders like George Bell.

Once back in Britain, Janet Lacey was appointed youth secretary of the British Council of Churches (BCC) in 1947. In 1952 she became Secretary, and later Director, of its faltering Inter-Church Aid and Refugee department. In 1957, during the second week of May, she organised the first Christian Aid Week and renamed her department 'Christian Aid' in 1964. By the time she left in 1968, over 400 local churches and committees were involved. Together they were raising £2.5m (£42.5m in today's money) per year to fund development projects in forty countries.

Lacey was born in Sunderland, the daughter of a Methodist minister. On his death she moved to live with her aunt in Durham, where she saw something of the harsh realities of life in the nearby mining villages. After technical school she began her working life, training as a youth worker with the YWCA, first in Kendal and later, by 1932, in Dagenham. She was a founder member in 1958 of Voluntary Service Overseas (VSO). In 1959 she sat on the UK World Refugee Year Committee. She chaired the WCC's work on refugee service and in 1956 wrote 'By the Waters of Babylon', a WCC dramatic statement on the plight of exiles. An 'ecumenical ballistic missile' if ever there was one, she travelled widely, including on one of the earliest jet-planes, Comet II. After Christian Aid she became Director of the Family Welfare Association from 1969 to 1973 and, finally, reorganised the Churches' Council for Health and Healing. She was awarded a CBE in 1960 and a Lambeth Doctorate in 1975. She was the first woman to preach in St Paul's Cathedral. In 1970 she published her autobiography, *A Cup of Water*.[2] A photograph of her is kept in the National Portrait Gallery.

In her youth Janet Lacey trained to be an actor. She performed in the mining villages of northern England, but despite her talents as a playwright and performer, she decided not to pursue a theatrical career – though in one way she did! She was said to bring something of the art of an impresario to her working life. In retirement she could be visited in her basement flat not far from Sloane Square in London and, appropriately enough, close to one of its most pioneering theatres (The Royal Court).

But if Christian Aid began with this remarkable woman, it also began in response to an emergency in Europe, closely followed in 1948 by the flight from their homes of 700,000 Palestinian Arabs to the West Bank, the Gaza Strip and Lebanon. They fled never to return during a war triggered by the withdrawal of the British and the declaration of independence by the State of Israel. Since then have followed countless emergency appeals: Lacey spoke of twenty a year in the 1960s; Rowan Williams, then chair of Christian Aid, referred to 2015–16 as a year 'full of humanitarian crises'. Christian Aid's income could rise dramatically (in 1983–84, for example) and then go down (in 1986–87). In 1972 there were no emergency appeals, and in 1982 no major ones. All this required careful management, not least to ensure that supporters at home understood the fluctuations and that humanitarian aid in all its complexity and scale did not deflect attention from longer-term work, which, according to the annual figures on expenditure, it did not.

Many appeals have been in cooperation with the Disasters Emergency Committee, founded in the early 1960s. Although the agencies had worked together in 1959–60 to make World Refugee Year a success, in the early years there had been growing competition between them. It had given rise to considerable tension, not least when Oxfam adopted quite aggressive tactics or, as some would say, up-to-date marketing techniques, applying business methods to charitable activities. On one occasion Oxfam had appealed directly to the churches and was heavily criticised by Janet Lacey. It was Lacey who encouraged cooperation and coordination instead of competition. She proposed a committee with a view to making joint appeals and sharing the donations equally between its members. After informal meetings it was set up in 1963 by the Red Cross (which provided the administration), Christian Aid, Oxfam, Save the Children and War on Want. Later that year it became the DEC.[3]

The first DEC appeal was made in 1966 for victims of the earthquake in Turkey. By 2024 there had been seventy-seven appeals raising £2.4bn with a membership of fifteen charities governed by their CEOs together with independent trustees. A Rapid Response Network of national media, including television and corporates, helped to raise the alarm and set up easy ways for the public to donate. Members had to explain how they would use the money and then do so within a strictly limited period of time[4] and for the stated purpose of the appeal. Following the Boxing Day tsunami in 2004, for example, Christian Aid and its in-country partners promptly reached over half a million desperate people with food, shelter and health care. The Church's Auxiliary for Social Action (CASA) in India set up feeding stations by the next day (27 December) and the National Christian Council of Sri Lanka (NCCSL) was sending food to hard hit areas by 28 December; but it is not always easy to spend large sums of money quickly and well.

War, violence, disease, cyclones, droughts, earthquakes, storms, floods and famines pay little respect to geographical boundaries. All corners of the globe, from east to west and north to south, from Haiti in the Caribbean to Eastern Europe, have found themselves in need of humanitarian aid: Africa more often than others, with Asia not far behind. Together their stories and Christian Aid's story make up a tapestry of efforts to support desperate men, women and children doing their best to survive as they lose their homes, their loved ones, safe havens, health care, schools, drinking water, the means though not the ability to feed and take care of themselves, and more.

Through this tapestry of needs and responses, however, runs a thread. Although it became more explicit as time went on – and in 2022 very explicit, as we shall see – right from the start Christian Aid had a bias to the local or, as later referred to, 'localisation': a bottom-up rather than top-down approach to humanitarian aid and, indeed, to all aspects of its work. It was locally led. A generally non-operational approach[5] reflects this, but it is fundamentally a matter of respect for people and what they are well able to do for themselves; of finding out their needs from them and what forms of support will be of most use to supplement their own resources.

Whatever that may mean, from ready money to training, it definitely does *not* mean outsiders assuming what is best for desperate people and flying it in, acting *for* people and not *with* them. When it comes to accountability it is not only about agencies being accountable to funders, but whether according to local people they received the kind of support they needed and, in turn, whether they made good use of it.

Of course, it is not as if no other NGOs have acted in this respectful way or that a bias to the local does not have its problems, especially when people are too exhausted to cope or are uprooted and their communities virtually destroyed; but whether unique or not, this bias to the local can be traced throughout Christian Aid's story.

Some emergencies and the appeals that went with them, such as Biafra, Ethiopia and Rwanda, stay long in the memory. Others get forgotten as the world moves on, but are no less disastrous for their victims and important to agencies like Christian Aid, which try to stand by them. It goes without saying that in every case Christian Aid appealed for funds to its supporters, many – though by no means all of them – in the churches, and was never let down.

Biafra

In the mid-1960s Janet Lacey visited Echara in Nigeria, where work had begun on a tough training programme for young men in the hope that they could build up their bank balances and settle down to cooperative farming. Soon they were growing yams and other crops, and building greenhouses for storage. Christian Aid sent them a Massey Ferguson tractor, which helped to bring more land under cultivation. At the time Lacey was delighted with what she saw, but later commented, 'I expect it disintegrated when the tragic civil war rent Nigeria to pieces.'[6]

In Britain little was heard of that war, soon referred to as the Biafra war, which broke out in 1967, until the media published horrific pictures of starving Biafran children in June 1968. The fighting was between the federal state of Nigeria and the newly declared independent state of Biafra. Nigeria, dominated by Igbos, was under military rule after a coup in 1966, led by General Yakubu Gowon. Lieutenant Colonel 'Emeka' Odumegwu Ojukwu commanded the Biafrans.

One immediate cause of the war was the way in which the British defined the borders of the newly created federal state, forcing three former colonies into one with no reference to ethnic histories, so exacerbating division and challenging over 250 ethnic groups to find a way of living together. Control of oil fields, at first in the hands of the Biafrans and later recaptured by federal troops, was also at stake.

The tragic situation became even more so as trust fell away on all sides. Ojukwu, for example, refused to accept desperately needed aid coming by way of Nigeria, while Gowon, reluctant to let it through in any case, refused at times to allow airlifts over Nigerian air space and left tons of supplies stranded in Port Harcourt. In Britain the government was nervous about being seen to take sides in the conflict, while aid agencies were caught up in the familiar issue of how to remain neutral. Many suggested that they weren't, tending to favour Biafra, which critics claimed had exaggerated the suffering to win support. The DEC, including Christian Aid, caught between government caution, public outrage at millions of children dying from starvation, together with accusations of acting contrary to Charity Commission rules, decided to hold back until the International Committee of the Red Cross (ICRC) advised on how to proceed.

In sheer frustration at the delay, Oxfam decided to break ranks with the DEC, flying personnel and medical supplies directly into Biafra to the disapproval of the British government.[7] Eventually, and far too late, the aid effort began to move.

Christian Aid remembered the war fifty years later in January 2020 at a ceremony at Lambeth Palace. Brian Sheen, a veteran of Christian Aid's war effort, told his story. Apprenticed to the English China Clays company in Cornwall, he saw the war played out on the news and made it clear to his bosses time and again that someone (in other words, 'he') should go and do something about it. Eventually they recommended him to Christian Aid, and he was soon part of one of its medical teams sent to Biafra. As a mechanic he looked after the vehicles. As an increasingly able first-aider he cleaned ulcers and wounds. His humanity and the depth of human need were captured when he tried to help a young boy put on the trousers and T-shirt he had just been given, by then too weak to do it himself. Brian couldn't stop the war, he said, but he tried!

In 2020, 9.5 million Nigerians were still depending on food aid, with Christian Aid feeding over 400,000 people over three years.[8]

Hungary

The Hungarian Uprising, probably lingering less in the corporate memory than Biafra's war, turned Christian Aid's attention once again to Europe and the aftermath of the Second World War. The Warsaw Pact had been signed in May 1955 between the Soviet Union and its satellites, including Hungary. The uprising of 1956, in which students played a prominent part, can be seen as part of the struggle to break free from communist rule and the heavy constraints the Pact now represented. It began on 23 October and was crushed by Soviet forces twelve days later, on 4 November. Imre Nagy, a cautious but reforming leader, was arrested and the Soviet-backed János Kádár took control. Meanwhile, the British, French and Israelis were fighting the ill-fated Suez War.

Both events predictably raised the spectre of frightened and uprooted people fleeing for safety. In the case of Hungary, 200,000 of them crossed over no man's land into Austria, which, welcoming but overwhelmed, appealed to the United Nations High Commissioner for Refugees (UNHCR) for international help.

On 31 October the intrepid Janet Lacey was in Geneva attending WCC meetings when, shamefaced for what was happening in Egypt, she heard on the radio anguished cries for help from the Hungarian freedom fighters. By the next day she was in Vienna where she was soon joined by colleagues from the ecumenical family doing what they could for the frightened and wounded. Help poured in from all quarters. Christian Aid bought two mobile canteens; Sainsbury's filled them with food; volunteers staffed them for weeks, lined up with others on the border.

Britannia aircraft were soon flying refugees from Vienna to London and other European capitals. Britain accepted 21,000. Some were welcomed into people's homes (for Christmas). Some were accommodated in camps. Some eventually found jobs and settled. Some got a more mixed reception, suspected of coming for economic reasons. The notion of people who had human rights rather than a duty to be 'grateful' and 'deserving' was not yet, if ever, fully understood.

Many of the refugees eventually left for the USA and Canada. Besides raising considerable amounts of money, Christian Aid handled all the paperwork for those who went on to Canada in a small office in the

BCC's HQ in Eaton Gate, London. For three weeks refugees filled all the rooms in the building, plus the basement, and sat on the stairs awaiting their turn. Extra space had to be found nearby. Staff were left exhausted, having played their part in what was then described as the greatest refugee crisis in Europe since 1948 and one of the darkest moments of the Cold War.

Ethiopia

On 23 October 1984 the BBC broadcast a report by Michael Buerk describing a 'biblical famine' in Ethiopia, accompanied by horrific pictures of starving children. The famine affected 7.5 million people; well over 300,000 (some said 1.2 million) died; 2.5 million were displaced; many left the country.

Buerk's report evoked an immediate outpouring of concern and generosity. Agencies such as Christian Aid and the DEC were inundated with money. The RAF delivered food by air. Bob Geldof and his newly formed Band Aid organised a huge concert at Wembley on 13 July 1985, complemented by one in Philadelphia, USA, on the same day. There were 72,000 paying £25 each to go in, along with David Bowie, Queen and U2. It ended with everyone joining in a rousing chorus of 'Do they know it's Christmas?', later criticised for portraying a false image of Africa as a broken continent. The concert and other related events raised £145m.

In September 1985, Martin Bax, Christian Aid's Acting Director up to almost the very day, took a very new recruit to join a huge lobby of Parliament by Christian Aid supporters among many others, demanding a significant increase in the aid budget to 0.7% of GDP.

The area worst hit by famine was Tigray, squeezed between Ethiopia in the south, Eritrea in the north, with Sudan to the west. The problem was not just that the rains had failed. The Ethiopian government, known as the Derg, had a long-standing policy of keeping Tigray poor by paying low prices for grain to peasant farmers, debarring them from non-agricultural jobs, confiscating their land, forcibly resettling them in villages for administrative and security reasons, and withholding official government relief. On top of that was an acute environmental crisis.

Grasslands had been ploughed relentlessly for cash crops. Fewer and fewer trees only accelerated soil erosion.

On top of everything else, there was war. The Tigray People's Liberation Front (TPLF) had rebelled with an attempt to overthrow the Ethiopian regime. The Derg's soldiers, tanks and MiG fighter jets were sent to destroy them.

Christian Aid took unprecedented action. *Argo Challenge* and *Argo Glory* were two small ships that set out from Ipswich and were met by a member of Christian Aid's staff in Port Sudan. They carried 5,000 tonnes of wheat destined for Eritrea: unprecedented because Christian Aid hired the ships and covered 60% of the cost.

In the spring of 1985 Max Peberdy, a member of Christian Aid's staff based in Oxford, joined a convoy of 10-tonne trucks loaded with wheat, flour, cooking oil and lentils at the depot of the International Committee of the Red Cross in Kassala, Sudan, heading for the lowlands of western Tigray. It was sponsored by an ecumenical consortium, mainly of European agencies including Christian Aid, called Ecumenical Relief Desk (ERD), based in Khartoum. Peberdy also carried a large leather bag containing £300,000 in cash (in Ethiopian birrs). The trucks were owned by the Relief Society of Tigray (REST) and guarded by the TPLF. The convoy was held up for days under threat of attack, moving only by night. Eventually it crossed the dried-up river Gash and then the border into Tigray.[9]

The convoy and its mission raised a number of controversial issues not entirely new or confined to this particular emergency. NGOs, concerned for the safety of staff and to maintain access, tended to guard their reputation for neutrality in situations of conflict and for respecting the sovereignty of states, in this case the government of Ethiopia. A convoy travelling against the wishes of the government and taking sides in the struggle clearly ran contrary to both. Crossing red lines as well as borders signalled a determination to engage with the real causes of a disaster and not just its apparent symptoms. The debate as to how far to go with this approach divided the ERD, which nevertheless allowed some of its members to go their own way.

Back at HQ came the tension between, on the one hand, the need to use images that evoke sympathy and raise money in a highly competitive environment, and, on the other, the need to educate supporters on the realities of power and the need for respect, solidarity, advocacy and campaigning. There was also serious unease among some as to how far giving oxygen to fighting forces was compatible with deeply held beliefs about reconciliation and peacebuilding.

Peberdy and Christian Aid had two further issues in mind when he set out, apart from feeding starving families. One was to put another dent in the widespread assumption that emergencies like this were a case of generous, well-off Westerners coming to the aid of hapless Africans incapable of helping themselves. He knew that nothing could be further from the truth. In fact, it was the local people, organised and led by REST, who were running the relief effort, organising the convoys, mending the trucks, taking care of the displaced from the even worse affected areas in the east, distributing food in the camps and reception centres, and setting up a system of local government in the form of village committees. It was REST who ran clinics and hospitals, often camouflaged or underground, orphanages and schools. If the West supplied the wherewithal in terms of cash and food, it was the local people who supplied the know-how, the determination, the hard workers on the ground, not to mention courage and defiance in the face of potentially overwhelming odds.

The second issue had to do with the doubts too often expressed, that food aid and money did not always get to the right people; that all too often they were misused, even to buy guns. Christian Aid always insisted that it knew where its money went and the safe hands that received it. Peberdy set out to demonstrate that in this instance that was definitely the case, with a photograph of the handover to prove it.

Farmers in western Tigray had a little sorghum to spare after feeding their families and often a displaced family as well. REST collected these small amounts. Peberdy bought them: 10,000 quintels (one quintel = 100 kilos) with money from Christian Aid and its counterparts in Holland and Norway. The farmers could then buy a few necessities such as salt and tea. The sorghum was enough for REST to redistribute and feed 100,000 for a month.

Years later, on 3 March 2010, that photograph came back to bite not only Peberdy and Christian Aid but the humanitarian agencies in general, and Band Aid (now a trust) above all. Breaking news on Ethiopia once again, the BBC published evidence, supplied by what turned out to be a malcontent backed by the CIA, that 95% of all the funds raised in the 1980s had been spent by the TPLF on weapons. Peberdy's photograph was said to show one of its members disguised as a representative of REST selling Peberdy not sorghum but mostly sand. Beyond Tigray, the Derg was accused of spending Live Aid and Oxfam money on its forced resettlement programme.

The report and its sources were investigated by Band Aid, Christian Aid and others and subsequently dismissed as 'misleading', 'preposterous', 'unsubstantiated' and 'untrue'. In November the BBC apologised.

The risk of aid falling into the wrong hands is well recognised and guarded against as far as possible, Rwanda being another example. The impression created by the BBC report did not, however, entirely go away. There were, as always, blurred edges. The need for reassurances remained.[10]

Rwanda

Anyone who went to Rwanda and Goma (Zaire) in the summer of 1994 would not easily forget what they saw. The genocide of that year was probably the most brutal episode in a long story of prejudice, oppression, racism, violence and war between Hutu agriculturalists in the majority, Tutsi cattle breeders, widely seen and envied as an elite favoured by the colonisers, and Twa, descended from the earliest inhabitants of the land.

In 1990 the Rwandan Patriotic Front (RPF), led by Paul Kagame, invaded from their base in Uganda. They were largely Tutsis driven into exile by earlier conflicts. Their guerilla-like tactics to regain power had no lasting success, and on 4 August 1993 a peace deal, known as the Arusha Accords, was signed by the Hutu President Habyarimana and the RPF. The peace was short-lived. The fragile situation was not helped by the radio station Radio Télévision Libre des Mille Collines, set up by the President and his wife, relentlessly pumping out propaganda targeted at Tutsis. Within a year Habyarimana was assassinated when his plane was shot down over Kigali airport on 6 April 1994. The killings by soldiers, police and militias began the next day. An estimated 600,000 Tutsis were slaughtered, many by machetes at the hands of their neighbours.

Between a quarter and half a million women were raped, many infected with HIV. In one instance 1,500 Tutsis sought refuge in a Catholic church in Nyanga. The Interahamwe ('Those who fight together'), made up of armed and murderous youths, bulldozed the building killing everyone in it. The priest assisted the killers and was later found guilty of genocide. According to Human Rights Watch, all the churches, whether Catholic or Protestant, tended to support the powers that be, and by failing to condemn the genocide gave it a measure of moral legitimacy. Ecumenical relations between those involved became strained.

According to UNHCR, which set up the refugee camps, over 2 million people fled for their lives.

Setting off on my own journey in May 1994, I left behind colleagues vastly experienced in the sights and sounds of human tragedy who nevertheless had been thrown off balance – some might say traumatised – by what they had seen and heard in Rwanda, even driving over corpses to get to those they needed to support.

After landing in Kigali, where Christian Aid had set up its first overseas office,[11] I travelled in a tiny plane to a camp in Goma, Zaire (now the Democratic Republic of Congo). Dennis Potter called one of his television plays, much admired at the time, *Blue Remembered Hills*; as we approached the landing strip, I could not help but think of it. These hills were blue: turned blue by the standard blue plastic sheets handed out by the UN to refugees for shelter.

I met and talked to two members of Christian Aid's staff from London funded by the DEC appeal, launched in April and raising £37m. They were working on the ground day and night with Rwandan organisations in the camp. Conditions were crowded and squalid. The stench of fear and abject misery was everywhere. The ground turned into thick mud after rain and, when the sun came out, to hard volcanic ash, extremely painful for bare feet. Hundreds died from cholera and dysentery. Supplies of food, limited as they were, could be sold to buy guns. Leaders of the genocide were controlling the camp while plotting to return to Rwanda and regain the upper hand. By 1996 the RPF was attacking the camp and the enemy within, forcing large numbers of its inhabitants to return home, supplied by Christian Aid and others with seeds and tools in the hope that they could grow enough food to feed their children.

The sharpest memory I took away was of a young woman completely alone but for a tiny child trying to feed at her dry breast, with nothing to call her own but her pleas for help and her one blue plastic sheet – for me, an unforgettable 'icon of sorrow'. What many others took away, apart from their own memories of the violence and the suffering it had caused, was a humanitarian response wide open to criticism. Precisely due to a lack of attention to views of local people, the food supplied, a lot of it by evangelical organisations, was inappropriate. The quality was poor. NGOs failed to coordinate. Standards in general were low. Lessons had to be learned. According to NGO worker Nick Guttmann,[12] what swiftly followed was something of a 'seismic shift' marked by the adoption in 1995 by NGOs, including Christian Aid, of the 'Code of Conduct for the International Red Cross and Red Crescent Movement and NGOs in Disaster Relief'. Several of its ten core principles are compatible with Christian Aid's 'bias to the local'. The so-called 'shift' went further in 2016 at the World Humanitarian Summit in Istanbul with its Grand Bargain to put 'localisation' high on the agenda not just of policy discussions but in practice.

By 2022 the reputation of Rwanda's government was somewhat rehabilitated. The British government was at its wits' end to stop 'illegal' migration into the UK above all by way of small boats crossing the English Channel. It made an agreement with President Kagame that migrants who were refused permission to stay in the UK would be sent to Rwanda as a safe country.

Tsunami 2004

According to later, mainly positive evaluations, one key feature of Christian Aid's response to the devastating tsunami that struck on Boxing Day 2004 paid off. Its commitment to working with local organisations and people made sure that the response was swift and appropriate. In Tamil Nadu, for example, CASA, working from the bottom up, once again followed the advice of the local community, supplying what it said it needed and encouraging it to stand up for itself when dealing with government officials.

But it was Indonesia that bore the brunt of what in this instance might fairly be called 'a natural disaster'. Of an overall total of up to 2.5 million people affected, 170,000 lives were lost. The Yakkum Emergency Unit (YEU), with ready money from Christian Aid, was on site in Rajabasa, a village in South Lampung, within days. With it came a medical team and essential supplies. Some 6,500 people had been affected.

Swiftly following relief efforts came the work of recovery. For centuries the sea, despite its dangers, had been adored by the coastal communities along the shores of the Indian Ocean. Now it had turned into a monstrous enemy. Their main interest was to get back to fishing again, feeding their families and earning a living in the marketplaces.

Striking statistics are one thing, from the strength of the underwater earthquake (9.0 on the Richter scale) and the size of the great waves (up to 10 metres high and reaching 3 kilometres inland) to the number of people killed, injured and made homeless. However, counting the number of small steps taken in the right direction quickly becomes more important. Two million homes were destroyed. Christian Aid and organisations like Habitat for Humanity were soon building new ones, more resilient to stormy weather (Christian Aid funded 24,000 over the next five years). The little ships with their nets were being mended so that fishing could begin again. Children were going back to school. In Sri Lanka their teachers tried to ease their traumas by dancing with them and performing plays. Less helpful were the mainly American missionaries offering 'Jesus' along with food aid in a mainly Buddhist country.

Tim Hetherington, a world-renowned photojournalist, saw the news at home on Boxing Day. Within ten days he was on the scene in Sri Lanka, where 35,000 had died. He returned later to film his documentary *Every Time I Look at the Sea* and produce for Christian Aid those hard-to-find images that are evocative but also respectful of people and the truth about their own efforts to rebuild their lives. Striking among them were telling images of those very same dancing children with their painted faces and masks.

Hetherington was killed in Libya in 2011. His images lived on and were seen by many in an exhibition, *Tsunami: Ten Years After The Wave*, mounted by Christian Aid in 2014 and toured round the UK. With those images came the inevitable stories. If I found my 'icon of sorrow' in a refugee camp in Goma in 1994, Hetherington seemed to have found his one morning on a forsaken Sri Lankan beach strewn with debris. Among it lay a father trying to sleep alongside the body of the boy he had lost and just buried in the sand.

Typhoon Haiyan

Janet Lacey's lively account of Christian Aid's early years, unsystematic as it may be, consistently demonstrates the conviction, even in those days, that everyone now signs up to, namely that emergency relief and humanitarian aid can never stop there. They have to push on as soon as possible, hand in glove with rehabilitation, longer-term development and, quite explicitly in her writing, the political engagement required to tackle the structures that make people vulnerable.

That necessary push, at least towards rehabilitation and development, was well illustrated by Christian Aid's approach to the mayhem caused by Typhoon Haiyan in 2013 in the Philippines, when winds of up to 195mph (and gusts reaching 240) blew devastating waves onto land, killing 6,000 and uprooting 4 million more. The DEC raised £47m within two weeks.

When Christian Aid reported back to its supporters three years later about what had been achieved, working with at least seven local organisations, it chose not to focus on the deliveries of rice, noodles, clean water and temporary shelters – much needed as they had been – but on stories of recovery, of which Jinggoy's was one. Fearful of the approaching storm, he had moved his family to higher ground, and then returned with his elderly father-in-law to guard their property only, in his words, to be 'washed' out of it, 'spinning like noodles to be stirred'. He clung to his father-in-law and an oil can for five hours until, exhausted, the older man asked to be let go and was not seen again.

Jinggoy tells his story, however, from a newly built house set back further away from danger. Working with local organisations like the Urban Poor Association (UPA), life and 'aid' had moved on. He is earning a living again. Lessons have been learned from this and other disasters, not least about the need to be prepared and prevent the worst wherever possible, and Jinggoy is somewhat reassured by the early warning systems and evacuation routes now in place. Of course there is a more complicated background to Jinggoy's story, involving longer-term efforts to create new sources of income and markets for selling goods, as well as strengthening the resilience of his and other communities even further. Building Disaster Resilience Committees was one example, able to receive readily available funds from a Shared Aid Fund for Emergency Response (SAFER), a fund set up after a change in the law by the Filipino government following successful lobbying by Christian Aid and others.

Ukraine

One problem for Christian Aid as a 'non-operational' agency became somewhat pressing when Vladimir Putin and his armies and mercenaries invaded Ukraine in the spring of 2022 and cries for help came from bombed and ravaged communities, not to mention the Ukrainian government. Yet again Christian Aid and the DEC sent out their appeals and money came pouring in. The DEC rules and a sense of urgency required it to be spent sooner rather than later. Christian Aid was short of feet on the ground. Good working relationships, however, were soon up and running. Crown Agents (now defunct), a not-for-profit international development company with strong government connections, provided Ukraine's Ministry of Health with urgently needed incubators[13] and front-line medical aid kits. The Alliance for Public Health, a Ukrainian NGO concerned mainly with HIV/AIDS, gave medical assistance and used its little vans to help people escape from immediate danger. In addition, Christian Aid channelled funds through its sister agencies in Hungary and Switzerland with their long-standing presence in Ukraine. World Jewish Relief and Blythswood Care were also very much in the picture. Blythswood Care, a Scottish charity, helped Christian Aid support Heritage Ukraine to provide shelter for displaced people in Odesa along with cash grants, leaving their communities to decide how best to spend the money.

Devolution

In August 2022 Christian Aid published 'Ripping off the Band-Aid', and in March 2023 'Letting go of control'. Both reports advocated an approach to humanitarian aid that had gestated for a number of years among NGOs and had echoes in policies pursued by the WCC. It had been nurtured and clarified by Local to Global Protection (L2GP) funded by Christian Aid and others, and put to the test notably in Haiti and then Ukraine. True to its instinctive bias to the local, Christian Aid now loudly advocated and enthusiastically adopted the approach as its obvious 'niche', as Michael Mosselmans, head of Christian Aid's Humanitarian Division at the time, called it, in the vast humanitarian enterprise. It was named 'SCLR': Survivor- and Community-led Response. In essence it advocated what NGOs find so difficult, namely letting go of power and control and devolving accountability and funding to local actors, including small grants to 'pop-up groups' to design and implement their own immediate responses. Why? Because beside the all-important principle of respect for people, there is the plain, practical reality that local people can respond more quickly, they can mobilise and network between communities so maximising resources, they have the necessary skills and better local knowledge, they can take a more holistic approach and they are cost effective.

On the surface, humanitarian aid is as non-controversial as mother's milk. Scratch it, however, and it soon becomes apparent that that is far from the case. There are issues and problems galore. Some have been touched on. A constructive relationship and balance between aid, development and structural change has to be carefully nurtured and managed. The images that raise money can misrepresent the people needing support and play down the kind of support they need. While NGOs such as the Red Cross have good reasons to maintain neutrality in conflict situations and respect the sovereignty of states, even when they harm their own people, others such as Christian Aid know that for them that simply cannot always be the case. Care should be taken to be prepared for disasters and prevent the worst happening again. Rehabilitation can easily rehabilitate people back into situations that remain fundamentally unchanged and did much to cause the crisis in the first place. Money and food can get into the wrong hands, exchanged and sold for weapons, damaging the reputations of agencies in the process. Preventive measures can improve matters but carry their own costs.[14] Local organisations cannot always meet expectations. There are inevitable tensions between well-meaning people working for the same cause. The report 'Missed Again', published in 2014 by Christian Aid, Catholic Agency for Overseas

Development (CAFOD), Oxfam, Tearfund and ActionAid in the wake of Typhoon Haiyan, complained about the continuing lack of coordination between government, international, national and local players.

Emergencies with their immediate causes come and go, the underlying causes remain. From the start Christian Aid seems to have understood that, if the poor and vulnerable are to be lifted higher, those causes have to be tackled, from long-held hostilities and injustices to climate change.

When I needed a neighbour

When I needed a neighbour were you there, were you there?
When I needed a neighbour were you there?
And the creed and the colour and the name won't matter,
Were you there?

I was hungry and thirsty, were you there, were you there?
I was hungry and thirsty, were you there?
And the creed and the colour and the name won't matter,
Were you there?

I was cold, I was naked, were you there, were you there?
I was cold, I was naked, were you there?
And the creed and the colour and the name won't matter,
Were you there?

When I needed a shelter were you there, were you there?
When I needed a shelter were you there?
And the creed and the colour and the name won't matter,
Were you there?

When I needed a healer were you there, were you there?
When I needed a healer were you there?
And the creed and the colour and the name won't matter,
Were you there?

Wherever you travel, I'll be there, I'll be there,
Wherever you travel, I'll be there.
And the creed and the colour and the name won't matter,
I'll be there.

Sydney Carter, written for Christian Aid 1965, © Copyright 1965 Stainer & Bell Ltd, 23 Gruneisen Road, London N3 1LS, www.stainer.co.uk. Reprinted by permission. All rights reserved.

‘When I needed a neighbour’

2
Afghanistan

In May 1992 Timothy Goggs was challenged by his vicar, Toddy Hoare, to have his shoes shined as part of a fundraising effort for Christian Aid Week. To his embarrassment, when he came to pay, he had no money in his pocket. Twelve months later Tim's will was read after he lost his life in Afghanistan. The entire proceeds from the sale of his house in Newcastle, amounting to £35,000, had been left to Christian Aid. There was, evidently, a strong connection between the two.

After two years in the Territorial Army, Tim had given up his place at Sandhurst to work for the Halo Trust, clearing landmines in Afghanistan. An estimated 10 million were scattered across the country. He had come to love its people, had learned some of their many languages and got on well with their leaders, often quoting the Qur'an in conversation.

Using an old Russian tank built to withstand explosives as it trundled along, he and others set out to defuse a mine blocking a road to the north of Kabul. Unbeknown to them, the mine was attached to two others. The massive explosion set the tank on fire. Tim jumped clear but then returned to rescue a colleague from the flames, losing his own life in the attempt. His bravery was recognised posthumously with the award of the George Medal.

The vicar and Tim's family raised a further £250,000 in his memory to add to Tim's bequest. Christian Aid used it, for example, to plant over a million trees, train rural midwives and increase the work skills of the orphaned and injured.

In 1994, despite mines clearance and attempts to raise awareness, at least 9 million mines were still buried in the ground – the highest number in the world – with hundreds of people being maimed and killed every month.[1]

Coming to the rescue

Afghanistan proved to be a minefield in more senses than one and Christian Aid's determination, right from Janet Lacey's days, to always push beyond humanitarian aid towards longer-term development to improve people's lives and make them more sustainable and, further still, to tackle the root causes of their distress, was severely tested. Repeated emergencies meant it had to join with local organisations over and over again and come to the rescue.

There were several reasons why. Afghanistan had a long history of war. In 1978 a communist-inspired rebellion established a socialist state. Opposition to it provoked the Russian (Soviet) invasion of 1979. After fighting the Mujahideen (fighters for Islam), the Russians eventually withdrew in 1989. Civil war between warlords followed, with the Taliban[2] gaining control of Herat in 1995 and most of the country soon after that. Christian Aid was advised by the UK government to evacuate foreigners but stayed and had to return government funding as a result. In 2001 the war against Al-Qaeda, following the 9/11 terrorist attacks, had enormous negative consequences for the country as the USA invaded in the search for its enemies while protecting something like a civilian government under President Hamid Karzai (2002–14). The USA, along with the UK and others, left in 2021 when the Taliban returned to power, ending – however unsatisfactorily – twenty years of war during which, and even before that, Christian Aid had navigated its way through the changing times and regimes.

Violence, however, continued, often with ethnic[3] and religious overtones. Disputes were often over scarce resources, like land and water, and the production of narcotics, by then officially illegal. Added to the toxic mix were 'natural' disasters including earthquakes and drought, disease and the Covid-19 pandemic of 2020.

In the early 1980s Christian Aid supported hundreds of thousands of Afghan refugees in Pakistan by way of the WCC's ecumenical networks. David (known as Dave) Hampson set up Christian Aid's own programme in 1994, working mostly with International Non-Governmental Organisations (INGOs) in the west of the country and, as they gained strength, local ones. In 2001 disaster piled on disaster. The drought, caused by a lack of rain over three years, 'when the wheat stood withering in the fields', sent thousands fleeing to the cities from the countryside or, once again, over the border into Pakistan.[4]

In that same year Al-Qaeda attacked New York's World Trade Center and the Pentagon in Washington. The hunt for the killers was on. Vengeance brought another invasion of troops, only intensifying the suffering of vast numbers of Afghans who had nothing at all to do with the fanatics. Christian Aid wrote to Tony Blair, rather naively perhaps, warning against opting for punitive action against Afghanistan rather than principled, constructive engagement with the Taliban.[5] As sanctions were tightened, any attempt to provide aid became increasingly difficult and dangerous. Christian Aid and others campaigned for a 'humanitarian pause' in the bombing. Chris Buckley, a staff member, wrote an article in *The Independent* on 14 September pointing to the dire situation faced by farmers, for example, cut off with no seeds to plant and banned from opium production, and how many NGOs, there to help, were being forced to pull out. He emphasised that talking was better than fighting and insisted that stopping the flow of aid was equally immoral to the killing of thousands of Americans. As if that wasn't enough, the INGOs faced the challenge of resettling nearly 2 million refugees as they were hastily 'repatriated' or pushed back out of Pakistan and Iran. Wheat, ghee, lentils, salt, seeds and tools were in high demand. Christian Aid played its part.

Christian Aid Week publicity for 2017 highlighted the plight of yet more Afghan refugees, this time stranded in Greece. One mother spoke of 'one hundred and eighty days of hell' after crossing the Aegean Sea from Turkey – in a small boat – almost drowning on the way.

On 15 August 2021 the Taliban returned to power after a sudden takeover and the chaotic withdrawal of US and UK troops and foreigners, followed by desperate attempts by the Afghans who had worked for them to escape reprisals. Many were left to their fate. Of the remaining Afghans, 97% were in poverty within a year following economic meltdown as aid was suspended and new sanctions imposed. Women began to disappear again, setting the clock back and undoing the work of twenty years. Fewer were working outside the home or seen in the marketplace. Their education was cut off above primary level. Christian

Aid decided to stay, but paused activities for a few weeks to protect staff and partners.

Issues that had surfaced in 2001 once more reared their heads in 2021. Governments were unwilling to engage with the Taliban. Sanctions were imposed. Humanitarian aid was cut off. The difficulties for Christian Aid and others trying to deliver it only mounted. Counter-terrorism measures and punishing the Taliban threatened to undermine any attempts to do so.[6]

The difficulties were only intensified by the virtual collapse of the banking system, so that money transfers – that is, getting money into the country – became almost impossible. The UN could hardly fly in planeloads of cash – but it did! How otherwise were salaries to be paid or, more importantly, how could money be put into the hands of the penniless to buy the basics or pay them cash for work?

All of this sorry story was punctuated by emergency appeals such as Christian Aid's Afghanistan Appeal from 2001 to 2006 which raised almost £4m from supporters in the UK and Ireland,[7] and the DEC crisis appeal of 2021, and then finding ways to get the money to Christian Aid's programmes.

Beyond aid

There are several references in Christian Aid's documents and reports to the challenge of moving on beyond humanitarian aid 'where the environment is not favourable for development'[8] and to the bleak and gloomy outlook for Afghanistan. Was there anything more constructive that Christian Aid could do?

In the 1990s, Jenny Borden, a leading member of Christian Aid's staff from 1979 to 2000 and responsible for Africa and the Middle East at the time, instigated discussions about whether or not, given the circumstances, to open an office in Afghanistan. In 1995 I visited Herat with Hampson with that question in mind. The journey there did not augur well. Our small plane came near to serious trouble as it attempted to land diplomats in Kabul on the way, circling down between the mountains in the mist. Much to their annoyance it failed, and they were forced to journey on with us to Herat.

I have vivid memories of walking the roads of that ancient city of culture with the Taliban in control. A huge crane, used to hang dissidents, interrupted the skyline as it brooded over the football ground. I was invited to a meal in a colleague's home. I saw nothing of the women beyond the hands that served us food through the narrowest of divides in a curtain. Outside, if they went out at all, the women were completely covered in heavy, pale blue burkhas, banned from paid work other than health care. Why open an office here when Save the Children were closing theirs? I attended meetings where women would arrive completely covered, until the burkhas came off and blue shadowy figures turned into strong, bright, smartly dressed, talkative human beings who proceeded to give the men a very hard time! Why *not* open an office, when this sort of talent and energy was ready and eager to go, asking for our presence and support?

CAID

Christian Aid's office in Herat was opened in 1997. A sub-office was opened later in Kabul. The openings were not, of course, the beginning of the story. Christian Aid's involvement in Afghanistan went back twenty-five years earlier, to the early 1970s. It originally worked through the WCC with the International Afghan Mission (IAM)[9] run by Christian ex-pat volunteers and a paid staff of growing numbers of Afghans. In 1971 Christian Aid contributed £50,000 towards IAM's plans to establish a hospital in Kabul to fight eye disease, backing up medical teams working out in the villages. One of Christian Aid's many emergency grants to support half a million Afghan refugees in Pakistan was made in 1980; others followed between 1982 and 1984. By 1986 Christian Aid had moved away from funding the IAM, though working contacts remained for some years, to working with local partners on, for example, vocational training for children orphaned by landmines, tree-planting as refugees returned to barren lands, and new opportunities for girls no longer allowed to go to school.

On the opening day in Herat in 1997 there were six paid staff, all but one of them Afghans. Working conditions were far from easy. Security issues disrupted visits to and from London. Perceptions could differ and mutual understanding was not always what it might have been: 'par for the course', some would say. Great care had to be taken not to shout too loudly about Christian Aid's Christian identity, also about its public face in a country where leaders could be hostile to Christianity. Perceived links with the USA could also spell danger. Strict security measures had to be taken at times. An ex-pat country manager was forced to live behind closed doors for a while. Staff moved about in unmarked cars and wore traditional clothes so as not to attract attention. At its worst, 'insecurity' meant the murder of aid workers by the Taliban as 'missionaries' and enemies of Islam. Christian Aid became known in Afghanistan simply as CAID (not for once an acronym!), though still registered with the government as Christian Aid.

By way of contrast, Christian Aid's path was eased by relatively good relations with the Taliban, much to the credit of Hampson and, following him, Barmak Pazhwak who, with Kate Straub, were responsible for the newly opened office. Both Hampson and Pazhwak had asked to meet with the Taliban leaders in Herat. Pazhwak was an Afghan himself and belonged to a highly respected family, counting the Poet Laureate among its members. He secured a letter from the Taliban, who knew his family, authorising him and CAID staff to travel and work.

Hampson was one of the few ex-pat aid workers who refused to leave when the Taliban were advancing on Herat in 1995, fearing that he might not get a visa to return. He was a familiar figure riding round on his bike doing all he could to help set up programmes in support of local people, especially women. He remembered his meeting with the Taliban's second in command, Mullah Rabani, meeting a foreigner for the first time, lying on a bed, dressed in dirty robes in the middle of a long room lined with men and machine guns. Having explained what he was up to, Hampson handed over his business card, which the Mullah proceeded to use as a toothpick. On leaving he offered to provide a note of the meeting in Pashtu. Declining the offer, Rabani commented, 'We have our Qu'ran, we won't be needing any other paper'. Despite the rebuff the outcome was generally positive. Where the official cars of visiting dignitaries had to queue at checkpoints for clearance, Hampson and his bike were waved through!

CAID did manage to push beyond humanitarian aid to some extent. It adopted its by now traditional and principled ways of working. Local people were listened to, often by way of Participatory Vulnerability and Capacity Assessments (PVCA) carried out by themselves. Local organisations like Rehabilitation Association and Agricultural Development for Afghanistan (RAADA) and the Rural Rehabilitation Association for Afghanistan (RRAA), to name but two of many,[10] appreciated open and frank dialogue and a generally respectful approach. After consulting with them, three interrelated themes seemed to emerge and stick,[11] namely 'Resilience', 'Peacebuilding' and 'Strengthening the hands of women'.

Resilience

'Resilience' became a familiar word in Christian Aid's vocabulary and it's a big one, sweeping up a range of activities, some of which might be thought to go beyond it. What did Christian Aid mean by it when, by 2011, it accounted for 75% of the country's programme budget, funded by the UK government's Department for International Development (DFID)?

In the opening paragraph of 'Building Resilience in Fragile States',[12] Christian Aid defined resilience as 'enhancing the ability of individuals and communities to anticipate, organise for and adapt to change', where the state lacks the ability or the inclination to do so. Put bluntly, it appears to be about surviving when vulnerable people come into harm's way.

The threats to them are many and varied. There are wars, internal conflicts and attacks by warring factions all too ready to use extortion, kidnapping and drug-dealing to enrich themselves and fuel their cause. The International Security Assistance Force of 2011–14 and the Afghan National Security Forces set up in 2013 failed to make much difference. Adding to insecurity came climate change, earthquakes, droughts and sandstorms, acute shortages of land and water and the lack or complete absence of health care and education. All of them, separately and together, had to be prepared for where possible, defended against, adjusted to and survived.

The measures taken were equally many and varied, helped by good working relationships established between CAID and local organisations. They included:

- flood protection, building canals, training in mines awareness and clearance
- improving roads and access to markets
- encouraging simple measures like handwashing
- education
- tree-planting, using climate-resistant seeds, animal husbandry, supplying tool kits, improving wood-burning stoves, protecting a pistachio forest
- job creation schemes and skills training, especially for girls
- plus ready cash, and cash for work.

Some of these measures came close to humanitarian aid and some at the time to showing signs of genuine development and change for the better. A story from the 2020s, told under the shadow of the Taliban, is about the village of Shar Shar, Badghis province, where, as in many, many villages, the women walked miles and miles in the scorching heat to fill a jug of water – until, that is, two reservoirs were built with forty-five taps, providing safe and accessible drinking water for over 700 families. 'It transformed the community's dynamic.' Time and money spent on water was now freed up for farming, cattle-rearing and paying the school fees, while 'a mother had time to tend her vegetable patch.'[13]

Peacebuilding

Peace was pursued by Christian Aid at several levels. A thoughtfully worded press release issued on 25 September 2001, following the terrorist attacks of 9/11, asked, 'Is Christian Aid in favour of war in Afghanistan?' It pointed out the clear risk of making an already desperate humanitarian crisis worse. It supported efforts to bring terrorists to justice and urged nations to work together to find a lasting solution and bring an end to the bitterness, injustice and alienation that fuel terrorism. It underlined the difference between a war on terrorists and a war on the Afghan people and stated a clear preference, realistic or not, for resolving matters by way of diplomacy and prosecution under international law.

It did not dodge the question about its support for the USA and its allies, including the UK, going to war as a last resort, but insisted that if they did so – and Christian Aid was in no position to have a view on that decision – they had to respect a number of principles, such as upholding the rule of law, minimising civilian casualties and not blocking humanitarian aid.

Internationally there were repeated efforts to make peace, including negotiations with the Taliban. A political settlement brokered by the UN's special envoy meant that 2019 began with high hopes, followed by a peace deal signed in February of the following year. Hamid Karzai won the election but the opposition rejected the result in favour of a coalition government, and things fell apart once again.

CAID's local partners showed little interest in negotiations at the national level or in 'messy politics', preferring to work for peace at the community level. It seems to have involved attempts to alter the tone of life there where people were listened to rather than ignored, treated each other with respect and tried to sit down and resolve their disputes – over water and land, for example – rather than perpetuate them; all of it was supported by the local mullah provided it stayed within Islamic law.

In practice, building peace and social cohesion looked very similar to building resilience. Once some of the problems were eased and the confidence to deal with them grew, some of the tensions were eased as well. Struggling and even fighting for water turned into joint efforts to conserve it and then share it.

Following the return of the Taliban in 2021 with their claim to have put an end to war, no one else would claim that Afghanistan was anywhere near a country at peace with itself. A comment made in 2016 still held true: 'The prospect of peace in the foreseeable future seems to be very gloomy.'[14] Women were again under attack. They were also central to peacebuilding.

Women

The plight of women in Afghanistan is well known. It was demonstrated once again in 2006. Money from the emergency appeal of 2001–06 was used to train women for work, which supposedly did not cross the red lines of the Taliban, and to create safe spaces in homes and gardens where they could befriend one another, socialise and work together.

Led by RRAA (Rural Rehabilitation Association for Afghanistan), many women were trained as health workers, birth attendants and paramedics in line with earlier work described by Kate Straub. By tradition babies were delivered by skilled older women but in ways that were unhygienic. The babies were delivered over cow dung since giving birth was regarded as unclean (reminiscent of the 'churching' of women after childbirth, with its roots in the Jewish practice of purification). The umbilical cord was cut stretched over the dirty shoe of the oldest woman in the village, ensuring longevity. Instruments were not sterilised. Cloths were not clean. Early breast milk, vital for protection against illness, was denied as being poisonous.

There was much to learn and share, but it was not without risk. Five health workers were murdered in April 2006.

Christian Aid, not for the first time, made the empowerment of women a priority. A married couple managing Christian Aid's programme in Herat from 2003 to 2005 (Tara Mascarenhas and Laurent Viot) took a highly unusual approach by offering internships to Afghan women in the offices of INGOs where they could gain confidence in the workplace and all-male offices could realise the benefits of having women working in them. Such an initiative would be banned by 2025.

In 2003 the Afghan government actually made a positive contribution to the empowerment of women. It set up democratically elected Community Development Committees (CDCs) and, later, district ones where men and women engaged with government officials over plans for their future. A report on work in 2023–24 records another consultative initiative in which a very different government was involved, namely five roundtables at which representatives of local NGOs like ACBAR and officials from the de facto authorities (that is, the Taliban) were present.[15] One outcome was the many PVCAs carried out in a lot of the villages with the help of CDC members, including women, where villagers explored their own issues and how they might be addressed. More significant, perhaps, was the growing acceptance of female participation in community life. Now they had opportunities to speak up about their concerns. Now, for example, in a process referred to as 'Reflect', reminiscent of Paulo Freire's concept of 'conscientisation', it became increasingly clear to them that their traditional role – silent, marginalised and submissive – was far from set in stone.

Empowerment, however, meant more than a voice to speak out about Gender-based Violence (GBV), human rights, inequality, lack of health care and much else. Economic empowerment was needed as well. One of the most attractive examples, at least to the outside observer, drew deeply on Afghan traditions around silk and saffron.

It was by no means the first,[16] but in 2024 CAID opened a project with the explicit intention of moving beyond an exclusive focus on humanitarian aid, and it had to do with silk and saffron. The skills required were not new, since practising them was culturally acceptable, nor was Christian Aid's involvement, but tighter restrictions meant new ways of working if women were still to have a chance to earn an independent living.

Four thousand women, many supplied with start-up kits, began producing silk as they introduced silkworms to mulberry leaves, their only food. Over 100 more began to produce saffron, planting the crocus bulbs, tending the flowers and harvesting their tiny stamens: three in each. Carpets, embroidery, clothing and dried saffron were produced and marketed, some of it abroad. A deep purple Afghan carpet from Herat lies at my feet as I write.

Resilience, peacebuilding and empowering women could never be discrete efforts. Whichever issue CAID touched it benefited the others, and although humanitarian aid was never enough, it was the major contributor – not only in kind – to all three.

The crocus

Visually, Afghanistan is associated almost wholly with the poppy, a potent symbol of the opium trade and the dark side of its history. Maybe the crocus is a better representative. It speaks of the beauty of a country made ugly by war and oppression. It is a tough little flower capable of looking after itself; but like its homeland, its three tiny fragile stamens are all too easily damaged.

South Africa's national anthem

Nkosi sikelel' iAfrika
(God bless Africa)
Maluphakanyisw' uphondo lwayo,
Yizwa imithandazo yethu,
Nkosi sikelela,
Thina lusapho lwayo.
Morena boloka setjhaba sa heso,
O fedise dintwa le matshwenyeho,
O se boloke o se boloke setjhaba sa heso,
Setjhaba sa South AfriKa, South Afrika.
Uit die blou van onse hemel,
Uit die diepte van ons see,
Oor ons ewige gebergtes,
Waar die kranse antwoord gee.
Sounds the call to come together,
And united we shall stand,
Let us live and strive for freedom,
In South Africa our land.

National Anthem of South Africa – Stellenbosch University Choir

3

On the campaign trail

Christian Aid has often referred to its 'prophetic voice'[1] and its readiness to 'speak truth to power'. It even ran training schools for young prophetic activists in the 2020s. The words conjure up images of Old Testament characters like Isaiah and Amos (reluctant as he was to be recruited), Nathan and Elijah and even Jesus, regarded by many as the last of the great prophets. They claimed the moral high ground, castigating rulers and priests, speaking up on behalf of the defenceless, often at considerable risk to themselves since the powerful and the public had their ways of 'shutting their mouths' when they didn't like what they heard. The imagery resonates well with supporters making connections between their Christian faith and their attempts to stand by the poorest.

It has to be said, however, that prophecy at this dangerous and audacious level has more often than not been acted out in Christian Aid's story overseas rather than in the UK. Admittedly on many occasions Christian Aid as an institution has been outspoken and severely criticised and wounded as a result, not to mention hounded in the courts. Attempts have been made to shut its mouth for being 'political' rather than 'charitable'. Revealing letters sent in the 1960s between Alan Brash, then Director of Christian Aid, and Richard Kirkley, then Director of Oxfam, and internally between Brash and Hugh Samson, responsible for Christian Aid's communications, show just how aware they were of the need to campaign and of the tensions that came with it. It did not always sit easily with fundraising, for example, and both supporters and the Charity Commission kept raising questions as to whether Christian Aid was a charitable or a political organisation.[2]

But generally speaking the prophets have been found elsewhere: among the landless and their leaders confronting the landowners, the likes of Oscar Romero, Steve Biko, Nelson Mandela and Chico Mendes, social movements determined to stand up to their oppressors, black and white people resisting apartheid, workers standing up for their rights, and forest dwellers obstructing the so-called 'developers' out to fell their trees, while Christian Aid has done its best to support them.

When it comes to 'tackling the root causes of poverty', another phrase constantly used by Christian Aid and certainly involving 'speaking truth to power', there is a much tighter connection between what is said and what is done, chiefly by way of its campaigns aimed at real and lasting change.

A very early example was the Freedom from Hunger campaign inaugurated by the UN in 1960 in response to growing public awareness of a worldwide scandal highlighted by mass starvation in Biafra. Many governments, international institutions and NGOs were swept up in a tide of public concern. In Britain, Janet Lacey from Christian Aid, along with Oxfam and War on Want, set up the British Freedom from Hunger Committee, while the government responded by setting up the Overseas Development Administration (ODA), later to become the DFID and later still, in September 2020, to be dissolved and its work absorbed into the Foreign, Commonwealth and Development Office (FCDO).

Action was very much in the form of funded projects that didn't stop at immediate relief, necessary as that always was, but tried to get at the causes of famine. The criteria for funding included paying careful attention to the situation on the ground since, although hunger was widespread, the reasons for it could differ from place to place. One size didn't fit all. Emphasis was placed on local knowledge and participation, a somewhat enlightened approach at the time, and on remedies – chiefly improved farming techniques – that were sustainable. The campaign went much further than just responding to emergencies, but not yet as far as questioning global economic and political structures and their capacity to create plenty and scarcity at the same time.

Financial issues

The questioning was soon to follow. Many of the issues had to do with finance and were taken up by Christian Aid, playing its part but never on its own, in campaigns on trade, taxation, World Bank and

International Monetary Fund policies and debt. Putting them briefly, world trading rules rarely went in favour of poorer countries. They supplied the raw materials the world needed but rarely profited from them as much as they should. They did not have the resources to process them themselves and so add to their value: a tin of pineapple is worth more than a fresh one. Adding value was left to the multinational companies well placed to buy at competitive prices in the South and then manufacture and market them in the North. 'Free' trade deals such as those between the EU and countries in the Caribbean, Asia and the Pacific, known as Economic Partnership Agreements (EPAs), were not mutually beneficial when import duties were lost and fragile businesses exposed to competition.

On tax, big businesses were accused of either avoiding (legal) or evading (illegal) them by creative accounting, underestimating their profits and hiding their money in low-tax havens. As a result, poorer countries were not receiving the revenues they were due and so had less to spend on health and education and general welfare. Things were not helped by the concessions they felt forced to make in order to attract business from outside, or at times by their own failures to avoid waste and corruption and by sheer bad management of the revenues they did receive.

The debt crisis going back to the 1970s, and still growing in 2025, only added to their troubles. Poorer countries were lent considerable sums of money for development or to deal with emergencies such as the outbreak of Ebola in Sierra Leone in 2014 or, more often, when large amounts of money were 'washing around' on the financial markets of the UK and the USA in urgent need of investment. They came to be known as 'irresponsible loans'. When the time came, the borrowers could not pay back what they owed. Loan sharks and 'vulture funds' moved in. They bought up the high-risk loans at cut prices and then insisted on repayment at the original rates with interest, so compounding the problem.

The WB and IMF did not help matters. Their Structural Adjustment Policies (SAPs) pursued in the 1980s and 1990s were designed to kick-start a country's way out of poverty and into growth and were made a condition of debt relief, either by rescheduling over longer periods or cancelling them in part or in whole. Vulnerable industries like farming had to be opened up to cheaper imported goods and the cold winds of world trade. The state and public services, with what ability they had to care for people, had to be shrunk with the job losses that went with it. The result was criticised for making matters worse rather than pulling countries out of trouble.

In short, the root cause of so much hardship was the global economic order. What then did Christian Aid do about it and what did it achieve?

In general and working with others, it carried out research to make sure it knew what it was talking about. It tried to understand how change happens[3] and act accordingly. It educated the public, including schoolchildren and the churches, allowing faith to illuminate the issues. It raised awareness through the media, often in highly eye-catching ways. It trained and mobilised supporters in their thousands to demonstrate and lobby policymakers, of which Jubilee 2000 (J2000) and Make Poverty History (MPH; see below) were outstanding examples. It stood in solidarity with comrades and networks all round the world. It increasingly understood that campaigns are obviously on behalf of the disadvantaged but that the disadvantaged are also agents in their own cause, acting for justice along with the rest, often at considerable cost, and educating the better-off in the process.

Trade

On trade, Christian Aid, Oxfam, the Overseas Development Institute and others published the Haslemere Declaration in 1968. It was put together by the Haslemere Group, which met in the small Surrey town of that name. It faded away a few years later but left a long-lasting legacy. The Group, which included members of Christian Aid's staff, pushed charities like Christian Aid to do more political campaigning. The Declaration had strong things to say about the realities of world trade, regarding them as fundamentally unfair. The General Agreement on Tariffs and Trade (GATT), later in 1995 to become the World Trade Organisation (WTO), was challenged to live up to its own rules laid down in 1947 calling for the abolition of tariffs and quotas. Poor countries should be allowed to sell their agricultural commodities freely in the rich ones and helped not only to grow coffee beans but industrialise and manufacture, say, instant coffee themselves and so compete on fairer terms.[4] The Declaration was firmly opposed to the UK joining the European Common Market, busy building protective walls around itself.

One way in which Christian Aid and Oxfam built on the work of the Haslemere Group was to set up the World Development Movement (WDM), becoming Global Justice Now in 2015, to educate and campaign on their behalf, free from the constraints of charity law. Another was to launch the *New Internationalist* magazine in 1973.

In 1992 came the Fairtrade Foundation. Its forerunner was Traidcraft, set up in 1979 by Richard Adams in Newcastle and Gateshead. It sold fairly traded goods and later a range of Christmas cards to raise money for Traidcraft, CAFOD, Christian Aid and the Scottish Catholic International Aid Fund (SCIAF.) One card, called 'African Nativity', featuring the Maasai people, substituted the camels with a giraffe, a warthog and an elephant. The sheep survived. By 2019 its revenues had risen to £8m but began to decline; sadly, it fell into administration in 2023. The challenge, however, was to shift sales from tables in churches to shelves in supermarkets. It led Traidcraft, CAFOD, Christian Aid, the Women's Institute and others to found the Fairtrade Foundation in 1992 to take up the challenge. Shoppers were encouraged to write on their till receipts ('Trade for change' vouchers) in support of fair trade and hand them in before leaving. They seemed to rather enjoy doing so. The Co-op was the first to respond by selling Cafédirect.

The Foundation's obvious public face, soon widely recognised, was its kitemark guaranteeing that retail products from wine and flowers to coffee and cocoa had been produced in line with internationally agreed standards such as fair pay and fair prices. Figures issued in 2020 indicated an income of £10m from licence fees, though some supermarkets have shown reluctance to pay for the careful monitoring that the licence helps to finance. The pioneering Foundation became one of over twenty-five similar organisations across the world.

Other issues lurked not far below unfair trade. The Rug Mark, founded in the early 1990s by Indian activists who linked up with groups in Germany and the UK, hit out against the use of child labour. The mark indicated a clean bill of health. Around the same time, Christian Aid along with the WCC, the Christian Conference of Asia and others, worked hard as members of ECPAT, originally meaning 'End Child Prostitution in Asia Tourism' and later 'Every Child Protected Against Trafficking', now a global network, with a UK branch established in 1994, committed to protecting children everywhere against abuse and trafficking. In 1998 the Global March against child labour crossed forty countries from the Philippines to Switzerland. It did much to bring pressure on governments to agree to the International Labour Organisation's Convention the next year, dealing with the worst of it.

Some years later, in 2000, Christian Aid and CAFOD were founding members of the Trade Justice Movement, which also grew into a worldwide coalition of up to sixty NGOs, trade unions, human rights campaigners and Fairtrade organisations providing information and expert analysis on trade issues. The Co-operative Movement joined in 2005. In 2003, Trade Justice organised a mass lobby of Parliament ahead of a WTO meeting, which it criticised for being more concerned to ensure that trade flowed freely than shaping it to raise living standards and improve lives. In 2005, along with Christian Aid and the Fairtrade Foundation, Trade Justice was a core member of the MPH campaign when thousands of Christian Aid supporters marched and confronted the G7 in Edinburgh, demanding once again meaningful action on trade, debt and aid.

An interesting feature of the trade campaigns was the games they used to educate and prepare schoolchildren, young people and adults for action. Andrew Croggon of CAFOD seems to have invented the first one. There were many versions: the Trading Game, the Paper Bag Game, the Chocolate Game, the Trainers Trading Game among them, all designed to show how unbalanced and unfair the 'game' was. Different teams round a room or church hall represented rich and poor countries and business interests trying to make a living by trading with each other. The raw material was often sheets of paper which could flood the market or be in short supply. The price varied, as did access to markets and opportunities to sell as groups closed in to protect themselves from competition. If the raw commodity could be 'manufactured' by cutting the paper into shapes, like a sports shoe for example, it increased in value, but not everyone had scissors or pencils. Participants learned what it felt like to be on the receiving end of unfair rules of the game with a biased referee and a far from level playing field. Sometimes tempers flared. Careful debriefing when the game was over clarified the lessons learned. On one occasion, during Christian Aid Week 1979, a version of the game – the Grain Drain – was played outside St Paul's Cathedral.

Tax

Perhaps the most eye-catching feature of a joint campaign on tax mounted by Christian Aid and Church Action on Poverty (CAP) was a red bus plastered with slogans, which toured UK cities for fifty-three days in 2012. It parked itself outside cathedrals and other prominent landmarks and attracted the attention of considerable numbers, from passers-by to bishops. They were invited inside to view an exhibition, or to chat outside if the bus was full, and learn at first-hand about yet another way in which the rich were benefiting at the expense of the poor: at first-hand because Savior Mwambwa was on board and spelling out the harm that tax dodgers had done to his home country of Zambia by not paying up. Christian Aid's Director at the time commented that some of those alleged dodgers were her friends!

Christian Aid and the Debt and Development Coalition Ireland (DDCI) launched their Trace the Tax campaign in 2010, which aimed at an end to secrecy and country-by-country reporting on tax havens. It criticised governments that allowed large international businesses and private entrepreneurs like Philip Green and his clothing retailers to avoid paying billions in tax. The Conservative MP Andrew Mitchell, supportive of Christian Aid in many ways, on this occasion accused it of 'political agitation' and not keeping to the business of a charity.

In addition to writing to all the FTSE 100 companies, the campaign set its sights on four groups: Vodafone, Unilever, TUI and Travel, and International Hotel Groups. They were challenged to be more transparent and to make sure their accountants followed suit. The campaign had what supporters liked to call two or three 'wins'. Vodafone accepted the challenge and opened up its books. A majority in Parliament had voted in favour of reform in 2008. The Big Four international accountancy firms included country-by-country reporting on investments as standard practice in 2010 and the government introduced legislation requiring the same.[5] In 2015 it agreed to publish regular reports of business activities in all British Overseas Territories, with legislation to come into effect in 2021.

Much of what needs to be said about tax campaigns can be found in 'Tax Justice Advocacy: A Toolkit for Civil Society', published by Christian Aid and the Centre for Research on Multinational Corporations (SOMO) in 2010. It was a collective effort headed up by Sally Golding working with a reference group from North and South and tested out in international workshops.

It remains a remarkable document of 130 pages and, as Golding herself commented, not to be read through at a stretch but for dipping in and out of for 'tips and tools' on how to develop an advocacy strategy on tax, or indeed on other issues as well. Sections deal with research, lobbying, communications, messaging and campaigning, with case studies to go with them. The section on developing a strategy helps with identifying issues and possible solutions: spotting stakeholders who can help achieve its goals, deciding on indicators of success, ensuring clear messages, and preparing both insider (negotiating with policymakers) and outsider (protesting) approaches.

While its own campaign seemed to falter around 2015 (see below), Christian Aid remained heavily involved in a range of less eye-catching but longer-lasting initiatives. In 2003 it became a founding member of the UK Tax Justice Network researching and briefing in support of advocacy. One of its particular concerns was the secrecy surrounding low-tax havens (countries with very low tax rates) where companies could register their HQs and their profits could be hidden away, estimated by the World Bank to be $13 trillion in 2012. The Network issued regular updates.

Sometimes the news was good. After a campaign in 2005 in Bolivia by civil society movements, for example, leading to reform, increased tax revenues led to a rise in spending on social services from $173m in 2002 to $1.57bn in 2007. All too often the news was bad. In 2007 billions of dollars of taxes were being lost worldwide. In 2010 the WB and IMF estimated the amounts lost were between $100bn and 200bn. In 2012 the Network reported that $660bn of taxes had been avoided by multinationals and $13 trillion deposited in tax havens. In its 'The State of Tax

Justice' report (2020), the Network reported that $427bn of potential revenues were being lost annually to tax abuse. In 2023 $4.8 trillion of tax was on course to being lost to tax havens.

The issues were clear, as they were from the beginning. Tax revenues, such as they were, had to be used for the common good. Their levels were too low, often to attract investment. All too often they were dodged and the takings secreted away in tax havens. A bright light needed to be shed on all of it.

Debt and Jubilee

While I was in office at Christian Aid, colleagues, keen as ever to tackle those 'underlying causes', presented me with a choice between two campaigns, both carefully researched and planned and more or less oven-ready. One was called 'Who Runs the World?' and focused on the structural adjustment policies of the WB and IMF. The other had to do with 'green' issues and the environment. Both highlighted dire consequences for poor countries.

I opted for 'Who Runs the World?' (though some work was done on 'trees'), most likely because I warmed to the challenge of raising awareness and concern about issues and institutions that were highly influential but little understood, and partly because 'green' issues seemed a rather easy wicket to play on at the time, about which most people would take little persuading. Hindsight would prove otherwise![6]

The campaign, followed by Change the Rules, was soon absorbed into Jubilee 2000 but it did provoke an Early Day Motion in Parliament on 19 July 1994, with ninety-eight signatories, including three Conservatives, calling for the 'replacement of structural adjustment policies with projects which meet the needs of the poor and promote sustainable, participatory and equitable development'. And the campaign did come up with some provocative posters about 'things looking up in the Third World', such as prices due to World Bank policies.

It also triggered a visit, at his request, from a WB official to Christian Aid's HQ. A small group of seasoned Christian Aid campaigners met with him. A note taken by one of them suggests that his account of things did not go down well and was criticised for being inaccurate and misleading:

a criticism which, in a moment of embarrassment, he appeared to partly accept. Another member of the group vividly remembers conducting the visitor out, still loudly bending his ear as they hastily made their way down the stairs, about how the WB should change its ways. Over the years Christian Aid has remained critical of the WB[7] but has also engaged with it, along with other NGOs, and had good working relations with many members of its staff.[8]

The J2000 debt campaign was launched in the Grand Committee room of the House of Commons on 13 October 1997: the Jubilee room itself turned out to be too small for the numbers wishing to attend on the day! Its origins go back to two visionaries: Bill Peters, a retired diplomat, and Martin Dent, a university lecturer at Keele with close links to Nigeria. The year of Jubilee is referred to in the Old Testament (Leviticus 25), when every fiftieth year slaves were freed and debts cancelled in an enlightened attempt to alleviate poverty, inequality and injustice. The two visionaries decided that the super-Jubilee year of 2000 was an opportunity not to be missed to bring the practice to life again on the same principles but in a very different world, freeing desperately poor countries and their peoples from slavery to debt. It was a vision that especially inspired the 'People of the Book': Jews, Christians and Muslims.

Christian Aid had begun talking about debt in 1989 when Paul Tyler, Head of Finance when not playing football, chaired a staff working group. In 1991 it sent egg-timers to all MPs with 'Time is running out' at one end and 'Cancel Third World debt' at the other. By 1997 it was high time to turn the vision of a Jubilee year into reality. Early steps were taken by Christian Aid in providing an infant Jubilee Debt Coalition with a small and inadequate shed on the roof of Inter-Church House, taken great care of by Tim Moulds, head of Christian Aid's area staff. Ann Pettifor was soon appointed Director and proved to be a brilliant and energetic leader. Ed Mayo of the New Economics Foundation became chair of its executive committee. No one expected it would grow as quickly as it did across the South, Europe and the USA, with thousands pursuing the same aims in their different ways.

The Coalition's challenge was to the IMF, held chiefly responsible for the debt crisis, the WB and their masters, the G8. The problem was the unpayable debts of poor countries built up as a result of financial practices already highlighted in previous campaigns such as structural adjustment policies, irresponsible lending and spending, unfair trading, and loss of revenue where taxes were avoided. The aim was to cancel the debts, especially those of the Heavily Indebted Poor Countries (HIPC).[9]

There were notable achievements along the way. Some cancellations began in 1996 but were limited due to IMF conditions, not easily met. More followed between 1999 and 2002. Since the millennium, $130bn worth has been cancelled.

One of the most striking events in all of Christian Aid's campaigning history was the never-to-be-forgotten demonstration in Birmingham on 16 May 1998, organised and led by J2000, of which Christian Aid was a leading member, with strong support from local staff like Christian Aid's Paul Place. The G8 were due to meet in Birmingham's International Convention Centre with many of its leaders lodging in the hotel next door and Bill Clinton spotted drinking a beer outside a pub by the canal. It was, however, as much 'The People's Summit' as the G8's as 70,000 people converged on the city from all over the UK (mainly from the north), from Europe, and from the South. They came on trains and buses, on bikes and rickshaws, on foot as pilgrims spreading the word on the way, and along the canals by barge and even a coracle. Christian Aid made sure that they also came from eight of the countries most in need of a Jubilee, namely Jamaica, Bolivia, Nicaragua, Bangladesh, Tanzania, Malawi, Mozambique and Ethiopia.

St Martin in the Bullring, Birmingham's parish church, was full all day with campaigners listening to a long list of speakers including trade union leaders, Daleep Mukarji, Christian Aid's newly installed Director, Johnny Hansen representing the Ghanaian J2000 campaign, and Clare Short, Minister of State for International Development. Outside, the G8 had swiftly decamped to Weston Park, well beyond the city walls, at least suggesting that, though they could avoid being surrounded by the crowds, they could not avoid the issue.

All was far from lost. Campaigners were determined to make their chain all around the city centre as a symbol not only of bondage and slavery but also of how joined-up hands and hearts can make a difference. Negotiating with the police, the ambulance service and the fire brigade was not easy, rightly concerned as they were about access in any emergency. They insisted that one major road should remain open, but when 3 p.m. came and time to join hands and keep silence, the police on duty quietly joined their hands with ours. The gap was closed and the chain was complete. Not long after, Tony Blair broke off from hosting the G8 summit and returned to Birmingham asking for a meeting. Three of us, led by Pettifor, talked with him for nearly an hour. I noticed a hole in his sock.[10]

No one imagined that after an exhilarating day the job would be done. MPH, a coalition of charities, NGOs, trade unions and more in which Christian Aid was heavily involved, took up the cause for a while. J2000 was a worldwide movement but in the UK MPH was strictly time-limited to 2005 to coincide with another G8 summit. It began on New Year's Day with references to it in an episode of *The Vicar of Dibley* on BBC television. Bob Geldof raised its profile round the world with another rousing Live-Aid style concert (called Live 8). Proposed TV adverts were judged by Ofcom to be too political.

In July the BBC estimated that 225,000 went to Edinburgh to challenge the G8, meeting at Gleneagles, to put an end to extreme poverty by taking meaningful action on debt, trade and aid. They wore white T-shirts and armbands marked MPH in black. They waved placards. One massive banner on Edinburgh Castle looked down over the city. They marched round and round in the scorching sun. There were bands, stalls and speeches. Kathy Galloway, heading up Christian Aid's work in Scotland at the time, was asked to represent the Scottish MPH coalition as a speaker. She found it 'exhilarating and terrifying' to step out onto the stage before people stretching in front of her 'as far as the eye could see'!

Many did it all again in Cologne the following year.

The verdict was mixed. Geldof gave the G8 10 out of 10 for aid and 8 out of 10 for debt. Less upbeat was the comment that 'the people have roared but the G8 have whispered'.[11] There was talk of re-creating MPH in 2013 when David Cameron, as British Prime Minister, was due to host the G8 summit, but little came of it.

J2000, however, never let the matter drop. There is a well-recognised fragility about campaigns. They can come and go, as did Christian Aid's on trade, tax, WB and IMF policies and debt. Its climate justice campaigning (see Chapter 13) may well prove otherwise. Campaigners can run out of steam or need a change. The world moves on, and the campaigning caravans and buses move along with it: many of the issues don't.

The Jubilee Debt Coalition, later to become Debt Justice, persevered. It continued to enjoy outstanding support from Gordon Brown, Chancellor of the Exchequer in Tony Blair's government and a staunch and effective ally from the start. A frail Muhammad Ali joined members of the Coalition one day at the memorial in Victoria Tower Gardens outside the House of Lords, commemorating the passing of the Slavery Abolition Act in 1833. (Afterwards, he performed his 'levitation' act for us!) Despite progress, countries were still being pushed into further debt. In 2000 the South was said to owe $2.5 trillion. Irresponsible lending continued through the financial crisis of 2008. In 2002 at the Lambeth Conference, World Bank President James Wolfensohn was enraged by a Christian Aid film on debt. In 2019 in Christian Aid Week, Debt Justice and Christian Aid announced a New International Debt Crisis. In 2022 they sent a petition to MPs protesting about Black Rock, an investment firm, and its refusal to reduce the interest rates on Zambia's debts or reschedule them. On the positive side, in 2010 Debt Justice successfully campaigned for a change in the law limiting the amount for which vulture funds could pursue the HIPC group in the courts.

Apartheid

Turning to a campaign of a very different kind, during the apartheid years South Africa's problems had little to do with its considerable debts since it was not a poor country. The focus instead was on a thoroughly racist regime and how to bring it to an end. During a state of emergency and long before that, the non-white population, mainly black people, suffered from dire poverty, low wages if any, forced removals from their lands, enforced separation, no votes, military rule, violent vigilantes in league with the security forces, censorship, high mortality rates, disappearances and hangings. Their community organisations and leaders were frequently banned, up to thirty at a time. Despite the oppression, they mounted non-violent consumer boycotts and defied the apartheid laws that banned black people from non-white areas except for work.

Steve Biko founded the Black Consciousness Movement. His killing in police custody on 12 September 1977 sent shock waves when announced to a Christian Aid staff conference. In 1985 a group of black theologians (unnamed) from Soweto issued the KAIROS document challenging the churches' response to apartheid and sparking furious debate around the world. Once again it was the oppressed themselves who spoke truth to power and paid the price.

There were long-standing connections between South Africa and Christian Aid, as there were between churches and trade unions. Christian Aid could count heroes of the struggle among its friends, such as Desmond Tutu, General Secretary of the South African Council of Churches (SACC) and later to become Archbishop of Cape Town; Beyers Naudé, a prominent but disaffected minister of the Dutch Reformed Church; and Frank Chikane who, after heading up the Institute for Contextual Theology, succeeded Beyers as General Secretary of the SACC. Joe Seremane was less well known. He served time on Robben Island, and his wife Esther, a social worker, was harassed by the Special Police. Joe was Director of the Justice and Reconciliation Department of the SACC, persuading young people to organise, be disciplined, and get skills and training.

Against this background and in light of British government policies, Christian Aid and the British Council of Churches organised a conference in London in February 1989, 'Britain and Southern Africa – The Way Forward', to focus attention on the suffering and oppression and the need for Britain to give clear support to those working for democratic change. Its Call to Action Against Apartheid looked to the UN to call for compulsory sanctions, and meanwhile for Britain and Commonwealth countries to impose a range of measures, including sanctions and clamping down on investments and loans, well within their power to do so.

The Southern Africa Coalition, born soon afterwards, brought together more than sixty organisations including churches, charities, NGOs, trade unions and local authorities with a long list of patrons. The Rt Revd Simon Barrington-Ward, then Bishop of Coventry, was its chair, and the General Secretary of the TUC was vice-chair. As Director of Christian Aid I chaired the executive committee, with Mike Terry of the Anti-Apartheid Movement as vice-chair. Mildred Neville, formerly Director of the Catholic Institute for International Relations (CIIR), was its remarkable coordinator. It was hosted by Inter-Church House in London.

The Coalition set out to mobilise public opinion. It educated and informed. On the ground Christian Aid's area staff worked hard to bring local churches on board. In February 1990 the Coalition organised a Southern Africa Week, culminating in a mass lobby of Parliament calling for a fundamental change of government policy towards South Africa by putting pressure on the regime, supporting and reinforcing existing sanctions and banning oil and arms sales. The government of the day, led by Margaret Thatcher, was not to be easily moved.

Meanwhile, economic pressures mounted on South Africa's government, which began to make promising noises. Cynics remarked that apartheid was becoming too expensive to maintain. Nelson Mandela was released from prison in February 1990 (ironically just before the lobby of Parliament in London in the same month!). The apartheid legislation was repealed in 1991. The first democratic elections were held in 1994 and Mandela became the country's President. Jenny Borden, one of Christian Aid's directors, happened to be in South Africa at the time of a service of thanksgiving organised by the SACC at the FNB Stadium in Soweto. She remembered Mandela thanking the churches (sadly not deserved by all of them) for their steadfastness in opposing apartheid, while Desmond Tutu danced in the aisles and a frail Trevor Huddleston confessed that his dream that he would not die before apartheid came to an end had come true!

Maggie Hamilton, with Christian Aid's support, created 'Counterpoint' (1993–2000), aimed at raising awareness of justice issues by collecting and singing grass-roots songs from across the world. She travelled widely, including in Africa, Asia, the Middle East and Latin America. One collection, from South Africa, *Sing Freedom!*, was published in 1993 by Christian Aid and Novello. In 1994 Maggie was invited to join the choir for that same service of thanksgiving. Looking across, she saw the organist playing from her song book.

Not everything changed. Inequality, injustice and violence persisted in South Africa even as political power shifted from white to black people.

Soon after the 1989 BCC conference, Christian Aid let loose one of its cleverest posters onto high street billboards. In effect it stated loud and clear that apartheid made people poor but went on to appeal for funds to help put an end to poverty! It was a notable example of navigating the well-known tensions between educators, campaigners and fundraisers. Campaigns and respectful pictures of strong people, however vulnerable, did not always tug sufficiently at heartstrings to raise money. On this occasion all involved seemed reasonably satisfied. The poster was also notable as an attempt, allusive as it was, to challenge government policies while remaining 'charitable'. The attempt did not entirely succeed when Christian Aid's chairman, Brian Young, discomforted but loyal to his wayward staff, its Treasurer, Geoffrey Smith, and its Director were cautioned at a hastily arranged meeting with the Charity Commission.[12]

4
Brazil

Folklore has it that when God created Brazil his angels remonstrated with him that no human beings should be so abundantly gifted. God replied, 'Just wait till you see the government I'm giving them!'

That's not the only contradiction which lies at the heart of Christian Aid's encounters with Brazil. On the one hand it could sometimes find a dynamic economy lifting millions out of poverty while acquiring the status of a middle-income country and becoming a leading member of BRICS (Brazil, Russia, India, China and South Africa).[1] On the other hand, it is a country as deeply divided by inequality as any other on earth, unaddressed by economic progress with a grim interdependency between the two.[2]

Those who suffer as a result include indigenous people, black people, women, quilombolas (descended from escaped slaves who had hidden in remote areas of the country), displaced and landless people, the urban poor and the LGBTQ+ community.

Social movements

Tackling chronic inequality requires serious social and political change. Always setting out to tackle 'root causes', it is no surprise that much of Christian Aid's work in Brazil from 1984 to 2020 was in solidarity with social movements out to do the same. They were not hard to find in a vibrant civil society. Notable among them were the Landless Workers' Movement (MST), involving hundreds of thousands of families fighting to secure their right to land where 3% of the population owned two-thirds of it, the Sempreviva Feminist Organisation (SFO), and the Movement of People affected by Dams (MAB).

Working closely with them was a progressive ecumenical movement. The National Council of Christian Churches of Brazil (CONIC) organised ecumenical missions to support struggling communities. The Anglican Church worked with women against violence and along with Christian Aid belonged to an ecumenical forum later to become ACT Alliance Brazil which Christian Aid joined officially in 2017. Sadly, the Roman Catholic Church, evidently turning its back on its earlier support for the liberation movements, and some Pentecostal groups, played a decisive role in shifting policies pursued under Bolsonaro in a conservative direction.

Funding social movements was not easy. Often made up of local groups dispersed in remote areas over Latin America's largest country and organised in a communitarian rather than hierarchical fashion ('bottom-up'), they lacked the ability to meet the requirements of funders in terms of accounting and reporting procedures. An attempt to address the issue came with Christian Aid's Power to the People project, supported by the Institute for Socio-Economic Studies (INESC) and other NGOs and by DFID from 2008 to 2013,[3] aimed at strengthening the voice of excluded communities and making more accountable governance work for them. It led to a national consultation in 2014 when over 7 million voted for reform. One aspect of Christian Aid's support provided funding, mainly from supporters rather than institutions, which could be used more flexibly for research and training: 'non-designated', it might be called, without too many strings attached, an approach reflected elsewhere as Christian Aid learned what partnership ought to mean.

A good example of this approach was a campaign supported by Christian Aid to make sure that the quilombolas, among the poorest in Brazil, remained exempt from rural land taxes amounting to £4m per year. The threat arose when land previously regarded as 'unproductive' was upgraded to become 'titled' and therefore usable and taxable. Challenging it in the courts cost money. It could not come from official donors but it could and did come from the churches, especially in Wales and Scotland. Helped by a Brazilian pro bono law firm and even the Public Prosecutions Department, the social movements chalked up a success. The exemption came into play in 2014 and was later reinforced in the courts.

Besides funds, Christian Aid helped the social movements create international links both for funding purposes and to add strength to their cause. A meeting with counterparts in Bolivia, Mozambique and the Philippines in 2000, for example, produced a joint reaction to current World Bank policies on agrarian reform. Another example brought InspirAction Spain on to the scene, initially to raise funds and later turning to advocacy. It was set up by Christian Aid in 2008 and closed in 2020.[4] Paul Spray represented Christian Aid on its board. Not 'rain' but Christian Aid in Spain! The timing of 2008, in the midst of a global financial crash, was terrible. It never covered its costs. Meanwhile in Brazil, Jair Bolsonaro, President from 2019 to 2023, was giving the green light to huge engineering projects affecting thousands of people and their livelihoods, without any consultation or regard for the local consequences. It emerged that a major shareholder in one construction company was Spanish. InspirAction Spain put in an information request. In the light of it, pressure was brought to bear on the company and at least one project was abandoned.

Among these threats to people and their habitats, two issues stand out: mining and deforestation (450 million trees were cut down in 2010–11). MAB was more easily associated with the first issue but many organisations with overlapping agendas worked closely together along with the churches and Christian Aid.

Mining and dams

The world is hungry for minerals, some of which, ironically, are needed to make the clean energy technology that may ease the climate crisis. Brazil has plenty of them, such as bauxite, and successive governments, along with international investors, have been keen to make money out of them. Mining, however, has profound effects on the communities living nearby and on their environs, whether in the Amazon delta or elsewhere. Like the heaps that once loomed over the pitheads of England's coal mines, looming, earth-filled dams called 'tailings dams' hold back huge amounts of toxic waste from the mineral mines of Brazil – and dams can collapse.

The best-known example is the Brumadinho dam, which collapsed in January 2019. Two hundred and seventy people were killed and tons of toxic waste were unleashed into the Paraopeba and Doce river valleys in the south-east state of Minas Gerais. In its wake came pollution, environmental damage, dead fish and threats to the ways of life of over 100,000 people. When men were brought in to carry out repairs, they violated local women. Up to forty other dams were thought to be vulnerable at the time, mainly in the Amazon. Christian Aid worked with ACT Alliance and MAB to support 3,500 affected families.

Later it helped MAB mobilise people to demand greater regulation of the mining industry. It produced a detailed report on Brumadinho, pressing for mining companies like Vale do Rio Doce, responsible for the damage done, to be prosecuted and pay compensation, which for years after, according to Christian Aid staff, was not sufficiently forthcoming.

Rubber tappers

The demand for rubber contributed both to Brazil's economic prosperity and inequality. Trade prospered for one thing, because cars needed tyres! It declined for a while when Ceylon, as it was then, learned how to produce it more cheaply. It prospered again when meeting the demands of war.

Through the economic ups and downs, rubber tappers in the Amazon worked for little or no returns, following their designated paths through the rainforest twice a day, bleeding the trees, catching the oozing sap in Brazil nutshells and collecting it later in the evening. Their returns were small partly because they had no choice but to accept the low prices offered by the traders. Things improved when Christian Aid supporters in Scotland funded the purchase of donkeys to take their wares to market themselves and bargain for a better deal.

Rubber tappers faced continual threats from ranchers, backed by government and large-scale agribusiness, intent on buying the land and clearing it, slashing and burning to make way for cattle pasture. When the trees went, so did the tappers' meagre livelihoods. In response, they organised themselves into unions. They resisted deforestation by literally standing in front of tractors and chainsaws to bar their way, a technique known as 'empate' or 'stand-off'. At the same time, with the support of the Massachusetts Institute of Technology's (MIT) outreach in Brazil, they fought successfully for the establishment of reserves where the forest could be managed and rubber tappers earn a living in a sustainable way.

In 2019 the Comissão Pró-Índio (CPI-SP), supported by Christian Aid, mounted a programme called Forest Custodians, aimed at protecting 35,000 square miles of forest and 28,000 residents from land-grabbing. It encouraged local communities to monitor illegal mining activities, logging and large infrastructure projects such as roads that opened up the forest to even more damage, and then lobby for their rights. Meanwhile in the UK, as wildfires raged in Brazil, Christian Aid lobbied the government to insist on measures to safeguard the rights of communities and the environment in trade and investment negotiations.

Unsurprisingly, in Brazil as elsewhere, the struggle was not without cost. Many died or were badly injured. In March 2019 Dilma Silva Ferreira (aged 48), coordinator for MAB in the region of the huge Tucuruí hydroelectric dam, was murdered together with her husband and a friend; and they were by no means the first or the last.

Chico Mendes was born in the Amazon and grew up as a rubber tapper. His father, along with thousands from the most deprived areas of Brazil, was deported there to boost the rubber trade. Chico was a devout Catholic, inspired by Liberation Theology. In the early 1970s he helped to organise the Xapuri Rural Workers Union and later became its President as well as national spokesperson for the rubber tappers. He won an international reputation for his environmental work, persuading the Inter-American Development Bank and the WB to endorse the idea of forest reserves and bring pressure to bear on the Brazilian government, which created the first of them in 1988.

Because Christian Aid was closely involved with the work of the Landless Workers' Movement (MST) and especially with the cause of the rubber tappers in Xapuri, I went to visit Chico Mendes in early December 1988. I walked with the rubber tappers through the forest. I watched them at work. I went with Chico to a Bible study group, or base community, where they sat in a circle, read out Bible passages and argued energetically about joining up faith and politics in the tradition of Liberation Theology. He pointed out the ranchers with their guns. He was well aware that he was a marked man needing police protection. He invited me to his modest home to share a meal with his wife and three young children. Two weeks after I bade him a fond farewell, he was shot dead by a rancher while his two guards played dominoes. I shall not forget his heroism, nor the defiant words of his friends: 'If Chico dies, a thousand Chicos will rise up and take his place!' Brazil remains one of the most deadly places in the world for environmental defenders.

In 1997 and for years after, Christian Aid's budget for Brazil was one of the largest of any country programme. By the early 2000s many donors and INGOs were leaving the country as it seemed to prosper under a progressive government. Christian Aid withdrew from Brazil in 2020 'in order to be more focused and go more deeply' in its work; though, realistically, it was mainly due to a drastic fall in income. It maintained links through a regional office in Managua. The issues it tried to address in the company of Brazil's social movements and ecumenically minded churches still remained. It didn't forget them. In 2022 it co-authored the report 'Profit before people and planet', highlighting the tax policies that enabled international mining companies to transfer wealth out of Brazil rather than a fair proportion of it going to mitigate the damage done to people and trees and to enhance their lives.

In 2024 the newly installed chair of Christian Aid, Sarah Mullally, Bishop of London, visited Brazil to mark the fortieth anniversary of the ordination of women in the Anglican Church. She was struck by the number of conversations she had about Christian Aid and its work: on women's rights and climate change for example, going back for decades.

Momento novo – 'A new moment'

Today God calls us to a new moment,
To walk with all people here together;
This is the time to transform what no longer works,
And no one can do it alone!

Chorus
So come along!
Enter the circle with everyone else!
You are so very important!
So come along!
Enter the circle with everyone else!
You are so very important! Come!

The power that makes life spring forth today,
Is living right here within this body;
Inviting all of us now to share in this work,
Of loving and joyous new song!

Chorus

Brazilian words by Ernesto B. Cardoso, Paulo Roberto, Déa Affini, Eder Soares, Tércio Junger, Darlene; English version by Sonya Ingwersen with adaptations by Maggie Hamilton

5

Christian identity, faith and theology … we believe in life before death

'We believe in life before death' was generally hailed as a brilliant strapline, appealing as much to secularists as to Christians. It was coined by Christian Aid's communications team in the late 1980s and was still on display outside Christian Aid's London office in 2024, before being temporarily replaced with a call for a ceasefire in Gaza on a day when the milestone of 40,000 Palestinian deaths in the conflict with Israel was reached. The strapline however had about it a certain ambivalence towards Christian Aid's 'Christian' identity, affirming faith but shifting the emphasis.

On the face of it, Christian Aid was upfront about its Christian identity from the start. CAFOD, Tearfund and World Vision were just as serious about their faith and made no attempt to hide it, but it was not quite so blatantly obvious to the general public. When it came to Christian Aid, no one could miss it and in the UK, where it all began, there was no reason why anyone should. In the 1940s, churches were well attended. About a third of children still went to Sunday school. Church leaders like William Temple were respected by the public at large. Free Church preachers like the socialist Donald Soper attracted large congregations. Britain was assumed to be a Christian country and caring for the poor, however misguidedly at times, was an obvious expression of its faith. No one would think twice about calling the infant organisation 'Christian': no need to be 'out and proud'![1]

Only as time went on did questions begin to be asked. Some were about charities in general, their overheads and whether they could be trusted to make sure the money got to where it was needed. Others, as with Christian Aid, related to Christian identity. They sprang up for a number of reasons. The Second World War had broken a number of social moulds. Churchgoing was in decline. Religion and its followers were being put on the back foot as secularisation began to bite inside and outside the churches, provoking books such as John Robinson's *Honest to God*.[2] Abortion and homosexuality were legalised, censorship was largely abolished, divorce made easier, cinemas and shops opened up on Sundays – all moves that the churches were perceived to resist, swimming against the tide. Opportunities to travel and immigration opened eyes to difference and diversity. Other faith traditions, once exotic and largely unknown, became the stories by which neighbours lived in an increasingly multifaith society: Muslims, Hindus, Sikhs and Buddhists among them.

At least one question about Christian Aid was easy to answer even if it did not go away: do you only help Christians?

The first visit I made abroad as Director involved a five-hour river crossing over a vast stretch of swirling water in a top-heavy ferry boat covered in people from prow to stern, only to arrive a mile away as the crow flies from where we started, to be greeted by the Muslim friends we were working with in Bangladesh. It was there I learned to eat rice with my fingers and sleep outdoors on a wooden pallet, before visiting the next morning a flourishing local industry that we had helped them set up. For the record, church partners, though prominent, have not always been in the majority: 50% around the world in the early 2000s and only 25% in 2024, the rest coming from organisations and communities practising other religions and none but, like Christian Aid itself, all committed to standing with the poor and vulnerable irrespective of their creed.

Far from being exclusive, Christian Aid would say that being a Christian movement means exactly the opposite. As it once put it, 'All shall be included in the feast of life.'[3]

Missionaries

The question about being missionaries was trickier. Some Christian agencies, Tearfund for example, equally dedicated to doing development well, were content for a while to be labelled in that way. Christian Aid was definitely not, despite its roots and connections. As a child of the ecumenical movement it partly owed its existence to missionaries eager to cooperate for a greater good. One of its early and senior members of staff, Carlisle Patterson, had been a missionary. Dame Diana Reader Harris once chaired the board of Christian Aid and also that of the Church Mission Society (CMS). Missionaries sat alongside Christian Aid at roundtables organised by the WCC, in Sudan for example where 'mission' and how to fund it could be on the agenda as well as 'development'. Janet Lacey described missionaries as 'the pioneers of service agencies' in her book *A Cup of Water*.[4] One supporter confessed to being inspired by Christian Aid to become a missionary carrying, he hoped, some kind of good news for the poor!

Nevertheless, from the mid-twentieth century there was growing evidence of the general decline of the missionary movement. The headquarters of some in Partnership House, virtually next door to Christian Aid's office in London, began to empty out. Many missionary societies started to forefront other work, such as their long-standing medical, educational, even development programmes. Spreading the good news of the gospel and living the reality of God's love were less closely tied to the need for conversions. Despite the changes, missionary societies lost support and found it increasingly difficult to survive.

Some of the reasons can be found in the social changes already referred to. Growing familiarity with other religious traditions, for example, raised questions about Christianity's supremacy and with it a reluctance to dismiss them as inferior and strangers to the truth. All religions, for all their deep spirituality, were seen to have their human side and the limitations and fault lines that go with it. Given this more level playing field, attempts to 'convert' seemed inappropriate in contrast to friendly invitations, critical engagement and a willingness to be interested in and learn from one another. So Christian Aid, from the outset, firmly declined to be a missionary agency in the sense of trying to convert people to Christianity.

Christian Aid's reluctance, not to say refusal, to support the building or repair of churches reflected its nervousness about being suspected of having missionary or proselytising motives. It overlooked, however, what the missionaries and certainly the debates about 'holism' within the WCC circles understood, namely that human well-being amounts to more than bread on the table, good health and education. It includes the psychological (starkly illustrated by the traumas following the Rwanda genocide) and the spiritual, along with opportunities to go to church, sing and pray and foster community.

Colonialism

Behind the growing wariness of missionary work, however, lurked another big agenda. If Christian Aid could distance itself from proselytism, it could not do so from colonialism. Missionaries, many of whom I knew and admired as a boy when they came to stay on furlough, could be great characters. At one point I was accepted to work with them overseas. The ones I met had good intentions. They were true to their faith and Christ's command to go into all the world and make disciples (Mark 16:15f.). They made sacrifices – as did their children! They cared for the poor. They ran schools and cared for the sick. If they were part of something darker, they were no more to blame than the rest.

Some claim that colonialism did some good things and that criticism of it might need to be more nuanced. Others couldn't disagree more and have hardly a good word to say for it. Either way, any account has to remain strident about the plundering of resources, the disrespect for people and their cultures, the enrichment of the few by the exploitation of the many, the racism, oppression both political and economic and, maybe above all, the slavery that went with it. In all of this the churches and their envoys were at best complicit and at worst active beneficiaries, despite a few prophetic voices.

With the demise of Christian missionary societies came the rise of Christian development agencies like Christian Aid and the transfer of financial support from one to the other; but if there was change there was also continuity. Under the guise of international development, wealthier nations, their governments, international banks and NGOs could still impose their political, economic and trading structures on poorer countries, serving their own interests while endangering fragile social and market systems, for example, along with the natural environment, and still denying millions their right to flourish. There remained the need for self-awareness and guarding against colonial attitudes of superiority, condescension as to who knows best, patronising talk of mutuality, in-house racism and disrespect, especially when the ability to be of help and 'give' aid was largely due to the wealth gained from old colonial exploits and to the neocolonialism that followed.[5]

Oxfam with hymns

Despite its Christian identity and its desire at times to be 'distinctive', it hardly needs pointing out that when the chips were down there was little difference in practice between Christian Aid and development NGOs like Oxfam and Save the Children with no overt religious associations even though founded and supported by many Christians, Quakers and Anglicans among them. The jibe: 'you're only Oxfam with hymns', had more than a grain of truth in it. The aims were the same, the values were the same, the analyses were the same and so were their ways of tackling the vulnerability of so many by way of emergency relief, long-term development projects, investment and campaigning for structural change. Even if Christian Aid had a different attitude to ex-pats doing hands-on development, the difference was not always as clear-cut as some imagined.

The similarities were not surprising, especially when it came to the practical questions of the how-to-do-it variety. Whatever faith has to contribute, such as broad moral principles, it cannot tell you how to answer most of them. 'Implementation' is not its forte. It may believe that agriculturalists should be able to improve their crops, but it cannot tell you how. It may believe that decent medical care should be available to everyone but it cannot tell you how to treat disease, rid the world of malaria or set up and run a hospital. It may believe that the current economic system should be radically overhauled in favour of equality and fair returns but it cannot tell you what an alternative would look like or how to make it work. It may insist that you love your neighbours but it cannot tell you how to act out of love in their best interests. This is where there is no such thing as 'Christian development' and believers and theologians have to give way to wise people on the ground (who may of course be people of faith) and professionals such as agriculturalists, medics, economists, trauma counsellors and sociologists.

This limit to what faith can do is not a failure on its part. If anything, it is an advantage since it enables Christian Aid and Christians in general to find common ground and cooperate with others, Christian or otherwise.

If then a Christian identity does not mean that Christian Aid exists only for Christians, or that it is an undercover missionary society, or completely set apart from other NGOs, what does it mean? Put simply, it means that it is a highly active arm of Christian churches with a faith that they wish to be true to in solidarity with poor and marginalised peoples.

Christian Aid is not a stand-alone organisation even though legally a charity in its own right since September 1990. It is the official agency of forty-one Christian churches in the UK. It was created by many of them. It acts on their behalf and is finally accountable to them. Therein lies what has been called its 'legitimacy', underscored by the numerous church bodies it works with overseas.

Out of the forty-one sponsoring churches, the Church of England has been the most prominent. Working closely with Christian Aid was not always straightforward, and in that it was not alone. It sometimes struggled, for example, with the competing claims of Christian Aid on the one hand and the worldwide development work of its own Anglican Communion on the other. Again Christian Aid's perceived stance when so-called culture wars caused problems for many churches gave rise to suspicion and hostility among Anglican churches in Africa and also among conservative evangelicals in the UK. Senior figures in Christian Aid, Rowan Williams as Chair of the Board among them, did their best to steer a delicate path between uncompromising support for LGBTQ+ rights in the public or civic realm, as a matter of justice and human rights, and pressurising churches about their own internal teaching and policies; and when it came to women's issues, between being clear about their reproductive rights and being seen as advocates of abortion. Not everyone was satisfied, including members of staff, some of whom believed Christian Aid had compromised and not gone far enough, others that it had gone too far!

Christian Aid was operational in the Republic of Ireland many years before Margaret Boden (CEO of Christian Aid Ireland from 1998 to 2012) established an office in Dublin in the late 1970s. In 2007, Christian Aid Ireland became a separate organisation responsible for work across the whole of the island of Ireland while retaining strong links with Christian Aid, sharing board members and remaining along with Christian Aid under the umbrella of Churches Together in Britain and Ireland (CTBI).

Not everyone has been entirely happy with these close ties with the churches, including at times members of Christian Aid staff, many of them not practising Christians. Some have felt there were more efficient ways of getting things done than being over-committed to working with churches at home and abroad. Some were ready to sign up to what might be called Christian values such as 'inclusiveness' but distanced themselves from the Church's institutions and churchgoing in line with the majority of their contemporaries. That cannot, however, change the plain fact of what Christian Aid 'is', for good or ill, and mostly let it be said for good, since another plain fact is that when it comes to raising huge sums of money, turning out in Christian Aid Week, marching and waving banners for justice and writing and signing letters to policy-makers, it is largely churchgoers who turn up. Where there are the inevitable weaknesses and failings, of Councils of Churches and their development arms, for example, part of Christian Aid's remit is to help put things right and bring the churches up to scratch, so realising the potential of a vast international network.

One person was even more unhappy, however, with what he could see as a trend. Charles Elliott, writing soon after his time as Christian Aid's Director, noted a certain restlessness with the churches and ecumenical loyalties, and a preference for values rather than any serious theological grounding of Christian Aid's work. Above all he bemoaned the cutting of ties with the missionaries and their faith, leaving Christian Aid without any serious Christian critique of its development work and exposed to the secular ideology of 'modernisation' (see Chapter 11) whereby the underdeveloped are helped to become 'like us'.[6] Elliott was far from a proselytiser and was well respected in development circles but insisted that something far deeper and more spiritual was required if the 'powers of this world' were to be redeemed.

Elliott wrote against a background story going back to the 1960s and early 1970s, full of voices increasingly critical of overbearing approaches to development, charitable rather than political: voices exemplified by the Roman Catholic Populorum Progressio encyclical of 1967, the growing impact of Liberation Theology (SCM published Gustavo Gutiérrez's *A Theology of Liberation* in 1974) and, in the UK, books such as *Unyoung Uncoloured Unpoor* (1969) and *Include Me Out* (1970), both by Colin Morris and published by the Epworth Press. Christian Aid took much of this on board, committed as it was to genuine partnerships and structural change.

Elliott, however, wanted to take matters even further. He gave guidance as to what that would mean and some practical examples, such as the American Witnesses for Peace. In Nicaragua the so-called Contras, backed by the USA, were fighting against the Sandinistas; one aspect of the McCarthy-like witch-hunt against Communism. World Vision, now a much-changed organisation working with Christian Aid, was suspected at the time, by Christian Aid and others, of being on the wrong side of history. On the other hand, the American Witnesses for Peace confronted the Contras inside Nicaragua at risk to themselves, not in a spirit of anger and condemnation but raising questions about the demonic systems at work at an even deeper level than the often referred to 'underlying causes' and the harm they do, exposing them to the light of Christ and working for total transformation. Elliott was well aware of the difficulty of identifying any positive outcomes.[7]

A faith to live by

Christians and churches nevertheless do have a faith and so apparently does Christian Aid. Throughout its history, on countless occasions, credal-like statements keep cropping up together with firm reassurances that Christian Aid not only has a faith but lives by it.[8]

You catch glimpses of this 'creed' in its many documents and publications and on websites.

We believe, Christian Aid confesses, that God is love, God is with us, everyone is made in the image of God, equal in God's sight, having inherent worth. We believe that creation is good and we believe in sharing its resources with equity. We believe in the priority of the poor, that God keeps promises and that the world can be transformed. No one should live in poverty, which can be brought to an end. We believe in fullness of life for all. We believe in values such as justice, dignity, respect, inclusiveness and equality. 'We believe in life before death.' Rowan Williams saw Amanda Khozi Mukwashi, Christian Aid's one-time Director, as a living testimony to Christian Aid's faith, which for her leaned heavily on Christ as a disrupter challenging the status quo.

Behind any such 'creed' however lies a splendid variety, growing as time went on, of Christian traditions: Nonconformist, Anglican, black-majority, Pentecostal, liberal and evangelical among them, healthy but not without its tensions or always easy to manage.

At least one attempt has been made to try to draw things together. 'Theology and International Development', issued by Christian Aid in 2010, was probably the most extended and ambitious piece of theological writing in its history. Paula Clifford, Christian Aid's theological adviser at the time, in consultation with the global North but not at that stage with the South, set out to chart a new direction by gathering up the charity's past theological thinking, some of which she described as 'flimsy', into an overarching and distinctive theology of development. She referred to Liberation Theology and Contextual Theology as 'viable alternatives' but, much influenced by Karl Barth, opted for what she called a 'Relational Theology'.[9] In short, it describes God's inherent nature as 'relational', demonstrated in the inner life of the Trinity and in God's relations with creation and, above all, in 'indestructible' relations with human beings made in the divine image. Where such relationships are broken, as they are between us and God and with one another, they need to be restored. No doubt reflecting contemporary discussions about theories of development, Clifford argues that respect for human rights is an integral part of what she means by a restored relationship,[10] as is love for God and one another. Even more so, however, is justice, to such an extent that 'brokenness' becomes virtually synonymous with 'injustice', where to be broken is to be unjust and to be unjust is to be broken – and 'unrelated'.

The next question was how to apply or implement this theology or any other in practice? What are the links between them? Again, garnering what Christian Aid has said over the years, it has had plenty of answers. Theology justifies what we do, it inspires us, supports us, motivates us, disturbs us, underpins and dictates all our work. A new policy framework called 'Vision 2020' was described as 'stemming from core theological beliefs'. To use Clifford's words, Christian Aid's actions are 'rooted' in and grow out of its Relational Theology. If just relationships matter that much to God, then they must matter to us. That word 'relational' gets well used by Christian Aid after that, though there is little reference to it in 'Partnership for Change', a major policy document that followed in 2012, and no reference at all in 'Standing Together', setting out Christian Aid's strategy for 2019–26.

In 2012, Clifford followed up 'Theology and International Development', which she always described as a work in progress, with 'Theology from the Global South'. In it she recognised that up to then Christian Aid's work had been underpinned by a Relational Theology formulated in the global North, now to be developed by reflections from theologians in the South but set within this relational framework. It is full of examples of doing theology around a whole range of issues: gender violence, HIV and AIDS, power, inequality and sustainability, to name but a few. Developing a Relational Theology seems to be by extending relational thinking into these different contexts in conversation with the South. It is not altogether clear as to how open those discussions were to a different approach altogether, or whether Relational Theology as a given 'framework' was a bit of a theological straightjacket into which the South was invited to fit after making any necessary alterations. What is clear is that the issue is not whether working on, say, the issue of power is relational and involves relationships, since it inevitably does, but what sort of relationships they need to be.

In 2017 Catherine Loy re-examined the role of theology in the work of Christian Aid. In her book *Development Beyond the Secular*,[11] she paid tribute to Rowan Williams, probably the most qualified and respected theologian that Christian Aid has managed to catch in its net. He took on the job of chairing the board, so he said, to prove he still had a moral compass after being Archbishop of Canterbury! He enriched Christian Aid with what Loy called his many creative explorations into faith and development from a theological and a spiritual (not the same) perspective. He took relationships seriously, nuancing the idea in terms of our respect for one another and, with it, our mutual giving and receiving, growing together in dignity. He wrote with his poetic touch about a 'fuller humanity as being Christlike, self-emptying only to be filled with the energy of gift and being fully alive, a humanity in which everybody's poverty and need ... of one another is recognised'. On a quite different subject, reflecting on Romans 8 as climate change rose up Christian Aid's agenda, he once commented on our failure to think of our world as in relation to God and not just as 'a mega-warehouse of stuff to be used for our convenience'.[12]

When interviewing staff, Loy found evidence of a disconnect between theology and practice and, despite references to Clifford's Relational Theology in plans and reports,[13] real difficulty in applying it. The 'how' question remained unanswered.

Loy's answer was to go back to basics and suggest a different theology, which, following Edward Schillebeeckx, she called 'Christology from below', focused on the humanity of Jesus. In effect it looked for guidance and inspiration to the stories in the Synoptic Gospels about the life and teaching of Jesus. Here could be heard the words of the Magnificat (Luke 1) and the Sermon at Nazareth (Luke 4), raising up the poor and putting them first. Here was the prophet and scourge of the religious and political establishments. Here was the charismatic healer. Here was a God-given hero firmly on the side of the poor with everything stacked against them, promising reversals of power and fundamental social change. Here was the forgiving, inclusive Son of God reaching out to the stranger, the despised, the enemy, the outsider and the disliked. Here were patterns of relationship lived out in the real world, able to critique and light up present practice. Here was the willingness to sacrifice everything for the sake of a new world and the hope it could be achieved. Building on this theology, Loy arrives rather curiously at a similar-sounding conclusion to Clifford, with an extended discussion of Partnership but now inspired by the radical actions of Jesus rather than a Relational Theology.

In many respects her critique reflected already familiar ecumenical discussions about resource sharing. They had much to say about power, not only challenging its unjust structures but fostering partnerships where distorting imbalances are recognised, not least by Christian Aid speaking truth to itself, and power is exercised not to control but to serve. Again referring to Williams, Loy highlights the mutuality of giving and receiving where the giving is not all on one side and receiving on the other, but all have something to offer, whether money or experience or spirituality, and something to receive, so enhancing rather than diminishing each other's lives. Both Loy and Williams emphasise the fundamental need for trust, more evident in how the sponsoring churches trust Christian Aid than in Christian Aid's reluctance at times to stand by poor churches overseas judged to be too weak to contribute to development in an efficient way.

'Response to Catherine', an internal paper with no indication of date (presumably around 2017) or authorship, appears to have been a staff response to Loy. It restates the charges: that Christian Aid had failed to articulate a theology that resonated with staff or supporters or the South; that staff were motivated by other theologies; and that Christian Aid did not talk about a Christological theology where development work is inspired and shaped by the life and ministry of Jesus. In their response the writers pointed out that Loy only dealt with a snapshot in time of Christian Aid's theological work, quoting 2014 as an example when it produced theological reflections on gender, climate change and tax. There was no mention by Loy of, for example, the 1987 manifesto 'To Strengthen the Poor' with, in their judgement, its clear, theologically informed emphasis on the imbalance of power. The response, however, tended to miss the main point that what was needed was not a theology for this and that, or a systematic theology, but a theology that 'resonated' or 'worked' for those encouraged to 'use' it.

If the disconnect between theology and practice in Christian Aid can, according to Loy, be considerably eased by paying attention to the Gospels in contrast to a more conceptual approach like that of Relational Theology, it can also be eased by a different approach to 'how' we move from faith to practice. It is often referred to as 'praxis', or 'theological reflection on practice', or the 'pastoral cycle', or 'participatory reflection' as Loy calls it. It is demonstrated in some Christian Aid documents, especially those more obviously influenced by theological voices from the South.[14] It has a home in Contextual Theology, which starts by taking very seriously the context in which the thinking and doing take place, acknowledging that it will have a distinctive effect on the outcome.

Liberation Theology has a similar commitment to taking the social reality seriously along with intensive interrogations of Scripture as practised in the base communities of Latin America.

The image of 'how' you get from theology to practice is no longer one of attempts to apply a preconceived, all-embracing theological system to what we intend to do by some sort of deductive process spelling out its implications. Instead, practice is there from the start. 'Doing theology' begins by looking at what we are doing now and the context in which we are doing it as carefully and critically as we can (analysis?) and then moves on to draw on insights and experiences coming from many directions, some secular, many professional, but unavoidably for people of faith coming from what their fellow believers have said and done from biblical times through years of traditions and pilgrimages across the world, until today. There are no rights and wrongs about the outcome, only what we seriously believe for the time being, in the light of listening and thinking carefully together, to be a better and more faith-full way forward until there comes the need to think again. It's like sitting in a circle and going through a cycle.

The lengthy statement (referred to above) called 'To Strengthen the Poor', issued by the British Council of Churches and the board of Christian Aid in 1987, was overlooked by Clifford and Loy but, on reading it, seems to have stood the test of time quite well. It spoke clearly about the close relationship between power, injustice and poverty, and recognised the need for Christian Aid to test everything it did by asking whether or not it contributed to empowering often powerless people to stand up for themselves. The document, part of a journey exploring Christian Aid's identity, had a strong whiff of theological realism about it. It did not, however, look for a systematic theological framework. Instead, it spoke about repeated cycles of reflection on action which questioned what was being done, tried to understand the context of it, drew on relevant expertise, gathered and pondered the insights of faiths and other wise traditions, trying to find out of it all a well-informed consensus about the next steps and faithfully carrying them out until, once again, searching questions arise and the cycle needs to turn again. Theology does not have to be connected to that because it is part of it.

Counting the cost

A Christology from below, or taking our cue from the hero of the Gospels, while helping us to find a theology that 'works', also confronts us with some daunting challenges. One has to do with those risks associated with confronting the powers that be, risks that Jesus was prepared to take and for which he suffered the consequences. Another is his readiness to give up everything for the cause, inviting his followers to do the same. Crosses come into view. It all made sense in the desperate but promising circumstances of his day to give all you'd got in a final push for a different kind of kingdom. If it makes sense today, few feel able to rise to the challenge and, according to the Gospels, Janet Lacey's cup of water is enough to see us through on judgement day! (Matthew 25:31f.)

When Charles Elliott was briefly the Director of Christian Aid from 1982 to 1984, it was not an easy time for him and for those around him. What may have been at stake were very different ideas about the kind of 'charity' or 'movement' Christian Aid could be. Was it enough for supporters to raise and give money in a 'transactional relationship', as he called it, and leave it at that – a travesty, of course, of the commitment shown by many in campaigning, praying and raising money well beyond one week in May. Was a more intensive, costly, spiritual response required? The title of his book *Comfortable Compassion?* could sound critical of Christian Aid and of Christians who do their bit while leaving their own quality of life untouched and the problems of the poorest unresolved. Whether his vision for Christian Aid, reminiscent of the Sojourners in the USA, was realistic or not – and probably not! – it evoked the uncomfortable challenges that flow from a 'Christology from below' and a reading of the Gospels.

Meanwhile, Christian Aid did not abandon its theological quest. A lot of work continued to be done. Susan Durber wrote substantial theological papers on human rights and gender.[15] Area staff, often led by Sue Richardson and enriched by Bible study, thought hard about Christian Aid's adoption of a 'prophetic voice' and the crucial issue of 'power', where the God of the Bible and the Galilean do not remain neutral but take sides.[16]

'Siblings of Shalom – theological perspectives on peacebuilding' (2021), by Wendy Lloyd, Christian Aid Ireland, with a Foreword by

Liz Hughes, chair of Christian Aid Ireland, took the more reflective approach to doing its theology, moving between stories about making peace from the Bible and Christian Aid's partners and written from the unique perspective of their involvement in the 'Troubles' in Northern Ireland: for Hughes and others, literally on the front line.

In 2021 'Christian Aid's Approach to Theology' went as a paper to the board for approval. It insisted that Christian Aid takes faith seriously, referring more than once to Clifford's Relational Theology inspired by a trinitarian God alongside Contextual and Liberation theologies. It describes how the organisation has been challenged 'to find a mechanism to ensure that our theological underpinning readily informs our work and practice in a genuinely joined up way', so addressing Loy's challenge. It makes reference to Susan Durber's paper 'A Theology to Strengthen the Poor – a reflection on theology at Christian Aid', written in 2017 and echoing the 1987 declaration referred to above. It adds that the organisation needs to be confident and clear enough about its theological underpinning to engage in public debate, presumably having in mind renewed discussions about the role of faith in the public square. A degree of complexity, if not confusion, emerges when it refers to Christian Aid's need to be able 'to articulate its key criteria by which we judge how to frame a core theology of development', especially when 'core theologies' may be best left aside. But perhaps it had those cycles of action–reflection in mind.

The board paper went on to outline a process for the year ahead that would attempt to rise to these challenges. It was to include extensive conversations and, structurally, setting up a theology steering group, a theology working group and a new external theology advisory group. True to its word, in May 2024 Christian Aid merged two internal groups into one to form its 'Theology Oversight Group', charged with improving understanding of Christian Aid's Christian identity and how it works out in practice. Externally Christian Aid re-established its Theology Advisory Group in 2023 with a more diverse membership and many more voices from the South, better able not to fashion theologies but to challenge and nourish Christian Aid's thinking with a broad range of insights.[17]

PS: Beware when things 'theological' or 'theoretical' or 'academic' are easily dismissed as having little relevance to everyday life.

6
Burma/Myanmar

The Burma Campaign (UK), a relatively small but influential organisation based in London, was co-founded in 1991 by John Jackson, a former member of Christian Aid's staff, and supported by Christian Aid for a number of years, adding a strong voice to Christian Aid's own advocacy work. It counted Glenys Kinnock and the murdered MP Jo Cox among its board members and found champions of its work among celebrities including Glenda Jackson, David Hare and Jon Snow (then of *Channel 4 News*). Its overarching task was to coordinate a campaign across Europe to free Burma and build a lasting democracy. It spoke up for political prisoners, exposed human rights abuses, helped to ensure aid to refugees, and strengthened Burmese organisations and individuals – an extremely sensitive piece of work if they were not to be exposed to reprisals.

For older people, however, the phrase 'Burma Campaign' is more likely to conjure up a very different picture, not of hoped-for democratic peace but of conflict, brutality and violence during the Second World War, when Burma sided first with Japan (though not without internal opposition) and then with the Allies. The war came to an end in 1945, but not the conflict. Burma gained its independence from Britain in 1948 under the Aung San–Attlee Agreement of the previous year. After Aung San's assassination in 1947 the country came under military rule, cutting itself off from the outside world and frustrating the hopes of many. The Karen were the first to rebel, soon followed by others. Since then, Burma has suffered one of the longest-running civil wars, between citizens and government, communists and democrats, ethnic armies, students, monks and the ruling powers. Overt military rule held its grip from 1962 to 2010 and again from 2021; in spite of this, Christian Aid stayed on, delivering programmes and offering solidarity to local organisations and communities.

In 1989 the country's name was changed to Myanmar by the ruling military junta. Its history has not only been blighted by conflict but also by poverty, gradually declining from a wealthy country rich in natural resources to one of the poorest due to mismanagement, corruption and land-grabbing by heavy industries from a largely rural community. In 1987 it was given 'Least Developed Country' status by the UN.

Throughout, minorities have been attacked repeatedly and remain the most marginalised and vulnerable. Among them the Shan are the largest, amounting to 10% of the overall population. Their people have been subjected to forced and low-paid labour, human trafficking and army raids on their villages. Like others, they have engaged in guerilla warfare as they struggle for independence.

The Kokang grow rice and have engaged in armed conflict with the Burmese army as recently as 2015. The Wa grow poppies for the drug barons but have been encouraged to produce rubber and tea instead in return for international aid. The Karen, 7% of the overall population, comprise disparate ethnic groups mainly in the south along the border with Thailand. Having fought the government since independence, once reaching the outskirts of Rangoon, they participated in a major uprising in 1988. As their villages continued to be burned, hundreds of thousands fled to refugee camps on the Thai border, a grim reality which became a major item on Christian Aid's agenda. The Kachin live in the rugged and remote hill country of north Myanmar. Over years of fighting, hundreds of thousands have taken refuge in camps on the Chinese border, where they have been far from welcome.

Religious differences within as well as between ethnic groups have added to the heady mix. Buddhism is the state religion of Myanmar. Its monks have often been at the forefront of the fight for better things. Christianity came with the missionaries. First to arrive were the American Baptists led by Adoniram Judson in 1813, overcome on arrival by the sight of the magnificent Shwedagon pagoda. They were followed by Anglicans and Methodists. The Rohingya are Muslims. They have suffered horrendous persecution allegedly involving crimes against humanity and genocide. In 1978 military operations against them led to 250,000 fleeing to Bangladesh. Christian Aid did not get involved due to lack of access and political sensitivities. In 1982 the Rohingyas were denied citizenship and regarded as illegal immigrants. In 2017 a further crackdown led to over a million fleeing, mostly again to Bangladesh, with vulnerable and unprotected women and children among them. Large numbers found a measure of safety in the newly created Kutupalong refugee camp in Cox's Bazar, one of the world's largest, where Christian Aid was soon hard at work.

Aid

Against this background it is small wonder that a good deal of Christian Aid's long-standing involvement with the poverty and suffering of Myanmar over four decades has had to do with emergency or humanitarian aid, supporting the struggles of desperate people to cope with one crisis after another. Much of the work has been in refugee camps working alongside the Burma Border Consortium (later the Thailand Burma Border Consortium and then simply The Border Consortium) with grants from DFID. Elsewhere it was with the Myanmar Council of Churches (a natural partner for Christian Aid) and other faith-based organisations often more trusted than officialdom and able to gain access to areas where others could not. Unusually, in Kutupalong, Christian Aid's staff were to be found working on the ground in the overcrowded conditions wearing CAID badges: 'operational' as it were, until it decided to withdraw from all direct implementation here and elsewhere. Many active groups remained, unnamed for their own safety.

A visit to Mae La, a camp not far from Mae Sot, gave me a big surprise, literally, at 'the end' of it. Visually it seemed to stretch up like a long finger pointing from Thailand towards Burma. It was inhabited and administered from day to day by the Karen. When I arrived, they were delivering food aid. Heavy bags of rice were being passed from one to another up and up the hill to families in their open-sided houses, many built on bamboo stilts above the mud and with 'thatched' roofs. I followed the rice until at the end of the camp it was delivered to staff and students of a Baptist theological college. That it was a college was not surprising since I had heard how various schools and colleges had been set up, providing education and training in challenging circumstances. That it was 'Baptist' was not surprising either, since most Christian Karen are Baptists. That it was a theological college, training future ministers for their churches, certainly was surprising and not just because I had once taught in one myself! It was yet another affirmation that, for all the hardships, life for them was going to go on and, it should be remembered, that meant trying to make something of it for year after year in camps like this one.

A very different call for help, and this time not the result of conflict, came when Cyclone Nargis struck in 2008, killing 140,000 people. The authorities did little. About the only good thing coming out of the disaster, if you can call it 'good' since it reflected the urgent and growing need for help, was more space opening up for civic society to act, bringing with it a not-to-be-missed opportunity for Christian Aid to find new organisations to work with inside the country and so make a bigger contribution on issues like health care, HIV, gender and livelihoods. It led to the appointment of an emergency programme manager, the recruitment of local staff and the registration of Christian Aid's office in Yangon (Rangoon until 1989) in 2015.

Covid-19, which struck a few years later in the early 2020s, had no redeeming feature whatsoever, spreading not only hunger, disease and death but an even greater measure of fear and mistrust.

Advocacy

Though understandably preoccupied with the immediate needs of desperate people, advocacy work was also high on Christian Aid's agenda. It meant speaking up on behalf of and, where possible, together with the Burmese people in efforts to resolve the underlying causes of their poverty and distress. Internally Christian Aid supported civil society 'under the radar', working alongside the Myanmar Council of Churches and the Karen Baptist Convention. Outside in the big wide world it was a task that required making a loud noise, urging corporates like Total and Premier Oil, banks and governments to disinvest, while being acutely aware of the need to go carefully in case of repercussions in Burma for the very people advocacy was designed to support. Christian Aid relied heavily on the Burma Campaign UK, which at times could go where Christian Aid in the earlier years (but not later) feared to tread. Joined by Desmond Tutu, the Dalai Lama and others, it adopted a strategy similar to that of the anti-apartheid campaign, with Aung San Suu Kyi seen as 'Asia's Mandela'. There were calls for sanctions against the regime, some of which were successful. Governments, including the EU, were urged to adopt policies in favour of strengthening civil society and standing up for the human rights of minorities, refugees and the internally displaced.

A less visible but fruitful piece of advocacy in 2007–2008 involved Christian Aid in efforts to shift British government policy. At the time it would not allow its funding to be used for cross-border purposes. Sovereign states and their wishes had to be respected. Meanwhile, vulnerable ethnic minorities in border camps had no access to health care and other services from inside Myanmar. The policy was reversed in 2009. Quiet diplomacy paid off.

In the same year Christian Aid approached DFID with a proposal to improve health services, especially for displaced women and children. Its unique feature, sometimes referred to as 'convergence', was to foster cooperation between organisations working across borders with those working from within Myanmar, including NGOs, government and ethnic health authorities. The result, it was hoped, would not only be better quality and more reliable services but also growing trust between the parties involved. Negotiations with DFID were lengthy but eventually successful, leading in 2011 to a substantial UK government grant.

The effort to improve relations and build trust was also apparent in programmes in several regions of Myanmar, supported by the UN Peacebuilding Fund both before and after the 2021 coup. They encouraged young people and their organisations to challenge provocations like hate speech, and to work for peace. Adopting what was referred to as the triple nexus approach, the programmes held together the three core areas of Christian Aid's work, namely humanitarian aid, development and tackling the causes of poverty, in this case conflict.

Aung San Suu Kyi

One of the best-known internal movements involved in that conflict was the National League for Democracy (NLD), forged out of the uprising in 1988 of students and monks and led by the charismatic figure of Aung

San Suu Kyi, daughter of Aung San who years before had signed the independence agreement and was later assassinated. It brought together people of all ethnic groups, including Burmans, the largest, in a not always easy alliance. Following a brutal crackdown in 1988, thousands fled to the border camps. Aung San Suu Kyi was kept under house arrest for years. The Saffron Revolution of 2007 was equally brutally crushed. Eventually local elections were permitted, followed by a General Election in 2015 when the NLD won a huge majority and Aung San Suu Kyi, barred from becoming President, became State Counsellor or Prime Minister in a government heavily watched over, not to say run, by the military. Eventually the generals turned against her once again and sentenced her to a life in prison after their coup in 2021.

Awarded the Nobel Peace Prize in 1991, Aung San Suu Kyi was once adored for her unending commitment to human rights and democracy. Several members of Christian Aid's staff were in close touch with her and from time to time able to visit her, finding their way down a normally deserted avenue to the gate over which she often spoke to crowds. On one occasion I managed to smuggle out a small black cassette with a filmed greeting from her to young people gathering at Greenbelt, an annual Christian festival in England, partly funded by Christian Aid.

During her years in government, Aung San Suu Kyi appeared to many inside and outside the country to fall from grace, failing to speak out and even defending her government when, once again and this time under her watch, the Rohingya were being ruthlessly persecuted and driven from their burning homes. The reason for her silence remains unanswered.

Oo Tiny Tay and Nui Lao

In any situation involving high-profile figures and where big words like 'massacre', 'persecution' and 'ethnic cleansing' are used, they can easily obscure the small-scale realities of people caught up in tragedies not of their making. Oo Tiny Tay was one of them, looking for a roof over her head, and Nui Lao (even tinier) was another looking for safety.

Oo Tiny Tay from the Irrawaddy Delta knew that she and her family of seven were lucky to survive Cyclone Nargis when 180 people in her village lost their lives and many more their homes. For a time after it struck, a tarpaulin was the only roof over their heads. Even before that, life was hard enough with only one of the children going to school and the others helping to mend fishing nets and labouring on farms to grow rice, earning between them a dollar a day. Now the pressure was on to build new and stronger houses. In a fine display of practical ecumenism, Christian Aid, along with a Muslim organisation and, in the lead, the Abbot of the local Buddhist monastery, were on the job, building low-cost housing from local materials for those who couldn't afford to build their own; but it would take time where time was in short supply as the dry season gave way to the rains.

Nui Lao was hardly born! Seven months old in 2008, she had just completed a month-long journey with her parents and her brother through the jungle, avoiding landmines and fleeing from the fighting between the Burmese military and the Karen National Liberation Army. She was one of a continual stream of new arrivals at the Mae Ra Ma Luang refugee camp in Thailand, 4 kilometres from the Myanmar border, where there was food and her mother felt that at least for now she and the family were safe with no need to run any further, but dreaming like many others of returning to a peaceful and democratic homeland.

Common ground

When the rain is falling, falling
And you're waiting for the sun
And at last the clouds begin to go away,
Take a walk into the garden
Or a tramp out on the moors –
Let the smell of drying earth transform your day.

Chorus
For the ground is grave and cradle
It is death and life to come
It is a gift for everyone to share around
It's a sign of understanding
To unite the human race
So that all of us discover common ground.

See the peasant toiling, toiling
In the fields from dawn to dusk
On land he'll never live to call his own
Or the pavement dweller scratching
Out a living on the streets
Without a plot of ground to build a home.

Chorus

Ken Forrest, in 'Common Ground: Songs for Christian Aid', © Copyright 1982 Stainer & Bell Ltd, 23 Gruneisen Road, London N3 1LS, www.stainer.co.uk. Reprinted by permission. All rights reserved.

7

Christian Aid Week ... the little red envelope

In Frensham, Surrey, three local vicars spent the morning washing up in the local pond, up to their knees in water. In West Wickham's public baths a dozen more took the plunge. On Merseyside, 81-year-old Miss Warburton earned £21 doing odd jobs for an elderly neighbour. In Kensington they stuffed as much money as they could into matchboxes. In London, John Singleton travelled through 190 out of 250 tube stations in a day without surfacing. The vicar of Brackley was out on his Aprilia 750cc motorbike with thirty more bikers roaring through 160 miles of countryside wearing red and white Christian Aid bibs; in Selby, Yorkshire, three Methodist ministers were doing much the same. The bishops of Swindon and Reading preferred to get on their bicycles, as did 58-year-old Nigel Porter from Essex, who pedalled for 800 miles round southern Ireland. Seventy people in Exeter didn't move an inch as they set out on exercise bikes for Senegal, clocking up 3,000 miles. Many preferred to go on foot on long country walks. Godfrey Meynell (aged 89) walked round and round a sports track covering the same distance as from Land's End to John o'Groats. Blind Mary Rees walked 22 miles to Guildford Cathedral with her 11-year-old grandson. Ian Cobb did 160 miles. For over thirty years, the fit and not so fit turned out to cross bridges from the Humber to the Forth and the Tay. In Dorchester they simply sat it out and had a picnic in the local park. In Liverpool you could say they floated by, when one float paraded through the city was graced by a beauty queen and the other carried a refugee's shack. Seventy-seven Oxford students lived for two days on 97p a day; thousands of others, from bishops to barristers, followed their lead. In Sandwich, Kent, they locked themselves up in a cage and starved, but not to death. In Lincolnshire, 138 women lost weight over five weeks.

In Lisburn, Northern Ireland, they tucked in to their bread and cheese lunches. All in a good cause!

Schoolchildren sold mud pies in Cardiff. Students at Oxford Brookes University set up a dating venue. Sue Pollard enjoyed a Quizaid night in Fleet and Graham Battenshaw from Otley hosted one, dressed up in drag as 'Brainy Brenda'. Scarecrows held a festival in Haxby and Wigginton, Yorkshire. John Sentamu contributed to a recipe book put together by a 14-year-old from Scarborough. Bach was played for fifteen hours non-stop in St Mary's Cathedral, Edinburgh. In Sheffield they read the Bible out loud for fifteen and a half hours.

Things got tough in Northern Ireland, where sixteen people were skydiving. In Clydebank, seventeen daredevils abseiled down a crane 46 metres high. In Essex, thirty-three did the same down Ingatestone church tower, including 65-year-old Pamela, only to be upstaged by 82-year-old Pam, a novice abseiler, in Cricklade, Wiltshire. Things got even tougher in Hull when Arthur Setterington, Methodist preacher and magician, lay on a bed of nails for one and a half hours. Danger loomed in Bangor when a local business executive was kidnapped and held to ransom. Coffee mornings and plant sales were safer territory.

Neil Kinnock, David Steel and Roy Castle got weighed outside St Paul's Cathedral on gigantic scales of justice. In a pop-up shop near Carnaby Street they were selling gardening tools, customised by the likes of Alan Titchmarsh, Bill Nighy and Jill Halfpenny. Another shop popped up in York. In Heckmondwike, seventy-two pairs of shoes were polished in three hours. In central London they used vacuum cleaners to blow up two 12ft-long buffalo-shaped balloons. Over on the South Bank they built a makeshift refugee camp out of old wood, corrugated iron and plastic. In Loughborough, car drivers were passing or failing their driving tests on motorised scooters and wheelchairs: Scooting for a Hoot. Roger Gayler from Dagenham shaved off half his beard as a reminder of how the other half lives.

In Wrexham, schoolchildren acted out on the streets the parable of the good Samaritan.

In Edinburgh, hundreds queued year after year outside the doors of St Andrew's and St George's, Church of Scotland, some famous authors among them. Inside, Mary Davidson, the inspiration behind it all, and her band of helpers, including several from HM Prisons, Scotland, were putting the finishing touches to a vast display of books for sale set out on 200 tables, all the pews and every nook and cranny of the church from top (in the gallery) to bottom. Most were modestly priced paperbacks. Some were more valuable. James Hutton's *Theory of the Earth*, for example, first published in 1788 and bought for a shilling, sold for £5,000. The first English edition, published in 1601, of the first modern world atlas, *Theatrum Orbis Terrarum* by the Flemish cartographer Abraham Ortelius, was found in a bag of paperbacks and also sold for £5,000. A *Doctor Who* script signed by David Tennant and Billie Piper sold for £3,000. And it was not only books but pictures, antiques, records, toys, stamps and postcards as well.

There were many successful book stalls up and down the country, but the Edinburgh Charity Book Sale, 50 years old in 2023, was probably by then the biggest in the world and, according to Mary Davidson, 'the largest single volunteer-led fundraising event for Christian Aid in the UK' having raised over £3m; and it all began when someone turned up at church with a carload of books.

From door to door

Meanwhile a middle-aged woman called Sarah, one of thousands of volunteers in villages, towns and cities throughout the UK, worked her way up and down several streets with her official badge on, delivering a little red envelope. Designed many years earlier, this envelope, with its flap wide open ready to be filled with what was mainly cash, became so well recognised that it found its way into popular radio and TV programmes like *The Archers* and *Rev*. In 2025 it still survived as Christian Aid's logo. Later the same week, Sarah would return to the same streets with her bright red Christian Aid bag, to collect what she had delivered and, she hoped, a useful amount of money. It was known as the House-to-House Collection (H2H). She had done it for years. And then she stopped.

Christian Aid Week was Christian Aid's flagship fundraiser right from the start. In January 1957 the Inter-Church Aid and Refugee Service (ICARS) of the British Council of Churches issued a very uninteresting-looking press release headed simply 'Information'.[1] It was a far cry from the eye-catching posters and other materials that would follow as the years went by. It announced the BCC's intention, in the face of ill-informed criticism of the churches' lack of action, to organise a national week in May to inform the public about its work resettling refugees and providing relief aid for all those suffering from political intolerance or natural disasters.

The chief instigators of the week were Maurice Rickards, an artist and activist, and Hugh Samson, a PR specialist, two independent consultants hired by ICARS and backed to the hilt by Janet Lacey, its Director. Eventually they both joined her staff.

'Samaritan Week' was a close runner to 'Christian Aid Week' in the debate about a name that could appeal both to churchgoers – always the backbone of Christian Aid Week – and to the humanitarian instincts of the general public, a debate that murmured on for decades. The first week, 1 May 1957, was launched by the Bishop of Stepney and the actor Kenneth More at the premiere of the film *Like Paradise* (not made by Christian Aid).

The educational side of the week included public meetings with well-informed and, mostly, inspiring speakers, widely distributed fliers, and films. Fundraising concentrated on H2H using the little red envelopes. In that first year (1957), £26,000 was collected in 316 towns. By the 1960s the total had reached £1m.

A 'post-mortem', as they called it, was held that autumn (1957), though by all accounts Christian Aid Week was far from dead already. There were grumbles about a shortage of envelopes (no such thing in those days as 'spares'), their late delivery, and not being sufficiently informative. Generally, the feedback was favourable and many churches unable to get organised in time for 1957 were busy signing up for 1958. A telling conclusion, and a surprisingly perceptive one so early on, was that things worked best in 'towns with an ecumenical life'.

In 1964 ICARS was renamed 'Christian Aid'. In the many years that followed, income from Christian Aid Week steadily increased, with some occasional jitters. By 1968 it had exceeded £1m. In 2007 it rose to a record-breaking £14.6m, representing 17% of Christian Aid's overall income. In 2011 there was a near catastrophe when it suddenly fell to

£12m, triggering painful cutbacks on programmes and staffing. Covid, which in 2020 completely ruled out H2H, only added to growing problems.

Christian Aid Week could be seen as a development project of its own. Materials for schools and churches and posters for the high street were developed and improved around annual themes. In 1957 it was 'Millions of hopes are fixed on you'; in 1970, 'Ignore the hungry and they'll go away'; 1971, 'Every second someone gets relief from hunger', against a background photograph of a corpse; 1974, 'Some people never forget Christian Aid Week', like an African boy in school; 1981, 'Soak the poor' with the clean water they so badly need; 1987, 'More Power to the Poor' to gain control over their own lives; and in 1991, 'Do you believe in Life before Death?' A number of special reports timed to coincide with the week and win publicity were equally challenging, exposing, for example, the exploitation of children in the carpet and sports shoe industries. More gently-does-it were short tapes for local radio featuring celebrities such as Glenn Hoddle and Rory Bremner telling life-changing stories.

Publicity took a brave step forward immediately after the law was changed in 1991 to allow charities to advertise on television. Christian Aid was quick to venture into an expensive, risky and punchy world. The very next year came pictures of 'hands' – two of them, receiving soil, seeds and rain until crops began to grow – and the red envelope appeared with Christian Aid's strapline: 'We believe in life before death.' In 1994 Chris Roles, head of fundraising, persuaded renowned photographer David Bailey to film the Christian Aid Week advert in Ethiopia but ran into difficulties. Bailey produced some brilliant work, but Roles had a hard time keeping him to his brief. In 1996 the word 'Survive' dominated the screen showing an old woman looking down on her baby granddaughter. She was recounting how much she herself had survived, including hunger, eviction, cholera and war, and wishing the child would not survive but live. In 2006 what was described as a rather Monty Pythonesque rickety multiplying machine was pictured set up in an African village where a single chicken went in at one end and lots of them came out the other. The same went for trees and pigs. 'You add and we multiply' was the tag line. The 2013 advert cried 'Bite back at hunger' and featured solar-powered freezers for preserving fish to eat and sell.

Not everyone approved when the red envelopes got bigger and better as Gift Aid was introduced with a sign-up slip to tear off and tuck inside with the money. For many it encouraged more thoughtful giving as well as increasing its value. E-envelopes to fill in online, introduced in 2018, and increasing use of social media, brought things up to date but, along with other measures, were not enough to stem decline.

Christian Aid Week often brought out the critics, including John Gummer, whom I found myself confronting more than once on the BBC Radio 4's *Moral Maze* with issues like arming guerillas, and being too political for a charity, swirling around.[2] For the most part, however, Christian Aid Week was regarded as a success story, the main measure of its success being the amount of money raised.

Money was important for all the obvious reasons, but there was a particular reason why this money mattered. It was non-designated, or what I liked to call 'free money', because it allowed Christian Aid to go where designated funds could or might not go and do what institutional donors might hesitate to do. New work could be opened up, new ways of doing development could be explored, start-up investments could be made which often went on to attract significant designated funding: £150,000 invested in South Sudan, for instance, led to a three-year contract worth £2.7m. Christian Aid Week money allowed Christian Aid to follow its deepest instincts and take risks while remaining accountable to the churches and the public by way of annual reports, readable annual reviews and in annual meetings with the BCC and its successors.

The stalwarts of Christian Aid Week have always been thousands and thousands of collectors and organisers – 400,000 in 1991, including Sarah, mostly but not exclusively from the churches. Supported by Christian Aid staff and especially area staff, they delivered and collected the envelopes in mainly, but not only, middle-class comfortably off areas. The majority did so for thirty to fifty years, well into their seventies and eighties. According to them, they mostly received a friendly reception on the doorstep, especially in communities where they were known and often 'expected'. A small minority could be rude, sceptical and even hostile. Their dogs could be very undiscerning.

Collectors had their tales to tell. A man from India now living in the UK, who well remembered Christian Aid's work in his village, opened the door and beamed a big 'Thank you'. On another occasion the door was opened by a former pupil grateful to her now retired schoolteacher. Daring to call on General Pinochet, under virtual house arrest, his guards were encouraged to give and managed to cough up 50p between them. More than one collector had to struggle home and on to the bank with a large jar full of small change. Emergency aid was called to one house when the chip pan caught fire as the envelope was being filled. A man refused to give when the spotlight that year was on Zimbabwe because he strongly disapproved of the regime. Wrapped only in a towel and dripping wet, a man found his envelope, made it rather damp and contributed generously. A happy mother and baby, both completely naked, were apparently indifferent to issues of modesty but equally generous. Blatantly obvious was the contrast between a man washing his Jaguar and giving 50p, and the generosity of folk in a nearby rundown neighbourhood, one of them giving £5. A small boy asked his father, an aid worker on leave from Haiti, who we were: 'A good thing!' he replied. The local Conservative councillor asked a lot more questions. A grumpy sceptic refused to give, and later chased us down the street with a well-fattened envelope saying he had changed his mind.

Collecting wasn't a particularly attractive job or always much fun, but this army of volunteers, going it alone or with friends, said they enjoyed getting out and about as they expressed their faith in a way they could tackle and make sense of, all in a good cause.

Down but not out?

Warning signals began coming well before the outbreak of Covid-19 in 2020. As far back as 1987 there were discussions about the fact that H2H was on the decline.[3] In 2017 Christian Aid Week brought in 5% less than the year before. Loyal volunteers were growing old. Sarah stopped collecting when she was 80, after fifty-four years and, crucially, as an older generation retired, their successors were increasingly hard to find.

Collecting was becoming more difficult and less enjoyable. There was a switch, accelerated by Covid, to delivering envelopes with instructions about where they could be returned, but no going back to collect them. The Covid-19 pandemic over, delivering was resumed to some extent but collecting was not. Two collectors tried writing letters to previous givers, some rather well-heeled, instead of calling on them, and got a good response. The complaint about a shortage of envelopes in 1957 now turned into complaints that there were too many, undelivered and going to waste; and why, some asked, new envelopes every year? Those envelopes were made to swallow up cash and cheques no longer used by a growing majority. Security issues loomed large. Doors were not opened after dark. The streets felt less safe. Hard-to-get-into flats and gated communities and increasing numbers of no-cold-calling zones and forbidding notices on front doors all got in the way. Fewer friendly faces were pleased to see you. Competition was increasing, not because of other H2H collections, but because of the bombardment of appeals through the letterbox and on social media. The red envelope could easily be thrown out with a sigh into the recycling bin along with the junk mail. Research found that people stop H2H collecting when the negatives of their experience outweigh the positives, including their motivations.[4]

Some of these problems, like the lack of cash, had underlying causes, which, when it came to emergency aid, Christian Aid was always keen to tackle. In the case of the missing cash, one underlying cause was the move to a whole new digital age. The observation, made way back in 1957, that things 'worked best in towns with an ecumenical life' proved to be perceptive. That word 'towns' conjured up a certain nostalgia for villages, market towns and stable suburban communities, where people knew each other, all mixed up with negative feelings, not always justified, about cities and estates where people were more wary of others and friendship was in shorter supply.

The reference to 'ecumenical life' is in part a reminder of shrinking congregations, particularly in what used to be called the mainstream churches so close to Christian Aid, and the disappearance of local Councils of Churches due to closures and lack of interest. By the turn of the millennium it was not so easy to remember or recognise the significance of the genuine excitement, now largely gone, in the pioneering days of Christian Aid Week when the churches came together in the youthful and inspiring ecumenical movement and found their unity in this piece of 'life and work',[5] appealing for compassion and justice without having to agree on what they believed.

As time went on, that word 'ecumenical' had more and more to do with relations between faith communities rather than Christian churches, as part of massive social changes during Christian Aid Week's long life towards an increasingly diverse population in Britain. It brought the black churches into membership of Christian Aid and some highs and lows on the doorsteps. The lows had to do with trying to explain an organisation, its culture and ways of doing things (like knocking on people's doors), that was totally unfamiliar. The highs included the genuine interest shown by Muslims, Sikhs, Hindus and others, eager to understand what Christian Aid was up to, sympathetic to its cause, respectful of its faith and generous in their giving.

Harder to pin down as an underlying cause of Christian Aid Week's decline were the frequent comments from collectors about a world, near and far, from refugee camps to urban streets, perceived to be increasingly dangerous, with its wars, migrants fleeing from poverty, persecution and the effects of climate change all adding to a sense of fear.

Several attempts were made to turn things around, like the big breakfast (Big Brekkie), Tea Time and Quizaid, all fairly successful but far from filling the gap left by the decline of H2H. Three reports, two in 2018 and one in 2023, began to map a way forward.

The first looked at nearly 200 internal documents dating from 2009 to 2017, unearthed by Christian Aid staff, indicating what they had been thinking about Christian Aid Week.[6] The evidence underlined the need for change and investment (despite budget cuts), a focus on recruiting new organisers and collectors, and an improved experience for over 550 existing organisers and, still, thousands of individual collectors.

The review's recommendations seemed rather tame, sounding like a bit more of the same, such as renewed efforts to recruit and experimenting with new 'products' like the Big Brekkie. It reiterated the ongoing tension around appealing both to Christians and non-Christians whether secular or, more recently, of other faiths.

A second report, hard on the heels of the first, called 'External Analysis for Christian Aid Week Transformation', was written, somewhat ironically, by Christian Aid's own internal CAW fundraising team. It upheld some observations of the first about the decline of the churches, the move away from H2H, the rising age of volunteers, the loss of a sense of community, and how contactless and online payments were replacing cash. It still believed that significant numbers of non-churchgoing Christians, together with older people and the general public, were more than willing to support charities like Christian Aid.

A third report, delivered in March 2023 by Aha Consulting,[7] seemed much more radical and creative. It had positive things to say about the status quo: £5m raised in a week was still well worth having! Christian Aid Week remained a huge community fundraising event. The worship materials continued to help anchor Christian Aid in thousands of supportive churches, despite their decline. On the other hand, it easily recognised the downward trend. In the past three years only 57% of what it called Christian Aid's 'warm audience' remembered receiving any communication whatsoever about the Week. In 2021–22 less than a quarter of churches on the database (16,562) raised more than £100.

The report spent less time on causes, some more familiar than others such as a rather opaque reference to a limited focus on 'acquisitions', concentrating its attention instead on where to go next. It proposed the slogan 'Seven days to make a difference', on which a whole variety of ways to take part could be hung, with a lot of play on the number 7!

The report called for five shifts:

- to one persistent clear message every year instead of changing them;
- from many fragmented 'asks' to a single one with a variety of ways to respond to it, and a digital solution to organising it, like a website or portal or hub opening up to a variety of journeys towards, for example, fundraising events, collecting, schools, campaigns and demos, speaking and preaching, signing up to and getting ideas, materials and support;
- away from too much administration and bureaucracy, so setting volunteers free to get on with it;
- from asking people to 'give' to asking them to 'sign up';
- from a mindset that it described as 'hamster-collecting' to one of being proud of a flagship product that staff could enjoy working on and even come to love – more like a festival than a chore.

The report's recommendations were largely accepted and began to be implemented in 2024 under the banner 'Seven days, so many ways', from a gift to a sponsored walk to a prayer and several other options. Did it make a difference? Not dramatically, but definitely in the right direction with organisers and staff reporting that the buzz had returned to CAW.

Back on the streets, the ongoing debate about appealing to Christians and non-Christians alike took an unexpected turn when the man of the house opened the door to announce that he was an atheist and would not therefore contribute to a Christian charity. The quick-witted collector replied that, if he really believed there was no God to help the poor, that was all the more reason why he should!

8
Haiti

In so many respects Haiti is a wonderful place with its art and culture, ancient traditions, unique cuisine, and natural wonders soaring from sea to mountain tops.

In stark contrast the UN sees ('categorises') it as one of the world's least developed countries. The British public, if it sees anything, most likely sees little more than gang violence, the breakdown of law and order in Port-au-Prince, and the scandal of aid workers behaving badly. Some, to the dismay of Christian Aid, see only 'the basket case of the Americas', blind to its rich heritage and the resilience of its people. Historians, however far back they go, may find it hard to see much beyond a succession of occupations by foreign powers, revolts and hostile internal relations between two halves of one island. Anyone thinking of booking one of many holidays still advertised in 2024 would see pictures of sun-kissed beaches (I swam from one of them), four- and five-star hotels and, on arrival, low-paid local workers and reassuring security guards.

For over sixty years, through the eyes of its staff, local partners and communities, Christian Aid has had to see Haiti's wonders obscured by poverty, violence and 'natural' disasters. These harsh realities have determined its agenda, whatever the official organisational priorities may have been. The three are difficult to separate out, each feeding off the others, and their depressing stories go back a long way.

Violence

Violence, always exacerbating poverty, was on the scene as early as 1492 when Christopher Columbus landed and called the island Hispaniola (Little Spain). The Arawakan people, including the Taino, who inhabited the island and called it 'Ayti' ('mountainous land') were soon wiped out as they were killed and fell foul of disease. France followed Spain (1697) and established a slave colony built on sugar, until former black slaves led by Toussaint Louverture drove the French out in 1801. Napoleon then sent in troops which were defeated by Jean-Jacques Dessalines in the renewed struggle of 1804. In 1804 Dessalines went on to establish the first black independent state in the Caribbean. War broke out between Haiti and the Dominican Republic (DR) in 1822. During the 1890s the USA furthered its commercial and military interests in Haiti until it dominated its economy. In 1915 the USA sent in troops following mass executions of political prisoners and installed their man as President. From 1915 to 1934 Haiti was occupied by US Marines, during which, in an election in 1918, a new constitution was introduced.

From 1957 to 1986, during their brutal regime, François Duvalier, otherwise known as 'Papa Doc', and his son Jean-Claude ('Baby Doc'), aided by the Haitian paramilitary Tontons Macoutes, executed 40,000–60,000 Haitians. Jean-Bertrand Aristide, a priest associated with Liberation Theology, brought hope but was twice overthrown by the army and militia (1991 and 2004). When the army was disbanded in 1994, a bold and necessary step after years of coups and human rights violations, it left a country awash with guns, some illegally trafficked from the USA, in the hands of unemployed ex-soldiers. The USA sent in troops again, which were later followed by a UN stabilisation force. The UN's withdrawal in 2019 left a highly volatile situation, with growing gang violence. In the early months of 2024, 1,500 were killed in Port-au-Prince amid a breakdown in law and order and renewed efforts to find a peaceful solution. And all of this is not to mention the violence of slavery (the slaves had been brought from Africa by the French), human rights violations, mass deportations from the Dominican Republic, the abuse of women, and looting, which at one time (2024) led to the closure of the seaport, followed by empty supermarket shelves and food shortages.

Poverty

Haiti enjoyed considerable economic growth between 1968 and 1981. There was little extreme poverty until the 1980s, even during the oppressive Duvalier regime. Two events stand out as making things worse. One was the financial settlement demanded by France when it was finally sent packing in 1804, creating the so-called 'independence debt' (1825), the effects of which still linger on. The other, in the 1980s and 1990s, was the introduction of policies by the World Bank and IMF, heavily criticised by Christian Aid and many others, laying down conditions for debt reduction and future aid. They insisted on the liberalisation of trade, where the protection of local industries was not allowed or greatly diminished,[1] and poor countries were opened up to what some believed would be the opportunities of the global market while others saw only perils. There were dire consequences for Haiti. At the micro level, all the chickens eaten in Haiti were supplied by local producers, with around twenty chickens each scratching away in their family fields. Subsequently scaled up and industrialised, the whole business was virtually wiped out in the face of cheap imports.

Wilbert George, a farmer in Plaine de Léogâne, grew sugar on his 2.5 hectares of land and delivered it to the nearby Darbonne factory. The factory closed down in 1987 when imported sugar arrived. George lost 80% of his income; his family went hungry.[2] Milk farmers were undermined by imports of powdered and condensed varieties. They fought back by processing milk into yoghurt. While a few importers benefited from liberalisation, for thousands more it was anything but, as the rural poor drifted towards the urban areas, trapped in slums with food shortages in place of self-sufficiency, and growing violence fuelled by poverty. What was needed was not free-trade zones and more tourism, but serious attempts to reduce imports and provide work by regenerating the agricultural sector on which 70% of the population depended.[3]

Disasters

Like the Philippines, Haiti is especially prone to natural disasters: tropical storms, hurricanes and earthquakes, compounded by deforestation and climate change. An earthquake in Port-au-Prince in 2010, measuring 7.0 on the Richter scale, trapped Prospery Raymond, then Country Manager of Christian Aid's Haiti programme, working at his computer in his office. After being stuck under a sofa for one-and-a-half hours, he was rescued by Christian Aid's driver and emerged to welcome colleagues into his home, including Sarah Wilson just arrived from London. They worked together round the clock for two days in Prospery's backyard on Christian Aid's response to the latest disaster, surviving on bread, coffee and one potato between them. The 300,000 who were killed and the 1.6 million made homeless were not so fortunate. Prospery's backyard continued to be a camping site for Christian Aid staff from the Dominican Republic (DR) and London for six weeks after the earthquake.

Following Hurricane Georges in 1998, widespread tropical storms caused death and destruction from 2004 to 2016. In 2016 came Hurricane Matthew, killing 546 and completely destroying whole communities, businesses, houses and all. Marcelin, a survivor, was left without a wife to care for their three daughters, fearful of their being abused in return for food. They huddled together in the concrete shell of a disused communal shower. Jocelyne, not far away, having lost her pigs, struggled to exist alone on very muddy ground with only a tarpaulin for shelter.[4] The gruesome statistics were only made worse by a second earthquake in 2021 in the south-west, this time with a strength of 7.2 and killing 2,248 men, women and children, injuring 12,762 and destroying 130,000 houses.

Christian Aid in Haiti

Several documents state that Christian Aid arrived in Haiti in the 1980s, but it was in fact involved well before that. As early as the late 1960s, Christian Aid was supporting the work of the Methodist Church there,[5] recommended for funding by CICARWS, the service arm of the WCC.[6] The Methodists were trying to improve education and medical care in the rural areas. They built simple but decent school buildings, trained teachers and provided them with houses in a not too successful effort to attract them away from the towns. They encouraged ecumenical cooperation with the Catholic Church and the Salvation Army through the Commission Haïtienne des Églises pour le Développement (CHED), which in 1975 fell prey to internal disagreements in what seemed like a struggle by local organisations for more control. In 1977 Christian Aid sent funds to the Methodist Church to support famine relief work following a severe drought affecting 300,000. Christian Aid continued to support the Church's agricultural work in Haiti and its Integrated Social Medical Programme into the early 1980s, when what was described as a terrible crisis in the Church brought the partnership to an end.[7]

Quite apart from its support for the Methodists, Christian Aid donated two trucks to the World Food Programme (WFP) in 1976 to help with the distribution of urgently needed supplies. At the request of the British chargé d'affaires, the doors of the trucks were painted with the slogan 'Gift of Christian Aid – London'! Vernon Littlewood subsequently wrote to the WFP explaining that this was contrary to Christian Aid's policy and ethos of helping as best it could but keeping a low profile and not blowing its own trumpet: a policy only rarely qualified.[8]

Through the 1980s and much of the 1990s, Christian Aid's work in Haiti was managed from London until it opened a programme office in January 1997.[9] Some accounts suggest that relations with the London office were not easy, with differing priorities and a top-down approach running counter to the bottom-up approach which Christian Aid was keen to encourage everywhere, involving local Christian Aid staff and the NGOs and community organisations they worked with. By 2017, headquarters regarded the programme on human rights as 'lethargic': in its judgement, Civil Society Organisations (CSOs) were not being sufficiently vocal about violations, especially on the border. In 2010 Prospery Raymond became Regional Country Manager across the Caribbean, managing work in four other countries as well as Haiti. Christian Aid's programme began to shrink, suffering with others the peaks and troughs of funding, until in 2020, while support for its partners continued, it was felt to be almost non-existent.[10]

On the border

The border between Haiti and the DR, splitting the island in half, runs for 392 kilometres from north to south, with thirty to forty crossing points, few of them legal or well managed. If two nations meet here, so do poverty, violence, the consequences of natural disasters and the felling of thousands of trees for fuel. Haitians are encouraged to go and find work in the DR, often in the sugar industry. Most lack any legal status, have no rights and suffer discrimination when they get there. Gender-based violence is rife. Many migrants stay for years. Large numbers return to Haiti, often deported by the authorities and left harassed and destitute on the border.

Following Hurricane Georges in September 1998 came mass deportations, leaving 400,000 living in warehouses, among them a grandmother, her daughter and child, all of whom were born in the DR but were now 'kicked out for being Haitian'. For a year from June 2014, the DR government allowed illegal migrants to apply for legal status on condition that they had been there for some time, had work and could produce their ID cards. Many were unable to do so because the Haitian authorities made little effort to supply the relevant papers despite pressure from Christian Aid and its partners such as the Groupe d'Appui aux Rapatriés et Réfugiés (GARR) and others. Between June 2015 and January 2016, another 129,000 left and a further 15,745 were deported. In 2024 there were an estimated 300,000 Haitian migrants on the border in danger of becoming stateless. GARR liked to have Christian Aid as a 'backing partner' because 'it doesn't go on the field to do things themselves, and allows people to do things their way'. The going was hard. The main focus was on Haitians returning from the DR. In contrast to all the hostility they met from soldiers and officials, GARR set out to welcome them, protect the women against gender-based violence,[11] provide for their immediate needs and help to form small communities where they could live, educate their children and find work. Instead of temporary camps with their lack of facilities and terrible smells, they tried to build real homes.

Talking of homes, great efforts were made, by many organisations including Habitat for Humanity and GARR, to build better houses: spacious with a backyard, well equipped, comfortable and above all secure, able to withstand wind, rain and earthquakes. After the 2010 earthquake, 820 were built around Port-au-Prince and 1,600 repaired, with support from Christian Aid. Training and tools were provided. Of the new houses built before 2016 (Hurricane Matthew), only one lost part of its roof. One householder was overjoyed: 'I feel wealthy, because when it rains, I don't get wet!' Another, Vilia, the face of Christian Aid Week in 2018, provided shelter in her house for over fifty frightened people. It was the only one in the area sturdy enough to withstand the hurricane.

On the other side of the border in the DR individuals and organisations were responding to disasters and risking their own safety as they confronted the government in the face of widespread racism, discrimination and human rights violations against Haitians. The Jesuit priest Padre Mario Serrano and Maria Servano, born in the DR of undocumented Haitian parents, to take but two examples, advocated tirelessly at both the national and international levels. Organisations like Onè Respe worked for 'honour and respect'. Christian Aid opened an office in the DR in 2006 and published its report, 'On the Margins', on the rights of migrants and Dominicans of Haitian descent.

Coming rather late in the day to the border, where programmes had been running since as far back as 2003, was Communities Living Peacefully, a three-year programme funded by USAID in 2022 to the tune of $1.5m and implemented by Christian Aid and Centro Montalvo, a faith-based organisation situated in the DR[12] with an emphasis on the commonalities rather than the differences, such as tackling deforestation and conserving water instead of fighting over it. Seven reforestation days were organised in 2023, when communities worked together planting some 4,800 trees and protecting shared water sources and canals around the Massacre River, named after its grim reputation. Meetings were arranged to encourage dialogue. In 2023 a rather large one, dubbed the Bilateral Communal Round Table, brought together forty representatives representing not only the communities, farmers and NGOs like Christian Aid, but also trade unions, government and local officials, even hoteliers. A wide-ranging agenda covered poverty, reducing tension, sustainable development, human rights violations, the need for well-managed official crossings, and efforts to promote trade and peace.

Natural disasters

Over the years Christian Aid built up a highly successful network of NGOs and local organisations working in Haiti. Numbering up to eighty, it became known as the Cadre de Liaison Inter-Organisations (CLIO). It aimed to map out who was doing what, avoid competition, and encourage cooperation and mutual support. It adopted the so-called Nexus approach[13] before it became more widely used, holding emergency aid, rehabilitation and development together. It raised its voice particularly on cross-border issues.[14]

Konbit pou Ranfòse Aksyon Lakay (KORAL) was nurtured into existence by Christian Aid before being 'set free to fly on its own' in 2007.[15] Some regarded it as somewhat secretive, with links to Voodoo. It was certainly a tightly knit community with a democratically elected committee. It helped its members to secure their livestock production by rearing goats as well as cows and chickens. It trained them in cholera prevention and general hygiene. It also played its part, along with many others, in coping with the repeated natural disasters that wore people down and made it harder and harder for them to get up again, all too often starting from scratch.

Better housing was of fundamental importance. So was 'being prepared' for the worst by clearing evacuation routes, for example, and providing cell phones to warn people in good time. Local organisations like KORAL pushed ahead with Christian Aid in Haiti as elsewhere with a survivor- and community-led crisis response (SCLR) to emergencies, respecting the ability of local leaders and communities to know best what to do in the immediate aftermath of storms and earthquakes and how to do it, and making sure they had the resources they needed in addition to their own, ready in hand. 'We didn't just watch things happening, but we were engaged,' commented one community leader.[16]

What the locals decided was best to do varied enormously. The most surprising was the decision to hold a four-day dance festival following an earthquake![17] Less surprising was to clear what had become an impassable road. What seemed increasingly sensible, but controversial, was the handing out of cash.

Homeless people fleeing from earthquakes into rural areas have immediate needs. Some of them, supplied by NGOs and local organisations, can take time to arrive. They have to be bought, delivered and then distributed. The needs are also diverse and include food, cooking fuel, health care, debt repayments and, longer term, schooling and restart-up costs for small businesses. Cash for Work schemes are badly paid and unavailable to the majority. Unconditional Cash Transfers, or UCTs,[18] were not the answer to everything, but they had distinct advantages. They offered desperate people the dignity of choice. They were simple and easy to set up. The money (at the time of the 2010 earthquake, around $26 per person per month) could be collected from well-established remittance agencies or handed out in envelopes. Cash to spend supported local markets where resilient traders would soon be functioning again. Four out of the six of Christian Aid's partners consulted, like KORAL, adopted it.

Always look on the bright side

When the late Prince Philip accompanied the Queen to Christian Aid's 50th Anniversary Service of Thanksgiving in a crowded Westminster Abbey, in conversation with supporters and visitors from overseas he was critical of my sermon which among other things faced up to the harsh reality that, despite all efforts, poverty and injustice still scarred the face of humanity. He didn't think that would do much to encourage the congregation to keep going. In other words: you should have been looking on the bright side![19]

Such talk may sound frivolous and inappropriate when it comes to Haiti. Nevertheless, there is a bright side. Close to Christian Aid, there are the likes of: KORAL and GARR busy rebuilding lives; VETERIMED, helping owners of one or two cows (there are lots of cows in Haiti) to produce yoghurt and milk for schoolchildren; Mission Sociale des Eglises Haïtiennes (MISSEH), encouraging ecumenical cooperation on social issues; and the National Committee of Human Rights (NCHR), brave human rights activists daring to speak out and working hard to get access to drugs for sufferers from HIV/AIDS. They represent the commitment of the many organisations in Haiti and beyond who refuse to go away despite the persistence of poverty and violence.

'There are so many treasures,' commented Helen Spraos, head of the Haiti programme for a time. Colette Lespinasse, Executive Director of GARR, was, in her judgement, one of them. 'The spark of that real commitment was incredible.' A former nun who had left her order to marry and bring up a family, Colette initiated much of the work with women and community leaders taken on by GARR. She wanted to see

1

2

3

4

1 Janet Lacey CBE 2 DEC appeal poster for Rwanda, 1994
3 Hungarian refugees, 1957 4 Yana, Ukraine

5

6 7

5 Tsunami, Southern Asia, 2004 6 Timothy Goggs, Afghanistan, 1992
7 Gul Shah, selling silk cocoons, Afghanistan, 2011

8

9

10

8 Human chain, Birmingham, 1998
9 Houses of Parliament projection, 2023
10 Dam collapse, Brazil, 2019

11 

12 

13 

14 

11 Chico Mendes, 1988

12 Lesley Williams abseiling, Oxford, 2016

13 Christian Aid Week poster, 1985

14 Edinburgh annual Book Sale, 2019

15

16

17

15 Supporters crossing Forth Bridge, 1980 16 The 'Tree of Life', 2005
17 March of landless people, 2012

18

19

20

18 Bezwada Wilson, London, 2025

19 Cholo Ngaramata, Ethiopia, 2024 20 'The Truth Truck', Nepal, 2015

21

22

23

24

21 Judi Dench filming for Christian Aid, 1968
22 Sabha, displaced during Gaza conflict, 2024
23 Mother and daughter, Bangladesh, 1998
24 Beekeeper Juanita Victoria Marquez, Honduras, 2016

25

26

27

28

25 Messah Brewah and savings box, Sierra Leone, 2019
26 Puppets, Greenbelt, 2016
27 The Twic Olympics, South Sudan, 2008
28 Christian Aid's 80th anniversary service, Westminster Abbey, 2025

fundamental change for the poor of Haiti. She fought for the rights of migrants. She radiated serenity, humility, kindness and decency. Spraos described her as devoid of ego and 'the perfect symbol of the best of Haiti'.[20] Violence against women is rife; they are beaten, disrespected and abused by their husbands with impunity.[21] Men feel entitled to sexual favours in return for their help. There is nothing 'bright' about that. Supported by KORAL, however, some women begin to find strength in one another and, working together, increase their economic power by forming cooperative groups,[22] making and selling small items like jam and peanut butter and 'investing' in livestock. With a degree of financial independence comes growing confidence to face down a deeply rooted patriarchal culture.

A brighter side to Haitian culture is what is known as 'kombit', a community spirit whereby poor farmers help each other, pooling what resources they have and, for example, going to work on their neighbour's land. A less happy example is known as 'restavek', a Creole word meaning 'to stay with', whereby a child of a poor family is sent to another where food, accommodation and access to education are exchanged for domestic labour. The practice is wide open to abuse. Kombit or 'solidarity' finds expression in Rara or marching bands, a tradition going back hundreds of years. Besides their communal farming, these tightly knit groups play at weddings and funerals, and even supply 'music while you work' out in the fields! They are less excluded than they were. In some cases, marching bands are now strong enough to bargain with local politicians, being willing to play for them in return for the chance to negotiate over local government policies – one of various efforts to gain representation at all government levels.

The *Freedom!* sculpture marking the two-hundredth anniversary of the abolition of the slave trade, marked in the UK in 2007, obviously had a bright side to it, but a darker one as well.[23] It was commissioned by Christian Aid and made by an artists' collective out of recycled junk metal found in the slums of Port-au-Prince. The artists and others ran workshops, including innovative art workshops, for children and young people, offering them alternatives to gang-related activities.[24] Their art works expressed something of what slavery meant and still means to them, as did the *Freedom!* sculpture, which can now be seen in the

International Slavery Museum, one of several international museums in Liverpool.

One young Haitian participant in the artistic process, Ronald Cadet, commented: 'People don't have chains on their arms and legs now, but people still have chains in their minds. When you have problems getting food, housing and education, you are not living in a free country.'[25]

9

Partnership … you'll never walk alone

The Christian Council of Mozambique (CCM) was founded in 1948. It is a member of the World Council of Churches and was a partner of Christian Aid for many years from 1984. Made up of over twenty mainly Protestant churches, it set out to foster political leadership and work for social and economic justice while providing humanitarian relief in the face of all too many droughts, storms and floods.

Its most notable work has been in reconciliation and peacebuilding, led for many years by its highly respected President, Bishop Dinis Sengulane.[1] First came the struggle for independence, which CCM supported without getting directly involved. Two years after Independence in 1975, with Mozambique Liberation Front (FRELIMO) now in government, came the vicious attacks by the Mozambique National Resistance Movement (RENAMO or MNR) from 1977 to 1992, out to cause nothing but chaos and maintain the power of South Africa's apartheid regime over its neighbouring countries. It killed 1 million people and displaced 5 million people in the process. It left men, women and children naked, beaten, raped and dispossessed.[2] CCM set up its Justice, Peace and Reconciliation Commission in 1984, facilitating meetings between FRELIMO and RENAMO. Peace accords were signed in Rome in 1992. War broke out again between 2012 and 2014 and more localised violent outbreaks have never entirely gone away.

From 1996 to 2005, CCM set about Transforming Arms into Tools. It collected 600,000 weapons in exchange for sewing machines, hoes, bicycles, construction materials and more, encouraging dissident rebel groups to stop fighting and start earning a living. In 2005, CCM with Christian Aid and DFID sponsored local artists to create out of those weapons of war a sculpture called *Tree of Life*. It went on display in the British Museum as part of a season of African cultural events.

Partners galore

CCM, however, is only one among many partners of Christian Aid, almost too many to count. They are not all of one kind.

In the UK there is, obviously, a broad spectrum of churches: forty-one were listed in 2025. Individual supporters, giving money, time and energy, run into thousands, including an interesting list of 'celebrities' such as Alan Titchmarsh, Beverley Knight and Omid Djalili.

Close working relations have long existed with CAFOD marked by inevitable differences of opinion and real camaraderie. Senior staff exchanged seats on each other's boards. Paul Spray, head of policy, represented Christian Aid for some time. CAFOD party invitations (and those of the Catholic Institute for International Relations), noted for their promise of generous hospitality, were soon snapped up.

Networks such as the British Overseas Aid Group (BOAG), Bond[3] and the Disasters Emergency Committee have been important parts of Christian Aid's life. Churches Against Poverty (CAP), funded for a time by Christian Aid, has complemented its work on the home front rather than Christian Aid venturing there itself. The *New Internationalist* magazine and World Development Movement, both of which Christian Aid helped to set up, have enhanced its education and campaigning work. Voluntary Service Overseas was funded and supported by Christian Aid in its early years, not a few staff members benefiting from the opportunities it offered. Not sufficiently recognised as 'partners' are businesses such as the Co-op, which funded Christian Aid Week for several years, and AquAid, which started in 1998 to donate 30p to Christian Aid for every 19-litre bottle of water sold. All too often under-recognised as supportive partners are government departments such as the ODA followed by DFID with its Programme Partnership Arrangements (PPA).

Beyond the UK, Christian Aid has worked with the EU, the Republic of Ireland, the States of Jersey (donating £30,000 for Gaza during the violence of 2014) and very closely with sixteen other church-based agencies in Europe as a member of the Association of Protestant Development Agencies in Europe (APRODEV), renamed Association of WCC related Development Organisations in Europe, later to become ACT Alliance EU, of which Martin Bax, previously Deputy Director of Christian Aid, was the first General Secretary.

Foremost among partners, however, are the in-country regional, national and local organisations Christian Aid has worked with all over the world, from Africa to Central and South America, Asia, Europe, the Pacific and the Middle East.[4] Literally 'first' in the 1940s and 1950s came Councils of Churches, including the WCC based in Geneva, all part of the burgeoning ecumenical movement. Alongside them have been other faith-based organisations: Buddhist, Muslim and World Jewish Relief. As time went on there was a tendency to move away from Councils of Churches to secular organisations, until they outnumbered the rest: an imbalance that Christian Aid later sought to redress.[5]

Selection is dangerous, but here are one or two attempts to bring a few more of them to life.

The Christian Council of Kenya, now the National Council of Churches of Kenya (NCCK), is Christian Aid's oldest partner if initial cooperation with the WCC before Christian Aid was fully formed is discounted. It has over thirty members and a long history of innovation and speaking out on political issues. Christian Aid got involved when in 1954, during and after the Mau Mau uprising, NCCK appealed to the WCC for help to rebuild the lives of those affected. Money was used to support detainees in government detention centres. Critics accused NCCK, and with it Christian Aid, of supporting the colonial government's policy of quelling Kikuyu discontent. Janet Lacey saw the main problem as people moving from one pattern of life (colonial) to another (independence),[6] the difficulties only intensified by their disillusionment exploding into the horrors of war. Since then, grass-roots development projects all over the country supported by Christian Aid have included pioneering work on leadership with young people, setting up village polytechnics, supported by the Kenyan government in the 1970s, and working with faith leaders on HIV/AIDS.

The S-Corner Community Clinic and Centre, Kingston, Jamaica, was featured by Christian Aid in its tent at the Pentecost 2000 Day in

Cheltenham. It had been a partner of Christian Aid ever since it started work in 1991, until 2009. Early projects, many of them breaking new ground in the country, tackled poor sanitation and access to clean drinking water, bringing pride and employment to deprived communities in the process. S-Corner built a formidable reputation for defusing tensions in the community where gang warfare had led to people going out fearful of being caught in the crossfire. Known and trusted by all sides, S-Corner set up peace committees involving gang members, community leaders and Jamaican reggae artists; it held workshops in streets and backyards on safe sex and health; it raised chickens; it helped 9–12-year-olds with homework and into school and college, and provided employment opportunities for adults.

Gonoshasthaya Kendra (GK), Bangladesh, was established in 1972 by Dr Zafrullah Chowdhury, a prominent physician and activist, against a background on the one hand of rural communities denied access to affordable primary health care and, on the other, of international pharmaceutical companies importing drugs at high prices when they could be manufactured more cheaply inside the country. Chowdhury stood up to the pharmas and worked with government on a national drug policy, while GK went on to provide health services to the villages, training up local female paramedics to ride bikes – contrary to village customs but crucial for getting health services to remote communities – and develop integrated rural development projects covering not only health care but also education, flood prevention, nutrition, agriculture and microbiology.

B'Tselem means 'in the image of', an allusion to Genesis 1:27 and to God creating humankind in his own image: the religious and moral foundation for respecting the human rights of everyone, Jew and Palestinian alike. Since 1989 and still in 2025, this 'Israeli Information Center for Human Rights in the Occupied Territories', a long-standing partner of Christian Aid, has been documenting, researching and publishing reports and videos on human rights violations and working with Israelis and Palestinians for a viable solution to what appears to be a never-ending conflict. Since 2007 B'Tselem has provided Palestinians with 160 video cameras to record their experiences. In 2009 it won the British One World Media special category award for its groundbreaking work in the field of citizen journalism.

Organismo Cristiano de Desarrollo Integral de Honduras (OCDIH), Honduras, focuses on the economic empowerment of women, including survivors of gender-based violence, helping them to know their rights and get legal support. Against the background of climate change, it works with them on sustainability and disaster preparedness and beekeeping! Juanita, a member of a beekeeping group providing technical and financial support for farmers, became the first commercial woman beekeeper in Honduras. She was trained by OCDIH to lead a group of vulnerable women to breed and manage stingless bees.

Returning to Africa, the All Africa Council of Churches (AACC), founded in 1963, stands out for the size of its membership (210 churches), its presence in forty-three countries, and the breadth of its work. It has observer status at the African Union. Christian Aid has worked with it on the Ebola crisis in West Africa, GBV, the empowerment of women, and almost everything else from emergency relief and development projects to advocacy and efforts to address the HIV/ AIDS epidemic and interfaith conflicts. Two smaller partners are the Zimbabwe Environmental Law Association (ZELA), supported from 2012, which focused on reforming the laws relating to mineral mines and the threats to communities and the environment that came with them, and the Eagles Relief and Development Programme in Malawi, from 2011, motivating well-attended church congregations to clarify and work to meet the needs and aspirations of the communities that naturally formed around them.

Partnership

Christian Aid has had a lot to say about partners and its commitment to partnership,[7] so much so that the words can become devoid of any real meaning. If it simply means 'working with others', then it's a feature that Christian Aid shares with any NGO you care to mention. In itself, this is nothing unique or distinctive. It is necessary and pragmatic, as Christian Aid's policy recognises.[8] Not even the most operational agencies, like World Vision, can do anything without those who find the money, publicise the cause, supply the information and implement the plans. Partnership is a matter of common sense.

Digging deeper, however, pragmatism soon gives way to something more like a matter of principle, and in at least three ways. On principle Christian Aid has been committed to solidarity, ecumenism and localisation, all of which find practical expression in 'partnership' undergirded at one stage in its history by a Relational Theology.[9]

Solidarity

Christian Aid professes to have stood together for over seventy-five to eighty years years 'in solidarity with our most marginalised global neighbours, of all faiths and none'.[10] In 2020–21 it even ran a series of solidarity training sessions for supporters. At times, what it meant by it was almost circular: 'By joining in partnership, we act in solidarity.'[11] For most of the time it meant standing programmatically with the vulnerable to eradicate poverty and injustice. Sometimes, as with other solidarity movements, it gained a sharper cutting edge, faced with some uncomfortable questions. It could well mean taking sides against the perpetrators of oppression such as an apartheid regime, or siding with the oppressed such as the Palestinians, challenging traditions of neutrality. It could also mean staying with people come what may, causing unease when, for understandable reasons, Christian Aid ends its support for an organisation or withdraws from a country altogether, as it did in 2019–20, under severe financial pressures, from twelve countries, including Brazil, the Philippines and South Africa, even though in some cases regional connections remained.

Ecumenism

It is one thing to be born into ecumenism, quite another to remain committed to it as Christian Aid has done. Having started out as a department of the BCC, in 1990 it became a charity in its own right but still reporting annually to its parent churches through CTBI, the successor to the BCC in 1990. It was no less involved from its earliest days in the international ecumenical movement, not least because Janet Lacey, its founder, was already a significant player as the WCC took shape.

'Faith and Order' and 'Life and Work' are the two best-known areas of international ecumenical endeavour. The first tries to unite the churches by overcoming their doctrinal divisions, including disagreements over baptism, the Eucharist and ministry.[12] The second tries to do so by cooperating on tackling poverty and injustice and all manner of human need. Christian Aid has had no real involvement in Faith and Order. It felt more at home in Life and Work within the growing ecumenical family. As time went on, more and more members of the family came to believe that cooperation of this more practical kind provided more fertile soil for Christian unity than Faith and Order.[13] 'Need not Creed', as Janet Lacey cried in the 1940s, or 'Doctrine divides, service unites', as many have cried since.

Life and Work went through a number of reincarnations from the original WCC Department for Reconstruction and Inter-Church Aid, formed in 1945, to Division of Inter-Church Aid and Service to Refugees (DICASR) in 1949, later to become Commission on Inter-Church Aid, Refugee and World Services (CICARWS), which in turn became Sharing and Service in 1992. Something of a sea-change came about when Church World Action was formed in an attempt to coordinate the ecumenical response to the crisis in Rwanda after the genocide. It was followed after much debate by Action by Churches Together (ACT), then in 1995 by ACT International, then in 2003 ACT Development, and finally in 2010 ACT Alliance.[14] The Alliance covered not only emergencies but development programmes and advocacy as well. It soon outgrew Sharing and Service and took on a life of its own. The agencies, as members, agreed to co-branding but were fiercely protective of their own public identities.

Life and Work, however, was by no means free from controversy. Organisational changes reflected shifts in thinking, stimulated by vigorous and at times divisive debates at assemblies, conferences and commission meetings in which Christian Aid's directors, later CEOs, and colleagues along with other ecumenical agencies played a full part, well aware of possible implications for their own work. Christian Aid's Director from 1998 to 2009, Daleep Mukarji, a pioneer health worker in India and founder of the Rural Unit for Health and Social Affairs (RUHSA) before joining the WCC, came to Christian Aid from the heart of them. In different ways these debates touch on the issue of partnership between Christian Aid and the WCC, and more often between the givers and receivers of funding within the ecumenical family.

At times there was a real need to build trust and confidence. Northern agencies, for example, could question the competence of WCC staff to handle large sums of money on their behalf. WCC staff in turn, along with Councils of Churches and others in the South, saw the agencies as themselves agents of Western governments, with their policies and eagerness to control. The Ecumenical Church Loan Fund (ECLOF), founded as early as 1946 by two Swiss bankers, and the soon to be WCC General Secretary Visser 't Hooft, did express the trust that was not always easy to find. The agencies, Christian Aid included, along with others, contributed funds with few strings attached from which loans were made, first in Europe and, by the 1970s (many now by way of microfinance schemes for investment), to national Councils of Churches. It was chaired for many years by Cees Oskam, CEO of the Dutch Interchurch Coordination Committee on Development Aid (ICCO).

Partnership was severely tested when the WCC inaugurated the Programme to Combat Racism (PCR) and, as an act of solidarity, gave financial support ($10m between 1979 and 1991) to liberation movements especially in southern Africa, one of which was the African National Congress (ANC), founded in 1912. Kenneth Slack, Director of Christian Aid at the time, felt unable to support the move as he tried to negotiate tricky waters between the churches, charity law, public opinion and the need for radical action in the face of apartheid. His decision to distance the organisation from PCR led to deep unhappiness among some members of staff, even to resignations. The incident lingered long in the public memory. Years later, Christian Aid Week collectors could still be confronted with accusations of buying 'guns for guerillas', whereas in fact Christian Aid had only sent a shipload of medicines to displaced women in the ANC refugee camps in Tanzania.[15]

Much of the discussion over the years had to do with the nature of partnership, even at times whether it was an unrealistic ideal. It was implemented in a number of ways. For years CICARWS's bread-and-butter job was to draw up a list of 'priority' projects screened by national Councils of Churches and listed by Geneva for agencies to fund, a system that proved to be workable but cumbersome. A WCC scholarship scheme, eventually discontinued due to a lack of funds, was administered by Christian Aid. National and regional roundtables were set up where the so-called North and South met and talked, and agreed plans and how best to give support. Great efforts were made to understand 'resource sharing' as two-way traffic. If funding went in one direction, gifts of insight, spirituality and a more holistic understanding of development (why not help to build churches?) could travel in the other. All 'partners' had something of importance to offer. Much was achieved.[16]

Threatening the ideal, however, were several harsh realities mostly related to power, even if benign. Funding agencies like Christian Aid received large grants from institutions, including governments. With them came constraints and the bureaucracy of accountability. Christian Aid could not pass on funds without asking questions about how they would be used, and were constantly pressed by back donors to do so. Some partners in the South bridled because they regarded funds as rightfully theirs to use as they saw fit, and felt that demands for oversight and compliance reflected a lack of trust.

The dependency of the South on the funding agencies was far greater than that of the agencies on the South, even though Christian Aid admitted it could do little without them. The brute fact of an unequal world could never be entirely overcome. In the last resort the funding agencies could call the tune, leading more than one frustrated round-table participant from the South to plead in my hearing, 'Don't call us partners!'

Despite countless good working relations, specific doubts were expressed from time to time by Christian Aid and its counterparts about some ecumenical partners. Staff could be reluctant to send money where they considered it was not being spent well, or even being misdirected or misused. In the early days one complained about a large car for the General Secretary of a national council of churches and refused to fund it. Later another pulled the plug when funds were used for a staff 'away-weekend' out of the country!

A second doubt was of more general concern. When in early 1985 I was interviewed for the job of Director of Christian Aid, a distinguished member of the panel (Mary Appleby) asked me about 'ecumenism and efficiency'. Not knowing the background to the question, I didn't answer it well! It reflected a degree of frustration among staff. They felt obliged to support an ecumenical partner when they believed it was not really up to the job, while an alternative organisation was in pole position to do things better and more quickly. Which came first: loyalty to ecumenism, or the most efficient way of standing by the poor? They had a point. It remained, however, part of Christian Aid's commitment to help realise the potential of the ecumenical network where some of its members were weak, though many others, let it be said, were and remained strong. Nevertheless, the number of faith actors, whether churches or faith-inspired professional development agencies, declined until later efforts were made to reverse the trend.

Localisation

A third way in which partnership became more than pragmatic recalls the familiar 'boast' that 'Christian Aid does nothing'. From the beginning, and deliberately keeping a low profile (according to its Annual Report for 1984–85), it set out to support others in their struggles, notably national and local community-based organisations, rather than sailing in and doing things for them itself. Even more so when it began opening offices overseas. Only rarely has Christian Aid been anything like operational. Once again there was a pragmatic side to this principled approach. Local people were essential allies in the cause. Their organisations had networking experience, confidence and know-how. They knew best what needed doing. There were cost benefits as well to employing local staff. Beyond pragmatism, however, were issues of respect for the equal dignity and intelligence of other people and their right to have their share of the world's resources and control them. They have their faults and failings as human beings and organisations, but so do those who set out to be of help. 'White saviours', whether missionaries or development workers, and over-confident organisations that think they know best, are not the answer. Wisdom and energy are to be found beyond, not just within them.

Ubumbano

In 2015 DFID ceased to fund programmes in South Africa as a middle-income country. Christian Aid closed its office there in 2015 and its programme in 2020. That raised a number of issues around partnership.

Withdrawal itself looked to some like a failure of solidarity, mitigated only by the determination of Christian Aid and others to find an alternative way of 'standing with' the poorest in an extremely unequal society, true to its commitment to solidarity, ecumenism and localisation. What eventually emerged was ACT Ubumbano. ACT refers to the international ecumenical network of ACT Alliance; Ubumbano translates as 'solidarity'. It is a network of thirty southern African and three European NGOs working together for economic, gender and environmental justice. Members meet annually in its 'solidarity hub': a safe space for open debate, reflection and planning. It is not primarily about funding but finding new and better ways of working together, which can then be taken up and moved forward by an advisory board. The chair, vice-chair and secretary are all Africans. Born out of controversy, it was officially registered in 2020.

The initial efforts of a consortium of European funding agencies to find a more 'efficient' model of partnership to replace the old was heavily criticised by strong African NGOs. It seemed contrary to all that had been learned about mutuality, simply perpetuating the old donor–recipient relationship. What was needed was described as 'a new form of anti-colonial partnership' designed, agreed and implemented by all concerned but firmly located in southern Africa.[17]

Christian Aid as a trusted friend did a good deal to save the day, though questions inevitably remained. One European partner pulled out for a time. Several others found it difficult to fit ACT Ubumbano into Northern donors' reporting requirements. They also challenged it to make further progress towards self-sustainability. Some even wondered whether it actually added value to an already vibrant civil society. Nevertheless Ubumbano remains an instructive example of partnership, a defining but evolving concept in the life of Christian Aid.

Welcome to the Feast

Light the candles, bring your presents, let us celebrate good days,
With rejoicing and thanksgiving, for great actions give God praise.
Now's the time for jubilation, lift your voice in joyful song;
Thanks for justice, Christ-like anger, friendships made through righting wrong.

In the shining of the candles, dust shows up – as in the sun –
Thus revealing all our failings, power misused and work not done.
In our praying: 'God forgive us', let's remember those reviled;
Folk exploited, women wordless, children who have never smiled.

Light a candle in the darkness, flames will penetrate the night;
Pass the brightness to your neighbours, 'til the world is full of light.
Act with justice, use your anger, be on God's side – choose the least;
God, in weakness, will receive us, calling us to share their feast.

Written and set to a Welsh traditional air for Christian Aid's fiftieth anniversary by Janet Nightingale, © Copyright 2001 Stainer & Bell Ltd, 23 Gruneisen Road, London N3 1LS, www.stainer.co.uk. Reprinted by permission. All rights reserved.

10
India

The messianic figure at the heart of Christian Aid's identity was notorious for breaking conventions and putting the socially excluded high on his agenda. He touched a leper. He took notice of a woman in a crowd fearful to admit she had touched him. He talked to foreigners and healed their children. He asked for a drink from a woman with a bad reputation. He ate and drank with publicans and sinners, generally regarded as riff-raff. He fed the hungry, put the poor first and was sympathetic towards the mad or possessed. He put his arms round those that others preferred to avoid.

Exclusion

It is no surprise, therefore, that when it comes to Christian Aid's story in India, following that inspirational leader, the excluded tend to dominate its agenda.[1] They include tribal people (Adivasi), women, Muslims treated with discrimination at the hands of the Hindu majority, and the 'Untouchables', a term abolished in the post-Independence constitution. Known legally as 'Scheduled Castes', they include Dalits ('broken' or 'crushed' people), or Harijans ('Children of God'), as Gandhi called them. They are not just at the bottom of the caste system but technically outside it altogether. Some have prospered especially in urban areas, most still doing the dirty jobs but others finding careers in public service and banking, for example, showing increasing assertiveness and even achieving political power. K. R. Narayanan was the first Dalit to become President of India in 1997.

In the rural areas and villages, however, it remains a different story. Millions live in poverty as marginal farmers and bonded labourers endlessly paying off their debts while surviving as 'scavengers', disposing of dead animals, sweeping, cleaning drains and sewers, collecting garbage and disposing of faeces from latrines with their bare hands or with coconut shells and acid.[2] Not that they are without spirit and determination. They can march and bang their traditional *thappus* (drums) in protest against their humiliation. In 2012, tens of thousands of landless poor marched 350 kilometres from Gwalior in Madhya Pradesh to Delhi demanding their fair share of land, a demand that the government accepted.[3]

What does 'exclusion' look like for these people who fail to be treated, let alone regarded, as human beings?[4] A lack of jobs, health care, education, nutritious food and even reliable sources of any kind of food all come readily to mind. In the primary school in Kesarpur, a village in Uttar Pradesh, the new 'cook', a Dalit, was not allowed in the kitchen when food was being prepared. She was left to fetch water and gather firewood. Elsewhere, due to discrimination, only 75 out of 358 children in the primary school were being fed.[5] Farmers could be evicted from their land if they couldn't prove it was theirs. Fishing people were not paid for work under a government scheme, Mahatma Gandhi National Rural Employment Government Act (MGNREGA), which guaranteed them a minimum number of hours of employment each year. Government health workers refused to visit Ayar, a village in Bihar, because they said the people were unclean and 'stank'. In 2014 Action Aid reported that in Madhya Pradesh health workers avoided 65% of Dalit settlements. In 2007 Human Rights Watch estimated that 200 million Dalits in India were living in these settlements on the edges of 600,000 villages, not allowed to fetch water from the village well – a situation often described as 'hidden apartheid'. Women were 'violated and all but forgotten'. Pratama Kumari from Phulwari Sharif in Bihar, desperate to continue her studies, was forced by poverty and her parents to marry at 15 and suffer at the hands of an abusive husband. She was far from the exception.[6]

In the West we can be inconvenienced by occasional power cuts. In Pipralic village in Madhya Pradesh, the population of mainly Dalits was without electricity all of the time, unable to work, or sew, or study after dark and needing to travel to other villages to recharge mobile phones, crucial in an emergency. The village was remote, with high hills on one side and a river without a bridge on the other. Poles were erected in 2012, but the electricity supply lines were never connected. When asked why, officials gave vague answers and sent the villagers away.

They were not the only ones in the dark. In 2014, Climate Action Network South Asia estimated that among the Dalits in India over a third of families were without electricity, and that those who did have it, had it for only short periods of time. That meant relying on kerosene lamps and, for cooking, firewood, animal dung, leftovers from crops and, if near one of India's many coal mines, coal dust – all of them with negative implications for the environment and health. Where electricity had arrived, it was mainly generated by coal and gas. Switching to renewables and away from coal seemed a long way off.[7]

One thing Dalits have never been excluded from is the aftermath of cyclones, typhoons, monsoon rains, floods and tsunamis. They suffer along with the rest, but more so, and even here discrimination soon creeps in. On 26 December 2004, what became known as the 'Boxing Day tsunami' wreaked havoc along the coast of Tamil Nadu, as elsewhere. Ten thousand people died and 650,000 were displaced. Dalits were pushed aside, excluded from the makeshift shelters provided and left with minimum protection near graveyards and rubbish dumps. They were not allowed to draw water from the donated tanks because upper-caste Hindus feared they would pollute it. They were, however, expected to recover dead bodies without protective equipment as emergency services officials stood by in their protective clothing.[8]

Belinda Bennet, Christian Aid's India Country Director at the time, along with her colleagues could see the glaring inequalities and within weeks challenged the organisations she was working with to investigate. One senior figure, adamant that his organisation left no one behind, came back to admit that one community of Dalits living outside a village hadn't received a single drop of aid three weeks after the tsunami.

Response

Christian Aid's response to the treatment of so many of India's poorest was along the familiar lines of humanitarian aid, longer-term development projects and getting at the roots of structural problems. As always, it supported and accompanied other organisations rather than doing it all itself. They make a long and colourful list! Some, like the Church of South India (CSI), the Church of North India (CNI) and the Voluntary Health Association of India (VHAI), Tamil Nadu, were long-standing and go back to the very beginning of Christian Aid in the 1940s. All were focused on India's most excluded.[9]

Of the many, Church's Auxiliary for Social Action (CASA) stands out for me, as it played a key role in saving my life in the early 1990s when I fell seriously ill with a somewhat dramatic bout of cellulitis while opening one of its famous cyclone shelters. CASA is a natural partner for Christian Aid. The two are alike in so many ways. CASA was created by the National Missionary Council in India, which was founded in 1914 and later became the National Council of Churches in India (NCCI) in 1979. It was born at much the same time as Christian Aid in the 1940s in response to much the same issue: for Christian Aid the plight of refugees in post-war Europe, for CASA the vast numbers uprooted by Partition in 1947 when the newly independent Indian government asked it for help. Committed to stand by the poorest, both their agendas cover emergency relief, long-term development and tackling the structural causes of poverty and injustice. CASA may be more hands-on, but like Christian Aid respects the wishes, knowledge and skills of local communities which it works to empower. Clearly an agency of the churches, CASA describes itself as 'non-religious', reflecting a degree of sensitivity about its identity that Christian Aid can well understand. Major J. K. Michael was an outstanding Director, in post for twenty-four years from 1977 to 2001, leading with almost military precision and giving the lie to any supposed incompatibility between ecumenism and efficiency. Mainly for domestic political reasons, for a period from 2023 to 2024, CASA lost its registration under India's Foreign Contribution (Regulation) Act (FCRA), an ongoing issue to which we will come.

Documents dating back to the early years of the 1950s and 1960s suggest two ways of describing Christian Aid's work in general at the time.

First, it was thoroughly ecumenical. Letters between the WCC and Christian Aid by characters such as Janet Lacey and Leslie Cooke, the one heading up Inter-Church Aid and Service to Refugees at the World

Council of Churches in Geneva and the other heading up Inter-Church Aid and Service to Refugees at the British Council of Churches in London, give the impression not of two organisations but one. There are similar close ties with the National Council of Churches in India.[10]

Second, Christian Aid's contribution can be described as largely concerned with humanitarian aid to refugees and with one natural disaster after another.

Refugees

The Partition of India in 1947 sent 3.5 million Hindu refugees into the already overcrowded border city of Calcutta. By 1963, three years after World Refugee Year, Calcutta still had one of the worst refugee problems in the world, placing huge responsibilities on the Bengal Refugee Service, an agency of the NCCI, supported by Christian Aid. Elsewhere, in 1964, Christian Aid sent funds to help support refugees crossing from East Pakistan into Assam.

And then there were the Tibetans. The Dalai Lama wrote to the WCC in August 1960 expressing his sincere gratitude for the help received from the NCCI, part of 'the splendid efforts' from all over the world 'to render every possible assistance to the unfortunate Tibetan refugees'. In 1964 Lacey visited some of them. They were children being looked after in a school in Mussoorie, opened by His Holiness in March 1960 and run by the Tibetan Homes Foundation. She thought it was well run but objected to Miss Norman, the Principal and a missionary, teaching Christianity to children of another faith, so ignoring an understanding with the Dalai Lama that they should be allowed to grow up in the Buddhist religion.[11]

Natural disasters never seemed to go away. The tsunami of 2004, where help was extended for the first time to the coastal islands of Nicobar and Andaman, has already been mentioned. Before that, Christian Aid had appealed for funds in 1955 because of the cyclone and flooding in the south Indian districts of Tanjore and Ramnad, and again in 1960 due to floods in Bengal and when drought and famine broke out in Bihar in 1966–67.[12] Such was the need that in 1975 the Indian government agreed with the UK to allow relief supplies to be imported duty-free. In 1993 an earthquake struck in Latur and Osmanabad in western India, followed by the super cyclone in Orissa of 1999 and the Gujarat earthquake of 2001. After 2004 came an earthquake in Kashmir (2005), cyclone Hudhud in 2014 and the floods of 2017–19. The deadly Covid-19 arrived in 2020 when there could be half a million new cases in a day, with hospitals overrun and oxygen and medicines in very short supply or completely unavailable to the poor. And that is not an exhaustive list!

Following the 2004 tsunami, help came in a variety of guises, some predictable, others less familiar. That desperate people were rapidly supplied with food, clothing, clean water, shelter, health care, toiletries, cooking pans and the like almost goes without saying. Families were helped to find the missing, alive or dead. Along the coast, fishing boats, outboard motors, nets and other tackle were being mended and replaced. Christian Aid, always wary of providing 'spiritual' help, nevertheless accepted the point often made by colleagues at the WCC about 'holism' and the need for mental as well as physical support; so it provided trauma counselling and, for the children, therapeutic activities such as sports and games, along with makeshift schooling.

Development

Immediate help soon turned into rehabilitation and longer-term efforts to prepare for the worst, and at the same time to make life better. CASA and others continued to build their lifesaving, multi-purpose, disaster (or cyclone) shelters and more durable housing able to withstand storms, floods and quakes. Coastal farmers faced problems of their own where land was contaminated by salt water. Desalination programmes went alongside experiments with seeds and plants to see what might flourish despite the salt. Every effort was made in India, as elsewhere,[13] not just to repair the damage but to put communities at the centre of disaster management and strengthen their ability to be ready for the next one when it came along – even to stand up to it and fight back.[14]

Over time, Christian Aid helped sustain hundreds of programmes all over India. An early one in 1975 provided the Poona Blind Men's Association with skills training to get blind people, another marginalised group, into work and supplied them with micrometres, measuring equipment for writing Braille.

Gold digging had been going on in Kolar, Karnataka, 60 miles east of Bangalore, for some years, attracting many from nearby Andhra Pradesh and Tamil Nadu who saw great opportunities for work for unskilled and uneducated people. For a time the mines had been prosperous, but those days were long gone when the Kolar Gold Fields Development Society decided to set up an exploratory project in what was now a neglected and depressed area, to find out the needs of large numbers of unemployed and all too many women and young people with little prospect of work. A group, many from the Scheduled Castes, got together and put their ideas to Christian Aid, which made two grants in 1976 to cover salaries, housing allowances, travel and administration: an interesting example of where a concern about overheads is meaningless, and transparency about itemised expenditure makes far more sense.[15]

Also in 1976, Christian Aid funded research by the Intermediate Technology Development Group, still at work in the 2020s as Practical Action, and its Indian equivalent – the Appropriate Technology Development Association – into a new type of cotton-spinning machine or *charkha*. It was powered by something rather like a bicycle. The prototype proved successful and *Christian Aid News* reported in 1981 that plans were in place to manufacture forty a month and supply them to villagers in Uttar Pradesh.[16]

When Gordon Brown visited New Delhi in 2011, finding work was still high on the agenda. He met with the National Confederation of Dalit Organisations (NACDOR), supported by Christian Aid, busy training up female street vendors and rag pickers in electrical skills to work in a local subsidiary of Tata, the steel-making giant. He thanked Tata for getting involved and encouraged other businesses to open up employment opportunities in a similar way. Christian Aid's Country Director, Anand Bolimera, was invited to join the Affirmative Action Council of the Confederation of Indian Industry (CII).

Roohi lived in an urban slum in Lucknow, Uttar Pradesh. She was partly paralysed by polio at the age of 6. Her father, of nine children, earned £35 a month running a tea shop. After three months' training, in 2015 Roohi was hired by Aegis (one of India's leading liquefied petroleum gas companies) as a customer service executive earning £90 a month. Gordon Brown would have approved.

One intriguing programme, in Turundu, Jharkhand, greatly increased the quantity of resin produced by insects on trees by replacing traditional methods with scientific farming techniques involving pruning the trees, controlling the pests, and improved methods of introducing the larvae to the plants. Elsewhere, up to 6,000 marginalised farmers learned about organic cultivation, resulting in increased yields and a more sustainable way of life.[17]

Tom Palakudiyil, looking back with others on his time at Christian Aid's office in Delhi, which he set up in 1998 and managed until 2002, spoke among other things of 'change'. It was along similar lines to the shifts in Christian Aid's approach to development across the board, such as empowerment, decentralisation and localisation, better described as 'trends', perhaps, since none of them happened all at once![18] One of those trends, towards self-reliance, might possibly be traced back as far as 1975, when Christian Aid made a grant to the Xavier Institute of Social Service working with tribals in the Chota Nagpur region of Bihar on conscientisation and the promotion of small-scale self-employment (or entrepreneurship, as they called it) in an attempt to move them away from dependency and welfarism.[19]

PACS

Years later, from 2009 to 2016, Poorest Areas Civil Society (PACS) went a great deal further.

It was an extensive programme which, according to Anand Bolimera, Director of PACS, built on the belief 'that chronic poverty in India is largely caused by discrimination due to social exclusion'. It covered seven states and ninety of India's poorest districts where a substantial proportion of the population belonged to marginalised groups. It reportedly touched the lives of 9.6 million people. Financing came not from a grant but a commercial contract with DFID carrying a budget of £32m, hard won in the face of fierce competition where Christian Aid could well have been seen as the underdog. It was the first such contract to make a surplus (of £600,000) and in each of its seven years DFID rated its implementation as 'A+', one official describing it as 'fantastic'. It laid the foundation for further government funding for substantial programmes in Sierra Leone and the Democratic Republic of Congo (DRC). This level of support from the UK government was not without its critics quick to point out that India's economy was one of the world's fastest growing, while downplaying the fact that 30% of the world's poorest were to be found among its peoples – a fact noted in 2011 by Andrew Mitchell, minister in charge of the UK's overseas funding at the time.

PACS was carried out by Christian Aid India and a consortium involving over 225 civil society organisations under the leadership of Bennet and Bolimera. It challenged exclusion and discrimination by enabling people to speak up for themselves, to be more confident, to mobilise, to be aware of their rights and, under trained leaders, to claim those rights by confronting the authorities or, far better, by working with them instead of being at odds.

A lot of good stories came out of it.[20] Returning to Pipralic village and its electricity supply, or rather lack of it, a community-based organisation was set up (a common step in the right direction) and, after training, developed enough confidence to ring up the Chief Minister's helpline and complain. Work resumed in four days. The power was switched on in 2014. Every house got lighting and a power point. Work and study could continue after dark. A local businessman set up a mill and everyone had flour to make chapatis.

In Ayar, Bihar, villagers became aware of their rights and submitted a petition to the authorities complaining about the health workers who refused to visit. The workers were 'punished'. A government mobile vaccination team and health care services soon arrived in the village. The health of the villagers improved.

In the village school in Kesarpur, Uttar Pradesh, where the new cook was excluded from the kitchen, three years' work with the mothers led to them taking a degree of control. There, and elsewhere, they stood for election to the school's management committee and made sure that cooks were allowed to cook; very poor children were not discriminated against when it came to school meals; and schools no longer reinforced, even 'taught', untouchability by the way they treated their students.

In 2005 the government passed the MGNREGA, which guaranteed everybody 100 days of paid work a year. The women in the remote village of Teghariya, Bihar, now summoned up the courage to apply and were employed to build an all-weather access road into the village to replace the muddy and dangerous existing path. They had problems to overcome. One was corruption. Their first attempt soon cracked open due to the incorrect ratio of cement and stone to soil in the mix; but they persevered and lived to celebrate success.

In Taldevri village in Chhattisgarh, the Dalit women's self-help group was no less determined. Against an all too familiar background of sexual violence and abuse, liquor was the problem. The men spent their money on drinking it while the women, with what little they had, tried to pay for food, medicines and the school fees. They set out to eradicate the making and selling of liquor. Taking the law into their own hands, they patrolled the village with large bamboo sticks ready to deal with offenders.

Along came yet another bus![21] From December 2014 to May 2015, one was specially adapted to take thirty young people at a time on a six-hour journey – 103 journeys altogether. On board they took part in workshops dealing with gender inequality, violence against women, and caste-based discrimination. On their travels they visited and talked with people from excluded communities and pledged to put an end to prejudice in their own.

During PACS a number of social audits were carried out and the findings presented to officials. Video journalists, or 'community correspondents', were trained to report directly from the grass roots, where the unheard spoke up about their grievances. Fishing people, for example, and others employed by MGNREGA had not been paid; health insurance cards were not working; teachers did get paid but then paid someone else, unqualified, to mind their classes. Evidence-based advocacy was now being practised by Dalits, and to good effect.

The Forest Rights Act of 2006 reinforced the Indian Forest Act of 1927, whereby all land was government-owned, and forest communities, if unable to prove ownership, were permanently under threat of eviction. In 2007, 25,000 landless people joined the historic Janagrah land march walking barefoot for 350 kilometres from Gwalior to Delhi demanding land titles. In 2012, 50,000 from Janagrah did much the same. A Global Positioning System (GPS) helped them to plot their land accurately and then establish and claim their right to it.

Safai Karmachari Andolan (SKA), supported by Christian Aid, mobilised affected communities to campaign for the elimination of the degrading practice of manual scavenging in India. As PACS was drawing to a close in 2016, Bezwada Wilson, one of SKA's founders, was awarded the Ramon Magasayay Prize for his inspiring work. At the award ceremony, the Minister for Rural Development, responding to a demand from Wilson, offered an unconditional apology on behalf of the government of India for having allowed the practice to continue.

After PACS

At the end of the seven years, it was essential that the social capital created during the lifetime of PACS was fully invested in the future. Momentum had to be maintained, not lost. A host of more organised and confident marginalised people were ready to move forward. DFID, holding Christian Aid in high esteem, invested £1m over twelve months to ensure continuity, but things did not run entirely smoothly.

Christian Aid India's office and activities were closed down in 2013, caught by something of an administrative accident in the dragnet of an Indian government check on NGO compliance. PACS was at its peak. Pressure mounted when a change of government in 2014 saw an increase in the use of India's FCRA of 1976, updated in 2010, to severely restrict the activities of thousands of NGOs and several charities from minority communities. Unless they received registration from the government, they could no longer receive foreign funding. Finding a way forward was both technical and complicated. The result was two organisations, one 'for profit' and the other 'not for profit', referred to subsequently as 'the hybrid approach'.

Change Alliance (Change Alliance Pvt Ltd or CAPL) was set up in 2014 as a 'for profit' company with its own board, as it had to if it was to gain approval. Belinda Bennet became its first CEO (2014–17), followed by Anand Bolimera (2017–24). Christian Aid invested in it long-term. It was best described as a consultancy working for private and corporate clients and, most importantly, for many members of the PACS consortium. Christian Aid also 'hired' it to monitor and support its programme in India. Project funding from London went directly to FCRA-registered partner organisations.

Waiting in the wings was another organisation or foundation known as Partnering Hope into Action (PHIA). It had been set up and registered with its own board in 2005 by Christian Aid as a kind of 'insurance policy' able to generate income within India should Christian Aid be unable to stay. It was in touch with a network of civil society organisations similar to Christian Aid's, working on much the same sort of agenda, but it was largely dormant. With the closure of Christian Aid's office in India in 2014, PHIA, working closely with CAPL, stepped up to inherit and make good use of the PACS legacy.

Together, by way of example, they were much involved in the Gender Equality Programme (GEP) launched in 2016 by Marks & Spencer and the British High Commission, later joined by Superdry, Mothercare and Levi Strauss. It set out to tackle gender inequality in the garment industry. PHIA set to work in over twenty-five factories and was awarded the Sandvik India Gender Award in 2019.

When Covid-19 struck, migrant workers from Jharkhand state were left stranded across India trying to get back home. PHIA, with the help of 200 volunteers and the government of Jharkhand, set up a helpline enabling it to identify and assist more than 1 million migrants. It also activated a network of 127 civil society organisations to see that the migrants, wherever they were, got food and other essentials. PHIA won a good deal of publicity and praise in the Indian press.

Looking back in 2024,[22] PHIA was judged to be an outstanding success in an increasingly hostile environment. It raised £1.5–£2m from domestic sources every year from 2019 to 2024, to the point where it was virtually self-sustaining. The legacy of the PACS programme continued even though funding for PACS 2 never materialised. The hybrid model seemed to have worked, winning a great deal of interest and respect in the NGO sector. However, a good many questions surrounding CAPL needed urgent clarification. Was it a temporary measure in a crisis, or the direction of travel for the future? Was Christian Aid prepared to invest sufficient funds for it to widen its role, gain the appropriate business skills, increase its business and become profitable?[23] Did a 'for profit' enterprise having to go carefully on human rights issues sit comfortably with Christian Aid's general ethos where justice, not profit, was the priority? Was CAPL's board a manageable anomaly within Christian Aid's governance structure? And in the face of financial realities, where did CAPL fit into Christian Aid's future plans for India and elsewhere?

Visitors

Of the many visits to Christian Aid in India, Tom Palakudiyil remembers one he found more than encouraging by the then Bishop of Liverpool, James Jones. The bishop, an evangelical, had confessed to being somewhat wary of Christian Aid, fearing it was 'too radical', whatever that meant. He had the integrity to go and see. Arriving in doubt during his sabbatical, he spent two weeks travelling and seeing Christian Aid's disaster preparedness work, visiting West Bengal and spending time with CASA. He came away a believer, full of praise for what he had seen and sending Tom an 'effusive' letter of thanks.

The significance of an earlier visit is harder to assess. On 25 October 1997 an article in *The Tablet* was headlined, 'Queen touches the untouchables'! During a visit to India she had gone to St Francis Church in Kochi, Kerala, where she met Dalit women who had benefited from a Church of South India programme funded by Christian Aid. They presented her with a cooking pot they had made, regarded as polluted and unusable by any of 'high' birth.

One of the women was Laila, married to a labourer who beat her. Another was Gayathiri, at risk of being sold by destitute parents. Both had become financially independent. A third, Narasamma, the face of Christian Aid Week in 1997, farmed silkworms and hoped soon to study law and fight for justice. The gift, together with a silk scarf, was their way of saying 'thank you' to the British people and churches for their support through Christian Aid.

The Queen's 'touch', avoiding condescension, said a great deal about inclusion, as when Jesus touched a leper and Princess Diana a victim of HIV/AIDS; but maybe even more significant was what that evidently moving encounter suggested about the courage and dignity of the Dalit women.

11
Learning to care

In 1971 Eric Jay, Christian Aid's Education Secretary, wrote in *Christian Aid News* (April) about why Christian Aid was committed to spending 'a small proportion' of its income on education. The article had a slightly defensive tone, no doubt with an eye on those who wanted all their money to go directly to the poor while keeping a careful watch on 'overheads'. He argued that education was important because 'for the sake of the poor we need to know' the facts about poverty, not least by listening to the poor themselves, and asking who is doing what about it, from governments to organisations like Christian Aid.

Christian Aid was true to its word. Eric Jay mentioned 2.5% of income set aside in his time to help the poor 'indirectly' by educating the British public, something that ecumenical leaders in poorer countries had asked Christian Aid to do. During her time as head of education and then of the Churches Team which succeeded it (1984–94), Barbara Vellacott could speak of 10% of Christian Aid's income being spent on education and campaigning. Looking back, she commented that there was plenty of money about and that the department's profile was high.

Staffing levels at that time were generous and were maintained. Although an education department as such disappeared in time, the work went on but distributed between different teams such as a Churches Team and a Schools and Youth Team. Youth advisers, schools advisers, adult education advisers, a visual education adviser (briefly) and, in Bristol for one year, a student adviser were all on the payroll full-time and part-time. They were backed up by a considerable number of area staff across the four countries, part of whose job was to be educators, informing and empowering the churches, and beyond Christian Aid by serious cooperation with Oxfam, Save the Children and, above all, with

CAFOD. Their four education officers met regularly and worked together where possible.

Ever since Eric Jay stated his case, Christian Aid has produced a steady stream of resources for primary and secondary schools at least twice a year, such as lesson outlines related to the national curriculum and GCSE exams, and materials for assemblies. They regularly receive glowing reviews. One stalwart supporter in Yorkshire wrote to say that when she now looked back at the material for schools, 'I just can't believe how good it was.' She sent several well-preserved samples to prove it, such as 'Resurrecting Rubbish' produced for Harvest 1988, and 'Going, Going, Gone' for the following year.

Some from the 1980s and 1990s were still in use in the 2020s. They included film strips, songs and videos and often had a light touch about them. Sixth-formers could be invited to play a game simulating the evacuation of a village due to flooding ('Disaster Zone Game'), or the perilous journeys people have to make as they flee from conflict ('Safe Place Ludo'), or how to survive as a street seller on the streets of Kolkata ('Paper Bag Game'). 'Beyond the Bake Sale' encouraged them to use their education to take action, as did 'Courageous Advocacy', a programme designed to equip schoolchildren to be confident enough to write letters to politicians, mount their own petitions, protest about single-use plastics to supermarkets and their own school governors, and help with Fairtrade stalls and foodbanks.

Much of this work was firmly anchored in the Global Neighbours Accreditation Scheme sponsored by the Church of England, first in its primary schools (10% of them in 2024) and by 2023 in its secondary schools. All schools were welcome to join. They could gain bronze, silver and gold awards according to how many boxes they could tick with the agreement of an independent visiting assessor. The boxes covered a good deal of ground, including the general culture of the school, its anti-racism agenda, growing understanding among teachers and pupils of the root causes of poverty, time set aside for discussion and reflection, and giving serious attention to pupils' agenda-setting questions, all of it aimed at empowering them to become courageous advocates for justice.

In the autumn of 1976, Christian Aid contributed to an ambitious nationwide education programme launched in Liverpool presenting materials for schools contrasting the problems of Calcutta (*sic*) with those of Liverpool to illustrate the need for urban renewal, a cause taken up by Michael Heseltine, a government minister at the time. The plea was not for money but for understanding. 'Hands across the World', produced for schools for Christian Aid Week in 2019, highlighted the number of children (260 million) who had no school to go to and challenged those who did have one as to what it meant to be a 'global neighbour' to those who did not.

Christian Aid education staff were well aware that they had much to learn themselves and agonised about how to guard against racism within their own ranks, including the risk of stereotyping. Then an email arrived in January 2024 from the deputy head of a primary school in Leicester. She was full of praise for Christian Aid's materials but was pulled up sharply by one of them. Preparing for an RE lesson with 9-year-olds, mostly born in Britain, many with family roots in other countries, she looked at a Christian Aid video for a way into her topic only to see all the poor people needing help portrayed as people of colour and for most of the time those helping them as white. One and possibly both of the children presenting the video appeared to be well-spoken white British individuals.

Worship and prayer

The Christian Aid teams dealing with schools and churches also did a great deal of work on worship and prayer. Liturgies were written for Christian Aid Week and harvest festivals and carol services for Christmas, with words and music for choirs and congregations. Several notable books of prayers were published with SPCK – notable because they were widely used: *Bread of Tomorrow* (1992), *Companions of God* (1994), written to accompany pilgrims to the Holy Land, and *Dear Life: Praying through the year with Christian Aid* (1998), all of them authored, co-authored or edited by Janet Morley.

She contributed this Advent prayer to *Bread of Tomorrow*:

God, our hope and our desire,
we wait for your coming
as a woman longs for the birth,

the exile for her home,
the lover for the touch of his beloved,
and the humble poor for justice.[1]

All Desires Known, entirely written by Morley and first published in 1988, articulated a helpful understanding of what prayer is about, even in its title: 'desire' or what we long for. It proved to be such a rich source of material, including collects, litanies and poems, that it has been reprinted several times since, for example by SPCK in 1992 and 2005.

Worship and prayer are strictly speaking not about education but about our encounters with God, whether adoring, thanking, questioning, beseeching or responding to God's invitations; nevertheless, in order to pray in an informed way or preach sermons that connect the good news of the gospel with the bad news of the injustices heaped on the world's poor, education has an indispensable role to play. Christian Aid's worship materials included plenty of it.

In 2021, for example, to mark its seventy-fifth birthday, Christian Aid produced *Rage and Hope: 75 prayers for a better world*.[2] Each prayer, some very long, some short, is accompanied by a personal background note. Opening it at random (pp. 108f.), we find George Kopti, a Palestinian priest in the Anglican Diocese of Jerusalem, remembering how his family fled from Jaffa as refugees in 1948, his grandmother giving birth to his father 'on the road'. He went on to write this prayer:

> Lord Jesus, you experienced being a refugee. You had to flee from death and hostility. You have not returned home to your birthplace. You know the pain of refugees and their longing for their homelands and a better future.
>
> I pray that you may bless all refugees. Give them hope amid loss and sorrow. Bless them as they find comfort in you and believe in your justice. Make them a blessing wherever you want them to be. Guide and protect them in the power of your Holy Spirit.

Or take, again at random, '... till all creation sings', made available by Christian Aid for harvest celebrations in 1998. The prayer of confession is infused with stories about Chico Mendes (see Chapter 4) and how Theresa Solomon from South Africa, a so-called 'coloured', was forced to leave her home under apartheid laws. The material for an address refers to Sudan and Bangladesh, where harvests are far from guaranteed, and to Paul's reference in Romans 8:23, in an effort to bring hope to those with God's Spirit as being the 'first fruits', the guarantees of a rather different kind of harvest. Even the reference to 'debts' in the Lord's Prayer (Scottish version) is linked to the modern-day debt crisis and unforgiving banks.

Supporters of Christian Aid who went to church to say their prayers with the help of its many resources would learn a good deal about poverty and injustice.

Development education

Because Christian Aid was not only concerned about educating students and churchgoers but also the general public, it got involved in an interesting range of initiatives, either funding them or supporting them as a member, or in some cases setting them up.

In 1958 the Bishop of Portsmouth made a request in a London newspaper for volunteers to go to Borneo and teach English. Alec and Mora Dickson, Christian Aid supporters, read the article and in that same year recruited, funded and sent out sixteen volunteers, and Voluntary Service Overseas was born. By 2022 there were volunteers in thirty-five African and Asian countries no longer doing their best as willing amateurs for short periods of time, good value as they were, but as qualified and experienced professionals in their own fields committed to staying for two years.

The Joint Committee on Society, Development and Peace (SODEPAX) was an initiative of the World Council of Churches and the Vatican, the only joint programme between them at the time. It ran from 1968 to 1980 and brought together representatives of the main Christian traditions from twelve countries. The indefatigable Eric Jay, who co-chaired it for a time, called it 'The Big Agenda'.

SODEPAX questioned whether existing education systems were doing enough to bring about change and asked how to make influential decision-makers understand their responsibilities to the world's poor.

It had a massive educational programme in mind, aimed at mobilising a worldwide lobby for justice. It was one of those ecumenical forums, quite different from the more active project-funding committees, where radical thinking went on, aiming to inspire radical action on structural issues.

Coming nearer to home, the World Development Movement was 30 years old when Mark Curtis, Christian Aid's Head of Global Policy and Advocacy and an outspoken critic of UK government policy, took it over in 2004. Christian Aid had helped to get it going in 1970 in the hope that it would campaign in the UK where at that time, because of perceived Charity Commission restrictions on political activities, Christian Aid felt unable to go. It produced briefings on issues like world trade and IMF policies[3] and over the years, along with Christian Aid and others, helped to get several other movements going as a co-founder and funder of the Fairtrade Foundation, J2000, the Trade Justice Movement and the MPH Campaign of 2005.

The *New Internationalist* magazine was the brainchild of Peter Adamson of Third World First. It was originally co-sponsored by Christian Aid, Oxfam and the Joseph Rowntree Charitable Trust. Later, based in Oxford, it stood on its own two feet as a multi-shareholder cooperative. It set out to teach the public about development issues in an accessible way. Its first issue, in March 1973, carried an interview with Kenneth Kaunda of Zambia. The headline on the cover of the autumn issue in 2023 was 'Decolonise Now!' Maybe it became best known for the August edition of 1973, which drew attention to the irresponsible marketing of baby milk by multinationals in the Third World.[4]

For many years the week in October around United Nations Day became known in the UK as One World Week. It was founded by WDM, supported by all the churches and funded by Christian Aid and all the usual suspects. The first week was in 1978 and the theme was 'Just Living'. In 2022 it was 'Act Now for our Children's World'. The aim was to raise awareness and encourage understanding and action on global issues that affect us all. In 2022, as money and influence seemed to wane, the trustees decided to close it down, leaving the field to the EU's Global Education Week observed at much the same time of year. Neither has made a great deal of impact outside the churches.

Ken David, who left Christian Aid's education department to work in Central Africa, 'starred' in the much-admired BBC documentary *The Politics of Compassion*, broadcast and repeated in 1980, profiling Christian Aid and Kenneth Slack, its Director, apparently feeling more sure-footed about campaigning. In a way, the programme heralded the formation of the International Broadcasting Trust (IBT) in 1982, a membership organisation to which Christian Aid and Oxfam have always belonged. IBT helps the NGOs to work more effectively with the media to ensure coverage of global issues. It offers training in media skills, now in a digital world, and provides regular access to influential journalists, programme makers and editors. It played a large part in ensuring that the charter of the BBC as a public broadcaster maintained a strong commitment to covering global issues.

In the run-up to the UN's Earth Summit in Rio de Janeiro, Brazil, in June 1992, Christian Aid worked with the BBC, IBT and environmental agencies on a week of broadcasting making clear that it was the world's last real chance to save the planet!

Teacher, teach yourself

Learning is not only about Christian Aid's efforts to educate others. It has had its own lessons to learn as well.

I remember digging myself a hole trying to cope with one of them. Christian Aid had long opposed child-sponsorship schemes, which were good money-raisers but isolated the chosen ones from their friends and communities, treating them as objects of charity lacking initiative and requiring them to learn to write back grateful letters when they had far more pressing things to do. For reasons I forget I found myself trotting out these objections on a visit to the Bishop of London, throwing in for good measure that designated funds tied our hands and increased the cost of administration. The good bishop, a bachelor, promptly announced that he was sponsoring five children. We managed to remain on good terms. The lesson for Christian Aid to learn was how to respond to the natural desire, expressed by many, to reach out not only to the unnamed thousands they were asked to help, and did, but to particular faces and communities they could get to know personally and take an interest in without using people with multiple needs to meet their own. Stories about them were not enough. Christian Aid responded in a number of ways. Supporters were offered opportunities to visit overseas. Leaders from overseas were invited to visit the UK, expenses paid. Donors could to some extent request their money to go to a particular country or programme, difficult though that was to manage. In Their Lifetime (ITL) involved a considerable commitment of a donor's time and money (see Chapter 15 for an example). An interesting story from Yorkshire and Mali about building personal, long-term relationships can be found in Chapter 18.

The most obvious efforts at self-learning have been the endless reviews, report-backs, evaluations and impact assessments of Christian Aid's projects and programmes, often but not always carried out by independent consultants, many of them retirees from the NGO world.[5] An extremely comprehensive review of aid in general came in the form of Roger Riddell's *Does Foreign Aid Really Work?*,[6] surveying its successes and failures and suggesting ways forward. Riddell guided Christian Aid's policies from 1999 to 2004. An evaluation for DFID in 2010 of the Partnership Programme Arrangement (PPA) concluded: 'Christian Aid in the view of the evaluators does provide extremely good value for money' (Annual Report 2010/11). It led to a successful bid for another for 2011–14 with increased funding.

A notable example of an internal review came in 2020 after Christian Aid decided in 2019 to close down twelve of its country programmes and, in effect, leave.[7] Many of Christian Aid's area staff offices in the UK suffered a similar fate at the same time. Of the twelve countries affected, leaving reviews were carried out internally on six: Angola, Brazil, Ghana, Guatemala, South Africa and the Philippines. Information gathering was somewhat restricted. Covid-19 prevented any actual visits to three of them. The reviews tended to look at more recent times and mainly focused on one aspect of the story. Highly relevant as that was, it did not present a full picture. The Angola review looked at strengthening civil society; Brazil at challenging growing social and religious ultra-conservatism and its effects, especially on women; Ghana reviewed work on tax justice; Guatemala on fostering cooperation between fellow members of ACT Alliance. South Africa did go back to the apartheid days and after that examined the significant shift in North–South power relations. The Philippines review focused on the issue of resilience or pushing back in the face of disasters and climate change.

A summary of these reviews and their findings highlighted a number of lessons learned.[8] Christian Aid needed to be adaptable and learn when to stay in the background, as in the Philippines, and when to be far more upfront, as in Ghana where Christian Aid directly implemented some programmes, and in Angola by working openly with the churches on peacebuilding in the wake of a disastrous war.

Other findings were about strengthening a partner's agenda rather than Christian Aid's, by supporting innovation, fostering links between local and national organisations, using unrestricted funds to build capacity and making sure that localisation, where leadership, freedom to act and the wherewithal to do so were handed over to local communities, really worked and was not compromised by donors' heavy-handed concerns about accountability and compliance.

A sixth finding might have been the most challenging. In several countries local and national organisations had, thankfully, grown stronger. Some could raise funds themselves. The South Africans had turned old relationships on their head, well able to call the tune and hold their own on the global stage, as they made clear to Amanda Khozi Mukwashi, Christian Aid's CEO, when they met her in 2019. What then might be the future role of NGOs like Christian Aid? Will they still have a complementary and distinctive role to play or face redundancy and in the long term learn how to leave in an even more final way? Might the highly motivating but unrealistic slogan 'Make Poverty History' need to make way for 'Make Christian Aid History', not because poverty was over but because colonialism was being reversed and building capacity in the South had been taken seriously, and new forms of solidarity were on the horizon?[9]

Many marginalised communities were in no position to make their presence felt like the South Africans. How could their voices be heard and taken into account as Christian Aid tried to learn to do better? Along came the trucks and the cameras.

Seen and heard

'Picture power', they called it. In Kalawani, Makueni County, Eastern Kenya, Christian Aid's Thriving Resilient Livelihoods programme was hard at work with the local community learning to be proactive in the face of drought, conflict, hunger and climate change, to mention only a few of the threats they faced.

Village savings and loans schemes were established where, after saving for three to four weeks, the women (the men initially felt that dealing in small change was beneath them) could take out a loan at a 10% interest rate from the little tin cash box they shared. The loans were used to set up small businesses, which in time could offer employment to casual labourers, or to buy anything from rainwater storage tanks to a few 'start-up' chickens. More spectacularly, the men began to build sand dams for channelling water to their fields where mangoes, beans, tomatoes, kale and passion fruit soon began to grow. The women bought pumps and pipes with their loans to siphon off some of the water to their gardens.

But how could the programme be assessed and improved? What had really worked? How could Christian Aid find out and who was to say? In March 2015, Christian Aid's photo unit in London went out to Kalawani and trained two local men and a woman – Mary, Jackson and Justus – selected by the community, in basic photography, followed by two weeks taking pictures of local places and people where they went as 'photo monitors'. What photos they took was up to the community. The results were compared and contrasted ('triangulated') with the findings of more traditional assessments.

The outcome was variously described as 'more credible', 'revealing', 'moving' and 'powerful'. The photographers spotted, for example, the inequality in terms of access to water between those living near the dams and those further away. Large numbers of photos were displayed to the locals and gave rise to lively debate. The savings schemes and dams scored highly, seen clearly through the camera's eye to have made a difference.[10]

The Truth Truck was another effort to learn, this time by listening to the voices that mattered but who didn't find it easy to speak or get a hearing. The truck, made locally by helping hands and kitted out by a local production company, was a makeshift recording studio on wheels. Following the earthquake it travelled through eight districts of Nepal in late January and early February 2016 to find out what emergency aid had been helpful and what had not. Local people were invited to step inside this safe space where, left to themselves and a few pre-recorded questions, they could take their time to give their feedback. Eighty women and ninety-nine men took part. Supplies of sanitary pads, soaps and toothpaste were not helpful because people did not know how to use them. Corrugated sheets for building temporary homes came out on top but with a clear message about building safer houses in the future. The fact that the video recording of the interviews was self-critical of Christian Aid was a pleasant surprise according to Dipankar Patnaik, Christian Aid's Emergency Programme Manager in Nepal.

'Picture power' might also describe 'Positive Negatives', one of a number of photographic exhibitions nursed along by Joseph Cabon, Christian Aid's own highly gifted photographer. The compelling and personal photographs of their lives were taken by HIV positive women in the DRC. They were exhibited in Kinshasa in June 2000 and then in London six months later.

Grand designs

Miles away from these micro efforts to learn was the macro world of international development, to which Christian Aid belonged, with its grand theories about how best to overcome poverty, inequality and injustice, about which there was always much to learn and debate.[11] All of them, however, had contributed to Christian Aid's thinking. All had their limitations, some more than others. Not one of them was adequate by itself.

Modernisation, one of the earliest and most pervasive of the theories, insisted that underdeveloped countries should become like us, the so-called developed, by embracing modern science and technology, industrialisation, growth and education as understood by the West. The economic growth it stimulated would trickle down and raise living standards. Badly needed funds from governments, the WB and IMF, private banks, NGOs and investors were transferred on that basis. Neoliberalism was a close ally of modernisation, insisting on the benefits of the free market and of small states exercising less control and providing fewer services. The structural adjustment policies of the WB and IMF were in line with that theory and judged by many to have done more harm than good, driving many countries into debt with a heavy price to pay to get out of it.

Dependency theory was a reaction to the shortcomings of modernisation. It drew attention to a new form of colonialism whereby the old colonisers kept control and continued to line their own pockets at others' expense. Where a poorer country opened its doors to investors, in mining, coal and minerals for example, Transnational Companies (TNCs) moved in, often paying low wages, damaging the environment and making sure they enjoyed the lion's share of the profits. Free trade benefited powerful companies like the pharmaceuticals far more than their so-called beneficiaries who, according to free-market rules, were not allowed to protect or subsidise their own vulnerable industries. These gross imbalances provoked Christian Aid's campaigns on fair trade and tax dodging.

A different approach was taken and embraced by Christian Aid, focusing on human rights and entitlements.[12] An essential feature of any development programme must be to further human rights as laid down in the UN's Universal Declaration of Human Rights in 1948. They include the right to education, participation, food, housing, work, health and the right to the means to claim them irrespective of race, gender or religion. These rights were universal but regarded by some as 'Western' and individualistic. Ways of ensuring they were respected varied and could include efforts at empowerment, advocacy and taking legal action as far as the International Court of Human Rights. They were not crowned with success.

The economist and philosopher Amartya Sen, followed by Martha Nussbaum, preferred to talk about capabilities and what people needed to be capable of living a good life, understood not just in terms of poverty and wealth but in a more holistic way. Sen's writings remain complex. He gives some striking personal examples, such as the woman who needs to be 'capable' of appearing in public without shame, the man who needs to be able to read, and the disabled person who needs to be able to get about.

Neither the human rights nor capabilities approach could entirely supplant the needs-based approach probably exemplified by Christian Aid's emergency relief work where the poor need food and shelter, seeds and tools *now*, without waiting for their rights or enhancing their capabilities. Its promoters, however, remained well aware of their responsibility to dig deeper and ask *why* the poor were in such need of immediate relief in the first place.

One of the answers all too gradually gained profile with the growing awareness of climate change. It gave rise to a plea for 'limits to growth'[13] and to the theory of sustainable development with sustainable development goals to mark its progress or lack of it. The goals were reviewed and revised from one year to the next at meetings of the UN's Conference of the Parties (COP). Whether talking about the environment, the climate crisis, economic development or politics, the aim as stated in the Brundtland Report, 'Our Common Future', was to meet the needs of the present without denying the future the ability to meet theirs.[14] For Christian Aid, climate change and climate justice became big issues, as described in Chapter 13 below.

Another quite different theory of development, the result of another learning curve, became known as 'localisation'. It up-ends some of the earlier ones, especially modernisation, as poorer countries and communities rather than the powerful ones began to dictate the agenda. It builds on one of the most influential lessons learned when looking into causes, namely the discrepancies in power, local, national and international, crying out for the empowerment of the powerless: one of Christian Aid's oft-proclaimed key concerns: poverty, power and prophetic voice!

Ahead of the World Humanitarian Summit in May 2016, Christian Aid along with CAFOD and DanChurchAid (DCA) founded 'Charter for Change', committed to increasing funding for local action. As a result, nearly 200 INGOs and national NGOs signed up to a Grand Bargain agreed to at the Summit, setting up Start Fund to cut out the middlemen and get money directly to local people.

The Local to Global Initiative (L2G), in contrast to moving from global to local, taken by Christian Aid and others, developed the Survivor and

Community Led Response (SCLR). It recognised that the key players in an emergency were the self-help groups that already existed or soon emerged, usually before any other actors, including the UN, arrived. Incomers should learn from them, not the other way round. They knew better what to do and how to mobilise people to do it. They knew better how to make good use of the available resources. Christian Aid's job was to see that they had them readily to hand, and that included ready cash. This theory of development was put into practice in several countries,[15] including when war broke out in Ukraine in 2022. Like any other theory of development it had its problems, not least around issues of accountability, mirrored in long-familiar WCC debates about resource sharing, where there was a danger, already referred to, that heavy-handed reporting requirements of donors would compromise attempts to hand over control and responsibility so that the locals could go free.

An interesting indication of these shifts of thinking over time is the struggle to refer to the supposed beneficiaries of so-called 'development' in an acceptable way. There have been numerous attempts, such as: least developed countries, underdeveloped, developing, poor, Lower and Middle Income Countries (LMIC), the majority world, lean (versus fat!), Third World, Two-Thirds World, the global South, the South, and finally perhaps finding it best whenever possible not to generalise but simply to be specific about the peoples, communities, locations, nations and continents being talked about.

Gone fishing

Probably the most well-known theory of development, 'from hand-out to leg-up', hides in the aphorism 'Give a man a fish and you feed him for a day, teach a man to fish and you feed him for life', often attributed to the ancient wisdom of Lao Tzu who founded Taoism in the fourth century BCE. Christian Aid reproduced it on a poster in the 1970s.

A good exercise might be to revise it in the light of all that has since been learned about development, as Christian Aid tried to do in its TV advert for Christian Aid Week in 2013. It talked about dignity for one thing and getting rid of the old aphorism's patronising tones for another, since this fisherwoman (or man) does not need to learn how to fish even if she can always improve her skills. What she needs is the opportunity to fish responsibly where waters are clear, stocks are good and well managed and foreign trawlers haven't cleared the fish out before she gets there. After that she needs to keep her catch cool (Christian Aid got excited about solar freezers), markets where she can sell it at a fair price, and be able to educate her children on the proceeds, singing a few songs as she goes. Don't 'help' her, simply give her not a fish but a chance.

12
Palestine

On 14 May 1948, not long before Christian Aid got involved, a young Israeli nation declared its independence, only to be met with fierce resistance from the indigenous Arab population. Almost immediately war broke out involving neighbouring Arab countries: Egypt, Iraq, Jordan, Lebanon and Syria. During and after the fighting, at least 750,000 (about half) of the existing Palestinian population were displaced to Gaza or the West Bank or driven out to become refugees in Lebanon and elsewhere in the region, never to return. Half of those remaining became refugees in a country no longer their own. These extraordinary events were named 'Nakba' or the 'catastrophe', remembered by Palestinians every year on 15 May.

A large-scale immigration of Jews followed as they fled from the horrors of 'murderous prejudice'[1] in Europe. In 1947 the UK had handed back to the UN its mandate from the old League of Nations to care for Palestine. The UN then voted to divide the country in two.

War and peace

The rest of the story is not about two states, Israel and Palestine, learning to live side by side as planned, but of an unending cycle of violence punctuated by the search for a just peace. By 'violence' is meant missile attacks, suicide bombings, shootings to maim and kill, collective punishment, arrests without charge, demolition of homes and farms, military incursions, rape, murder and attacks on villages and settlements, a good deal of it on both sides though not in equal measure or with equal power.

The violence was ongoing but pockmarked by datable events. Here are some: the war of 1967, when Israel wrested control of the West Bank,

Gaza and East Jerusalem from Egypt and Jordan, triggering a second exodus of refugees; the breakout of open hostilities in 1973; the invasion of Lebanon by Israel in 1982 in an attempt to wipe out the Palestinian Liberation Organisation (PLO); the infamous massacres in the Sabra and Shatila refugee camps in the same year; the first Intifada or 'shaking off' the Israeli occupation by Palestinians in 1987; the assassination by Israeli extremists of Prime Minister Yitzhak Rabin and a suicide bombing campaign by Hamas in 1995, both out to undermine the Oslo Accords; a second Intifada in 2000, provoked by Ariel Sharon's visit to the Temple Mount; the building of a wall 8 metres high round and through land in the West Bank in 2003, following the Green Line agreed in 1949 for only 15% of the way and making serious incursions into Palestinian territory; the armed takeover of Gaza by Hamas in 2007; Israel's blockade of Gaza and armed offensive (called Operation Cast Lead) in 2008–09; more violence in 2012 and a ceasefire brokered by Egypt; fighting in 2014 and 2021; and in 2023 a brutal attack by Hamas on Israel and the outbreak of war in Gaza as Israel vowed to remove Hamas from the territory once and for all. Talk of 'ethnic cleansing' and another Nakba were on many lips as tens of thousands were killed before a fragile temporary ceasefire in January 2025, soon followed by renewed and worsening hostilities.

As for the search for peace, various attempts were made to strengthen the hand of the Palestinians in the face of an overwhelming imbalance of power. In 1974 and 1975 the United Nations General Assembly reaffirmed their 'inalienable right' to self-determination and conferred observer status in the Assembly on the PLO. Much later it proclaimed 2014 as an International Year of Solidarity with the Palestinian people.

A peace conference in Madrid in 1991 was a precursor to the signing of the Oslo Accords two years later in 1993 and the setting up of a functioning administration in the limited areas under Palestinian self-rule. It was meant to be a first step in a process but became more or less permanent. In 2000, attempts were made at Camp David, by President Bill Clinton, Prime Minister Ehud Barak and Yasser Arafat, leader of the PLO, to agree a final settlement involving areas that were wholly and only partly under Palestinian control. They were inconclusive. The Arab Peace Initiative of 2002 could be seen to have borne some fruit in the Abraham Accords of 2020, which normalised relations between

Israel, the United Arab Emirates, Bahrain, Sudan and Morocco, but did nothing for the Palestinians. With further negotiations breaking down in 2010, when Israel declared it had no 'negotiating partner' for peace, and Benjamin Netanyahu's declaration of outright opposition to a fully sovereign Palestinian state in 2014,[2] and the unprecedented events of 2023–25 involving not just Israel and Palestine but their neighbours, only adding fuel to the fire, peace remained a seemingly unattainable goal.

When Hamas attacked Israel in October 2023 a remark by the UN Secretary General that the attack had a 'context' provoked a furious reaction from Israelis. They heard it as an excuse, not to say a justification, for the killings and hostage-taking, for which there was none, whereas for others it was an attempt not to justify but to comprehend. That 'context', however, cannot be adequately described by lists of dates and events. There were long-running issues, and fundamentally it was and remains about communities and families, men, women and children, their dreams and their suffering as reflected in their many stories. Here are a few.

Stories

Sanaa and her three children live in her father's house in Jerusalem where she has residency status, rare for Palestinians, and the children go to school. Ali their father carries a West Bank identity card and is not allowed to live with them. He stays in a family house in Bethlehem. He sees his wife and children once a fortnight when they travel to see him. 'The children', says Sanaa, 'ask about their father all the time.'

The Edkedek family bought building rights in the 1990s in a neighbourhood in East Jerusalem. In 2018 they built two apartments on the roof of another family's home: one for them and the other for their son about to get married. Before they moved in, they received a demolition order from the local authorities. Elsewhere the house of Hamad, a 76-year-old farmer from Khan Younis, Gaza, was bombed in 2008, 2012 and totally in 2014. He was offered a caravan to live in and was told there was no money to rebuild. Eventually he rebuilt the house himself by buying materials on the black market and running up far too many debts which he couldn't repay. He struggled to feed his family.

Due to the blockade, Gaza hospitals lacked the medicines, equipment and staff to support their Palestinian cancer patients. When referred to hospitals in Jerusalem they needed travel permits which could be refused and appointments missed. Noor, a mother of four, fighting breast cancer and needing pain relief to ease the side-effects of chemotherapy, waited for three hours in the hospital in Gaza only to be told when her turn came round that the drug she needed had run out.

Yara lives in a tiny village south of Nablus in the West Bank. Aged 54, with six children, she has lived there all her life except for two years when Israelis from nearby illegal settlements forced them out. Every Saturday they would come down on horseback, point their guns at doorways, stone the windows, set the dogs on the chickens and the sheep loose on the hill. Everyone was terrified. They were able to move back when Ecumenical Accompaniers arrived (see further, below).[3]

Issues

Among the long-running issues were 'land', regarded by some as overriding all others, 'illegal settlements', 'refugees' and 'water', all raising questions about 'human rights'.

The land issue could be looked at from several angles. Whose was it between the river Jordan and the sea? Christian Aid explored the question carefully from a theological perspective, recognising that the Bible has been variously interpreted in favour of either Palestinians or Jews. In contrast, it voted for an approach resonant with Liberation Theology where 'the earth is the Lord's' rather than anybody else's and God wills for all peoples their exodus from oppression and a hopeful journey to freedom and safety.[4]

From a personal rather than biblical angle, 'land' for a farmer like Daoud meant his land: 42 acres in the West Bank bought by his grandfather in 1924 – which is where the issue of illegal settlements ('illegal' because they were occupied in contravention of the Green Line and the fourth Geneva Convention) loomed large for him and many, many others. In the 1980s and 1990s his 42 acres were gradually surrounded by these settlements, until half were under threat of confiscation and he was no longer allowed to build a house there or farm the way he wanted.[5]

Land-grabbing by settlers brought with it measures to protect themselves, like security zones involving demolitions, tearing down olive trees and building the wall of 2003, together with numerous guarded crossings and military checkpoints: 542 in 2012. Roads were built for their convenience with fast links into Israel itself, making life extremely inconvenient for their Palestinian neighbours. Journeys to farms or schools or for medical help became longer. Endless time could be wasted waiting at checkpoints – and worse. Roger Riddell, Christian Aid's head of policy from 1999 to 2004, witnessed young Israeli soldiers laughing at a Palestinian taking his thirty trays of eggs to market as they smashed them to the ground. Villages and families were cut off from one another by roads they were not allowed to use. Water[6] for irrigation grew scarce, while the Israelis who controlled it enjoyed a good supply.

In March 2018 Palestinians in Gaza began the 'Great March of Return', insisting on the rights of refugees to return home. It was met with a harsh response and did not of course succeed, leaving thousands in the camps where they were and still are, many of them unable to earn a living and heavily reliant on humanitarian aid. When Janet Lacey revisited Lebanon in 1954, she commented that there was practically no change in the refugee situation except that more babies had been born. A similar sentiment could have been expressed decades later.

Human rights and their abuse ran all through these and other 'facts on the ground'[7] like a scarlet trail: the right to land; the right to dignity and respect; the right to safety; the right to freedom of movement; the right to water, education and health care; the right to return.

Policy

Christian Aid's policy on Palestine remained fairly consistent and in line with many other searchers for peace. It favoured a two-state solution but, prompted by partners, acknowledged that choosing the shape of peace lay with the Palestinians and Israelis, supported by impartial mediators. The conditions for a 'viable solution' were set out in 2007 by William Bell, a member of staff with long experience in the area,[8] under eight points:

- an end to occupation;
- self-determination and sovereignty on all sides;
- good governance with respect to Israel acting with impunity and to the dysfunctional and repressive Palestinian Authority, Fatah and Hamas regimes;
- the protection of human rights including the right of return for refugees;
- security for everyone;
- freedom of movement within and between the West Bank, Gaza and East Jerusalem;
- control of natural resources;
- an end to dependency and a renewed respect for international law.[9]

In its attempts to turn the tide for peace and in the meantime respond in a flexible way to current realities as best it could, Christian Aid committed itself predictably to a programme of humanitarian aid, longer-term development, a human rights agenda targeting the causes of poverty and suffering, and advocacy.

Having set its course, what did it do?

Action

Strictly speaking the answer, as usual, is 'nothing'. Christian Aid was never operational in Palestine but supportive of a considerable number of local organisations and their programmes.

It helped to bring humanitarian aid from the start. In the early 1950s it was a member of ecumenical church networks which included the Middle East Council of Churches (MECC) and its Department of Service to Palestinian Refugees (DSPR) as they responded to the poverty and plight of thousands. Elsewhere the Palestinian Agricultural Relief Association (PARC) and the Palestinian Medical Relief Society (PMRS) provided emergency medical care. The Culture and Free Thought Association (CFTA), based in Khan Younis, made cash grants to displaced families. But all these and many more efforts to relieve people's immediate distress were overshadowed by repeated urgent appeals for money, not least in 2024 made by Christian Aid and then the

DEC after negotiations with a cautious BBC and others which seemed to take far too long.

During the war in Gaza in 2023–25 as the number of dead and injured mounted, PARC and the International Orthodox Christian Charity (IOCC) were among many to receive considerable funding from Christian Aid. All of Christian Aid's partners were under siege, forced out of their homes, their offices under daily bombardment and surrounded by tanks. Raji Sourani, Director of the Palestine Centre for Human Rights (PCHR), was pulled from the rubble of his house in October 2023. Together these organisations on the ground made incredible efforts to reach and support desperate people with bread and blankets, food parcels, fresh vegetables, drinking water, dried milk made into cheese, medicines, bathroom units, nappies, art sessions for children, mobile health clinics and hygiene kits. The IOCC provided shelter and food in St Porphyrius church in Gaza city. The Women's Affairs Center (WAC) set up shelters for women in Rafah. Human rights abuses continued to be recorded but otherwise humanitarian aid just about took over the whole agenda.[10]

Despite the billions spent over the years on longer-term development in Palestine, according to PARC, it came to look more like 'de-development'. Training work with farmers became more and more difficult, even pointless, as land was taken away or became inaccessible, greenhouses and crops were destroyed and restrictions put in place in the name of security for settlers. 'Resilience', an increasingly familiar word in Christian Aid's vocabulary, seemed a more feasible proposition. The YMCA ran a training programme for women. It had to do with coping mechanisms and more proactive strategies to help them stay on the land, together with community building and trained leadership. A good example was when women leaders in Rabud, near Hebron, built a culvert bridge over a stream of raw sewage coming from a nearby illegal settlement to regain access to their land. Another saw women training in IT skills and getting jobs on the digital job market.[11]

Advocacy went in several directions. One was the steady stream of evidence-based information[12] made available to Christian Aid's supporters, the media and general public, and to influential bodies such as governments, the EU, the UN and the International Criminal Court.

It made sure that no one, high or low, could say they didn't know, and provided a solid platform from which to campaign for peace and justice and the righting of wrongs.

During the Olive Tree Campaign in 2022, Palestinian farmers planted more than a thousand olive trees in occupied territory, one for every member of the Methodist Conference and the General Synod of the Church of England, and one for every UK MP, all paid for by Christian Aid to increase awareness and galvanise support.[13]

In January 2003, Christian Aid published 'Losing Ground: Israel, poverty and the Palestinians' by David McDowall, arguing that increasing impoverishment was no accident, following confiscations of land, construction of settlements, the control of water, curfews, military invasions and countless checkpoints subject to closure. Almost two-thirds of all Palestinians were thought to be living on less than £1 a day. Clare Short, Minister for International Development, spoke out at the launch of the report; 9,000 copies were distributed and 12,500 downloaded.

Alongside Christian Aid Ireland and the Irish government, Christian Aid had a long-running human rights programme going back as far as 1985 when a Christian Aid policy paper on Palestine indicated a shift of emphasis towards more intensive work on human rights violations. Over the years it had supported Israeli human rights organisations and the Palestinian Centre for Human Rights while working closely with the churches in Jerusalem and the UK. The shift led to a reduction of support to the MECC's DSPR, which up to then had received most of Christian Aid's funding for humanitarian work in Gaza and the West Bank. Other factors were in play as explained in letters to MECC, such as a fall in Christian Aid's income and bad exchange rates; but there were also differences over MECC's relations with its beneficiaries and with DSPR's ability at the time to change and innovate.

Human rights organisations were now to be prioritised for funding. Between them they encouraged individuals and communities to claim their rights and provided rigorous monitoring and fact-checked reports as a basis for challenging abusers in the courts. In 2011 and 2014, one-time staff members of Christian Aid joined the Ecumenical Accompaniment Programme in Palestine and Israel, an international initiative led by the

Palestinian churches and the WCC, designed to be simply a presence standing alongside farmers, shepherds and schoolchildren at checkpoints to improve their safety and, on return, to raise awareness at home. Christian Aid worked with the Quakers at the British end of the programme.

Sensitivities

It goes without saying that Palestine is an extremely sensitive issue where those who get involved must learn to tread very carefully as if on eggshells, partly to retain trust and credibility and partly to uphold the charity's duty to be impartial and its wish to be fair. Christian Aid consistently acknowledged that there had been atrocities committed by both Palestinians and Israelis. It was clear that there had been suffering on both sides of the conflict and that both had the right to live as equals in safety and in peace.

Nevertheless, the imbalance of power and the scale of poverty, suffering and humiliation had been stark, making it difficult if not impossible for Christian Aid's bias to the poor not to be seen as bias to the Palestinians. As a result there were run-ins with the Charity Commission about the old issue of being – or rather, not being – political, and more painful, uneasy and at times hostile relations with bodies like the Jewish Board of Deputies and the Council of Christians and Jews, critical of its stance.

The most bruising confrontation was with the Zionist Advocacy Center (TZAC) in the USA, dubbed by Patrick Watt, Christian Aid's CEO, as 'lawfare'. In 2017 it took Christian Aid to court, accusing it of obtaining funds from the US government by fraudulent means. It regarded the charity as having 'crossed the line' by providing support to terrorists. It was an attempt, according to Watt, to undermine Christian Aid's advocacy work. Beware anyone who sets foot in Palestine! The battle ran for five anxious years and, had it not been dismissed, would have cost the charity millions on top of the £700,000 spent on legal fees and the loss of income due to its self-imposed pause on applications for US government funding.[14]

By way of contrast, there are heart-warming examples of Palestinians and Israelis working together for peace and of where Christian Aid has funded Jewish organisations in Israel. Zochrot, an Israeli civil society organisation based in Tel Aviv, provided counselling to those affected by conflict, and in at least one case members of a synagogue in north Israel provided eye-witness accounts of settler activities and still do, using them to raise awareness among fellow Israelis of the plight of their Palestinian neighbours.

A prayer published by Christian Aid in 2017 has no need to tread on eggshells or strive for impartiality:

> Pray not for Arab or Jew,
> for Palestinian or Israeli,
> but pray rather for ourselves,
> that we might not
> divide them in our prayers
> but keep them both together
> in our hearts.[15]

Sent by the Lord

Sent by the Lord am I;
My hands are ready now
To make the earth a place
In which the kingdom comes.

The angels cannot change
A world of hurt and pain
Into a world of love,
Of justice and of peace.

The task is mine to do,
To set it really free.
O help me to obey;
Help me to do your will.

Sent by the Lord am I;
My hands are ready now
To make the earth a place
In which the kingdom comes.

A song of Nicaraguan origin, attributed to José Aguiar and translated by Jorge Maldonado

13

The Big Issue

The 'green' issue, which I set aside in 1994 (see Chapter 3) in favour of exposing the unhelpful policies of the WB and IMF, became unavoidable for Christian Aid by the early years of the twenty-first century, and an existential threat to the future of people and planet. Christian Aid was probably the first among its peers to make it integral to its approach.[1]

The main features of the crisis were by then well known, even if still denied by some. If global temperatures were allowed to rise more than 1.5 degrees above pre-industrial levels (by 2025 they were dangerously close), the consequences would be dire. Sea levels would rise as arctic ice melted, and coastal lands and islands would disappear. Extreme weather events would become normal, bringing with them drought, catastrophic floods and fire. Lives would be lost, and those who survived would go hungry and start migrating in growing numbers, solving nobody's problems. The social fabric of life, woven through with law and order, community cohesion and care, would break down.

The fundamental cause of it all was the rise in CO^2 emissions, first gradually and then all too rapidly eroding the earth's protection from the damaging rays of the sun. The relentless felling of trees, often for greedy commercial gain, with their ability to absorb emissions, only aggravated the problem.

These dangerous emissions were the result of burning fossil fuels: oil, coal and gas. It had to stop, and they had to be left in the ground. Energy must come increasingly from renewable sources such as windmills, waterfalls, solar panels, tides and reactors. Insulating homes and workplaces from the cold and heat and similar measures to save energy, along with recycling to save waste, and green technology, had useful contributions to make but could pale into insignificance if the main challenge to clear the air and create a sustainable future was not met.

Christian Aid accepted this analysis, with two additions. The first was a crucial matter of emphasis. Christian Aid was not alone, but was nevertheless relentless in almost everything it said and did in highlighting yet another example of injustice. Poorer countries and their people generally contributed far less to the damage being done than the better off, but suffered more. Years of underdevelopment due to exploitation, losing out on trade and tax revenues including (ironically) revenues from extractive industries, had left them not only highly vulnerable but without enough resources to recover from disasters or defend themselves against the next one, let alone adapt for the future. Christian Aid's response was not to campaign about climate change or the climate crisis but about climate justice: 'justice' being the goal and 'injustice' the reality.

A matter of faith

A second addition was the way in which Christian Aid attempted to deepen the widely accepted analysis of the crisis: a crisis threatening not only to reverse any gains the development movement had made over decades but any hope of learning to live peaceably together. Necessary negotiations about cutting emissions were put into theological perspective, no doubt to help churchgoing supporters, whom Christian Aid worked hard to influence and bring on board, to relate the crisis to their faith. Several of them evidently gave their MPs a hard time.

Paula Clifford wrote her paper 'All Creation Groaning' in 2007. It was a precursor to her 'Theology and International Development' written in 2010.[2] In it she insists that if Christian Aid is to make an adequate response to the injustices of climate change, 'it is imperative that theology offers a framework' rooting action in faith.

As in 2010, she proposed a rather general theology of relationships. They certainly needed to change. 'Dominion' over nature had long been justified in the Christian tradition with references to Genesis 1:26–8 and God's command to Adam and Eve to go out into the world and multiply and have dominion over it. It suited well the rise of science with its growing sense of control and was typified, for example, in the material wealth of the industrial revolution and its impoverishment and exploitation of the world's resources. Relationships also needed to change from seeing the natural world 'objectively' as over and against us, to seeing ourselves as an integral part of it. Nature is not all sunshine and flowers, revealing something of God (Psalm 19), but it calls out for understanding and respect for the way it works. We are called to care for it as, being part of it, we care for ourselves.

According to Clifford, our lives are characterised by interconnectedness between one another, the natural world and God. These all-important relationships – modelled by the Trinity, a Christian doctrine where God is understood to be three distinct persons, Father, Son and Holy Spirit, in one – have broken down and become essentially unjust and in need of repair. Put another way, 'sin' or what has gone wrong is structural or relational, not just individual, tying together society and God's creation for good or ill – and in this case, 'ill'. Hope lies in joint action by the churches, which in 2007 she judged to be sorely lacking.[3]

A second theological commentary on climate change had a different flavour, mainly because it came from the South. 'Song of the Prophets: A global theology of climate change' was written up by Susan Durber in 2014 but drew exclusively on what Christian Aid's partners in the South, from Bangladesh to El Salvador, had to say. Like prophets they faced up to harsh realities with harsh words, dreamed dreams and inspired people with hope.

The realities were familiar enough, except that they were now firmly landing on the 'prophets'' own home ground. Dalits in India, for example, who lived close to nature, exposed to rain, wind and sunshine every day, spoke about a profound sense of injustice and of how the attack on nature sounded the death knell for their coastal communities, forcing them to move elsewhere. Voices from Ecuador did not speak in a detached way about an economic system exploiting nature and the poor in general; instead, they spoke of a system that was further impoverishing themselves. Others spoke of changes, not of their making, to their already challenging lives, which left them demoralised and finding it hard not to despair. Like prophets they called for repentance and a turnaround in the way we relate to one another and creation.

They went on to put a surprisingly confident emphasis on hope. Prophets were not just in the business of telling people off and demanding better behaviour. They were also in the business of stirring our imaginations and bringing us hope. The document refers to a whole lot of biblical passages to prove the point.

The bow in the sky, for example, symbolises God's promise to Noah never to destroy the earth with flood waters again. Good guidance is to be had in Leviticus about how best to look after the land and the needy. Jonah, much to his annoyance, saw how a whole civilisation could change its ways and avoid disaster. Amos reassures Israel that its fortunes will be restored after its cities have been demolished and its farmers ruined. Psalmists sing praises to God for establishing the earth on firm foundations so that it won't ever be shaken. Jesus says the meek will inherit the earth, and the early Christians, 'hoping against hope', look forward to a new heaven and a new earth. Theology in general insists that God can bring fresh life out of death. All in all, there is hard work to be done against enormous odds, but there is also a song to sing.[4]

Durber's 'Song of the Prophets' offers a welcome antidote to the ongoing frustration with governments and the lack of meaningful action when hope itself can feel like 'whistling in the wind'.

When it comes to action, Christian Aid tackled climate injustice on all the usual fronts with at least two possible exceptions, one of which, as we shall see, was unique at the time.

Programmes

Christian Aid supported countless programmes of work sharing similar aims. Vulnerable communities had to be forewarned and better prepared for the storms before they struck. They had to change the ways they built their houses or grew their crops to withstand the extremes of heat and cold, rain and drought. They had to be more resilient, working together under trained leaders and conserving what resources they had. They had to marshal their own knowledge and skills and have them recognised and respected by those who set out to be of help. And they had to find and strengthen their own voice to speak out powerfully against injustice and for radical change.

The Enhancing Community Resilience Programme (ECRP) in Malawi from 2011 to 2017 is a good example of this general approach. It was supported by DFID and the Irish and Norwegian governments and carried out by Christian Aid and a consortium including CARE (Ireland) and Action Aid in eleven disaster-prone districts with a population of 420,000 between them. It aimed to increase the capacity of local communities and government departments to withstand the impact of climate change, reduce risk, improve lives and adapt for the future. The many 'interventions' covered early warning systems, water management, farming, forestry, conservation, loans and savings schemes, gender issues, low carbon technology and advocacy.

Representatives from all the areas involved in ECRP, together with members of the consortium, met in a hotel in Lilongwe in 2017 to take stock and learn lessons for the future, of which they listed forty-one. Among them were the importance of involving the communities and giving them a sense of ownership; developing good working relations with local officials and experts such as agricultural extension workers and solar technicians; and evidence-based advocacy drawing on statistics and documentation but crucially on personal experience and, a new development, the photographs they had taken themselves.

Reliable funding and accountability remained as ever of fundamental importance. Human touches came through the report as they noted how 'interventions' with short-term benefits generated more enthusiasm than longer-term ones, and that enthusiastic volunteers needed keeping in order. Not without its problems, the programme was judged to be a success by all concerned; DFID awarded it a top rating of A+.

From another part of the world came the Climate Monitoring Action Project (CLIMA) building on earlier ones, where, from 2020 to 2023, Christian Aid worked with Centro Humboldt and the organisation Security for Small Producers for Coffee Export (SOPPEXCCA), building the ability of Nicaraguan coffee, cacao and honey farmers to battle against climate change. Great emphasis was once again put on weather forecasting, along with diversification. Trees were planted to give the crops the necessary shade. Many were fruit-bearing and also boosted honey production. Centro Humboldt, a major player in the scheme, was closed down by the government in 2022 as part of a wider crackdown on civil society, causing major damage to the programme. Christian Aid's regional office in Managua was also affected and relocated to Honduras.[5]

Resources

In 2021 Christian Aid published 'Taking Action on Climate Justice: A church group discussion guide'. Among the contributors were Robert Beckford from the Black Theology Forum of the Queen's Foundation, Israel Olofinjana of the Evangelical Alliance, and Bob Kikuyu and Sue Richardson, both of Christian Aid. Its imagery (the discussion group pictured at the start is of black women sitting outside in the sun) and text underscore its opening remark that 'climate change, although something which will affect us all, is a deeply racialised phenomenon'. While fully making that point, it sets out to encourage church groups to talk about climate justice and offers a guide, drawing on Scripture, to help them do so and go on to take action. It touches on six 'key ideas' or talking points: God, desire, greed, righteousness, justice and action, with questions to get the conversation going. The guide is one of many resources, from worship materials to lesson outlines and 'tool kits', published by Christian Aid to help young and old, churches and schools to get involved.[6]

In 2008 David Thomas, a science teacher and Education and Campaigns Coordinator for Christian Aid Ireland, wrote about the importance of explaining the issues surrounding climate change to primary and secondary school pupils and the difficulties involved. The science could be quite complex. The crisis was challenging to young people on a personal level as their eyes were opened to the interconnectedness of their world where the plight of a Bangladeshi had a lot to do with them. Added to that was that recurring sense of defeat which had to be overcome (back to whistling in the wind). Had things gone too far already? Were India and China with their coal mines only making matters worse? What was the point of young people caring about the planet if adults were failing to back them up? Thomas and Christian Aid nevertheless ploughed on.

Not all of their efforts were appreciated. In May 2019 Paul Homewood posted on his blog ('Not a Lot of People Know That') an entry entitled, 'Christian Aid's Blatant Propaganda for Schools', criticising a teachers' study pack as 'so full of inaccuracies, exaggerations and significant omissions that it is hard to know where to start'.[7] Start, however, he did, claiming that if only Christian Aid had put things into perspective children might decide that climate change 'was not worth bothering about', followed by a piece of advice that kids should be 'acquainted with harsh reality' and told that nothing they do will make the slightest difference. Beside the defeatism that Thomas had warned against, some detected more than a whiff of climate denial about Homewood's critique.

Two other resources informing and motivating supporters were Christian Aid's updates and its annual lectures. For example, the 2023 issue of 'Counting the Cost: A year of climate breakdown' analysed twenty extreme climate disasters, not all in poorer countries, and revealed 'a global postcode lottery stacked against the poor'.

In the report, facts and figures about the impact of extreme events and what needs to be done at local, national and international levels are set out once again, but they are also given a human face. The people who are affected talk about how hard it is to restart a business or get back to school, or rebuild a house, or get ready for the next rainy day. From Malawi where Cyclone Freddy struck in 2023 displacing 500,000 people, there is anxious talk about taking to locally made canoes to get to safety, and a 69-year-old widow tells of how the storm destroyed 'the only house that we struggled to construct': rather like eventually paying off your mortgage only to see your uninsured home swept away by the flood.

Christian Aid's annual lecture series began in 2021 with an inaugural lecture by the economist Sir Partha Dasgupta on poverty and climate change. In 2023 the UN Deputy Secretary-General Amina Mohammed focused on 'horrific injustice on a global scale' as a renewed debt crisis, deepened by climate change, engulfed the South, and on how women bore the brunt of it in a male-dominated, patriarchal world: gender injustice only intensifying climate injustice. Amina Mohammed argued forcibly for far more funding from the international community to bolster the key role that women were destined to play.

Campaigning

Resources of whatever kind, from prayers to public lectures, were designed to lead to action. Since the early 2000s Christian Aid seized every opportunity it could to mobilise the churches and foster networks to drive home the message about climate injustice.

One of them, the Pan African Climate Justice Alliance (PACJA), now has 1,000 members in forty countries across Africa, with a strong funding base and a life of its own independent of Christian Aid. 'The sort of thing we do well,' commented Christian Aid's current CEO Patrick Watt to me.

Meetings of the COP were prominent opportunities for campaigning. The Conference first met in Berlin in 1995 and has since met annually, with one delay (COP26) due to Covid. It is the decision-making body of the United Nations Framework Convention on Climate Change (UNFCCC), set up by international treaty in 1992. The Kyoto Protocol, a legally binding agreement to limit greenhouse gas emissions, was agreed to in 1997 and renewed in 2012 to run until 2020. During that time emissions were not reduced. It gave way to the Paris Agreement of 2015, which came into force in 2016, aimed at intensifying and speeding up action. The target of limiting global warming to 2°C above pre-industrial levels was revised to 1.5°C. COP28 in 2023 finally called on the world to transition away from fossil fuels. After a worldwide campaign joined by Christian Aid it agreed to set up a loss and damage fund to help poorer countries where adapting to the climate crisis was virtually impossible. Promises were made but governments, including the UK, failed to pay up. COP29 in 2024 increased the money pledged, still regarded as insufficient in the eyes of the poorer countries.

When COP26 came to Glasgow in 2021, Christian Aid Scotland set up a striking picture by I. D. Campbell outside the Scottish Parliament. Harking back to Henry Raeburn's famous painting of the Revd Robert Walter on ice skates, it featured two young Scottish skateboarders skating past the Parliament building carrying the slogan 'Get your skates on' in a bid to get individuals and governments to work together.

In 2021, Christian Aid also participated in the UN Food Systems Summit, bringing with it its long experience of working with small-scale farmers. September 2023 saw a Global Day of Action in the run-up to COP28 in Dubai and a demand to 'Make Polluters Pay' by taxing industrial giants such as Shell and BP who were making what were described as 'exorbitant' profits out of fossil fuels, and using the revenues instead to fill the coffers of the loss and damage fund as a matter of justice. Christian Aid issued a detailed technical briefing about how the fund should be enhanced,[8] while Christian Aid supporters joined in with protest choirs, pilgrimages to polluting sites, lobbying, prayer vigils, art and street theatre.

Christian Aid latched on to other events besides the COP meetings. In October 2011, for example, campaigners took to the streets in Manchester along with CAFOD and Tearfund on the eve of the Conservative Party Conference, insisting that the government should do more to cut emissions and that the Prime Minister should ensure the extension of the Kyoto Protocol due to expire the following year. In June 2019, 13,000 lobbyists, with lots of Christian Aid supporters among them, met with their MPs along the river bank in London about the Climate Change Bill before Parliament, stressing the need for more urgent cuts in emissions. In October 2023 the Rugby World Cup provided a good excuse for highlighting the disparities between countries which all had players in the same tournament: the UK, Japan, France and Australia on the one side and Fiji, Samoa and Tonga on the other where economies were under severe threat and their islands could soon be sunk under water. 'Stop Rugby Sinking' was the slogan, accompanied by a photo shot of Pacific islanders performing a traditional dance up to their knees in the rising waters of the Thames. In the same year Christian Aid marked the coronation by reporting on the effects of climate change on poorer Commonwealth countries and the less than proud records of the better off. Compared to Malawi, the UK was emitting 64 times more carbon per head, Canada 179 times and Australia 188.

Glasshouses

The call for climate justice challenged Christian Aid to put its own glasshouse in order in more than one respect. In July 2023 it stopped banking with Barclay's after eight years, critical of its ongoing investments in fossil fuels, a move publicly welcomed by Rowan Williams. The climate crisis uncovered more than one scandal of injustice. The plight of poorer countries was one, but issues around gender and racism were two more, both of which spurred on a serious in-house commitment to take action on both fronts. It was blatantly obvious that, if Christian Aid as an organisation was going to throw stones at everyone else for their carbon emissions and failure to do enough to reduce them, it had better take urgent steps to reduce its own. Endless flights by staff around the world, costing thousands a year in air miles as well as money, hardly boosted its reputation. The numbers were drastically cut, along with measures to use less energy and paper, and encouragement (helped by Covid-19) of 'hybrid' working between homes and offices. By 2024 the number of flights had risen again and it became hard to see how targets set in the Carbon Reduction Plan, signed off in March 2023, could be realised.

Two pieces of work in 2023 had a somewhat unusual flavour. In September Christian Aid described how UK shoppers were at risk from climate change because nearly a quarter of their fruit, vegetables, pulses and meat came from highly vulnerable countries where crops could easily be destroyed, causing shortages and higher prices. 'Wake up and smell the coffee' (May 2023) put particular emphasis on the threat to coffee growers and supply chains. The messages carried an unusually heavy dose of self-interest in contrast to the usual appeals for generosity and disinterested concern for the less well-off. Do something about it or else you'll suffer the consequences! Christian realism would have approved of the tactic.

The long march

There have been long marches in history, from Jarrow, for example, and to Selma and Delhi, highlighting the conditions of the marginalised, and people have travelled long distances more recently in South and North to protest against climate injustice. A Caravan of Hope travelled for two weeks through ten African countries on its way to make its presence felt in Durban, South Africa, in 2011, bringing with it 300 activists. In 2017, prior to general elections in the country, a cycle tour organised by Christian Aid in Kenya made its way through 47 counties encouraging voters to demand clean energy as part of the Big Shift Global campaign, and calling on banks to shift their investments from fossil fuel industries to renewables. In 2021 the Young Christians Climate Network organised a march from the G7 in Cornwall to COP26 in Glasgow by way of Lambeth Palace and York Minster.[9]

Christian Aid's own long march, masterminded earlier by Paul Brannen, head of its campaigns, will not go down in history but was unique in its own way. The Hampshire-based *Daily Echo* (September 2007) was not the only newspaper to publish an article about twenty intrepid travellers who on 14 July 2007 set out to march to London. Among them was Merryn Hellier (aged 65) from Herefordshire, something of a veteran in these matters. They were part of Christian Aid's 'Cut the Carbon' campaign supported by Leonardo DiCaprio and 233 MPs (thirteen of them Conservatives, including Peter Bottomley, formerly on Christian Aid's board) who signed an Early Day Motion (27 February 2007) calling for UK companies to be required by law to account for their carbon footprints in their annual accounts.

The marchers met up in Bangor, Northern Ireland, and after a send-off took to the Irish Sea overnight in a small boat, landing at Troon the next morning. From there their route took them through seventy towns and cities via Edinburgh, Newcastle, Leeds, Birmingham, Cardiff and Bournemouth: 1,000 miles in all, 'the longest protest march in UK history'. Along the way, 50,000 people got involved, marching along with them for a while, or providing food and rest and organising events. On arrival in London on 1 October they were accompanied by Ken Livingstone, Mayor of London, and his deputy Nicky Gavron along the last lap by the Thames. John Sentamu, Archbishop of York, welcomed them on behalf of the Archbishop of Canterbury at Lambeth Palace before they handed in a letter at No. 10, urging the government to cut emissions by 50%, and finally took part in a service at St Paul's Cathedral.

Of more significance than its length, perhaps, was the fact that half of the long-distance marchers came from overseas: Rosalie Soley (aged 22) from El Salvador and others from Tajikistan, Kenya, Brazil, India, South Africa, Bangladesh, the Philippines and the Democratic Republic of Congo. Only because of marching companions like these, where advocacy is informed by lived experience, could Christian Aid claim to know that what it talks and shouts about is on a sure footing. More than that, their presence sent messages about respect and partnership and Christian Aid's commitment, running through all its work, to making powerful coalitions of civil society voices. These were the all-important voices, contributing to advocacy in their own countries as well as the UK, that needed to be strengthened, amplified and heard.[10]

14

The Philippines

In 1978 Jack Arthey, a member of Christian Aid's staff, visited the Philippines as the guest of the National Council of Churches (NCCP). He met Edicio (Ed) de la Torre, a Catholic priest inspired by Paulo Freire's book *Pedagogy of the Oppressed*[1] and committed to a theology of struggle. The meeting reflected Christian Aid's and the NCCP's close association with social movements for radical change, not to say 'revolution' rather than 'reform'.

In 2021, while reviewing Christian Aid's time in the Philippines from 1960 to 2020,[2] Kate Newman told of how, in 2013, the modest office of Christian Aid (CAPHIL), with a staff of five, was suddenly overwhelmed and its development work overshadowed by the demands of an emergency (Typhoon Haiyan). It was the most powerful and catastrophic that ever made landfall anywhere in the world. Staff, like thousands of others, searched for their loved ones. They could only weep, and then felt compelled to act. Haiyan was followed a month later by a 7.3 magnitude earthquake in the coastal island of Bohol. The arrival of twenty hastily appointed members of staff with, for Christian Aid, an unusually hands-on operational approach caused tension between the old and the new over what to do and how to do it.

The contrast seems stark between digging deep into the causes of poverty, as Christian Aid has persistently set out to do, and the humanitarian aid which meets immediate needs but otherwise scarcely scratches the surface. Had Christian Aid been blown off course?

Political change

When Arthey returned to the Philippines in the 1980s he had in his pocket 'To strengthen the Poor', a statement issued by Christian Aid in

July 1987 giving clear guidance (according to Arthey) to Christian Aid's programmes across the world. Its priorities were obvious, as were its sympathies with those struggling for radical social and political change. He discussed the statement with a number of interested groups as they looked to the future after 'people power' brought down Marcos in 1986. It apparently helped to shape the future work of CAPHIL.[3]

Since the late 1960s, Christian Aid had funded programmes of work recommended by the NCCP by way of the WCC.[4] Slum dwellers, for example, were organised to stand up for their right to housing as bulldozers demolished their homes to make way for large-scale investment schemes. Indigenous peoples' organisations tackled problems similar to those faced in Brazil when mining for minerals often left devastation in its wake as dams collapsed, rivers were polluted, people died or were uprooted and nature cursed.[5] In 1970 Ed de la Torre founded the Federation of Free Farmers, fighting for land. In 1982 Romy Tiongco, another Catholic priest who joined Christian Aid's staff for a while, galvanised over 200 farmers to form a cooperative and challenge the middlemen who were doing them down.[6]

In time these social movements became politicised, loudly challenging human rights abuses and hounded by the military. Ed de la Torre along with many others[7] was detained under martial law for several years. He went on hunger strike on Christmas Day 1974 in protest at the treatment of political prisoners. Christian Aid supported the human rights organisation Task Force Detainees of the Philippines as it stood by them and their families. It was founded by Sister Mariani Dimaranan, a diminutive, determined woman backed by local lawyers, whose highly respected reporting on political prisoners, extra-judicial killings and human rights abuses brought the world's attention to the realities of life and death under President Marcos.

Pedagogy of the Oppressed was an educational tool employed by Ed de la Torre and others. It had no necessary religious associations. It raised awareness as to why people were poor and helped them recognise poverty and powerlessness as social constructs – in other words, made by human beings, not given by God or some natural order. Things simply did not have to be that way! Liberation Theology, the child of Latin American theologians, disrupted long-standing Christian attitudes to the poor, together with the Church's preference for dealing with personal sin rather than the sin lying at the door of economic and political systems that benefited the relatively few and dispossessed the many.[8] This appetite for change was what Arthey and Christian Aid met again in Ed de la Torre and what had inspired Christian Aid and its Filipino partners for so long, even though as time went on energy tended to drain away, especially when Rodrigo Duterte was elected in 2016. His repressive regime began attacking the media, threatening freedom of speech and undermining civil society all over again while carrying out extra-judicial killings in the name of a war on drugs.

Well before, in 1996, there was concern that the radical character of CAPHIL's work and that of its associates was taking precedence over the expressed needs of local communities where the age-old issues around ownership of land, shanty towns and human rights violations were as real as ever. Questions were also raised about how funds were being used. Arthur Neame, appointed as Christian Aid's senior programme officer for South East Asia, including the Philippines, in 1996, shifted the emphasis to local struggles and reforming local governance to allow people to engage with state officials at the level where government decisions affected them.

So, did that dramatic day years later in 2013, when the typhoon struck and humanitarian aid took over CAPHIL's agenda, signal something new: at worst a retreat from all of that commitment to change, or simply a change to the current agenda?

Disasters and resilience

There was nothing new about the extreme vulnerability of 7,000 islands, big and small, especially along the eastern seaboard, to what were once generally called 'natural disasters' such as volcanoes, earthquakes, typhoons, floods and mudslides. The Taal Volcano, for example, erupted in 2020 displacing 500,000 people. On average twenty typhoons struck the country each year, destroying homes and crops and leaving little time to recover in between: 'You're fixing your roof from one hazard and then disaster strikes again'.[9] In 2009 Typhoon Ketsana flooded Metro Manila with 455 millimetres of rainfall in twenty-four hours. In 2013 Typhoon

Haiyan was only different because it was more powerful and catastrophic than the rest, killing thousands, affecting over 14 million and doing $500m worth of damage. Climate change was well under way.

If for many INGOs the response amounted to a relief operation, for CAPHIL and many others it certainly did not end there. Talk of 'relief' turned to talk of 'resilient' communities able to withstand repeated shocks and adapt. The two big questions were: how to prevent the worst happening again, and how to strengthen communities to be able to cope and, given a fairer wind, move forward?

Efforts to prevent the worst, or even to be better prepared for it, produced a long 'to-do' list. Better weather forecasting about what to expect would help, as would open roads and evacuation centres to get people out of harm's way. Longer-term measures such as 'building back, building better' houses, improving the management of floods, securing land that stayed put and was not washed away or taken away by evictions and land-grabbing – all had a contribution to make. The hazards of climate change, ranging from spells of intense heat to equally intense spells of rainfall, called for crops, especially rice[10] and in some areas seaweed, that could better weather the storm, and new ways of growing them. Solar power could provide more reliable and environmentally friendly electricity. Savings banks could improve the village economy. Communities needed bringing together to find cohesion and a voice. Leaders needed training to maintain morale, ease tensions, take tough decisions, organise and see fair play. Traumatised people needed understanding and support.

Joined-up action

But how could all of this and more be brought about where communities born out of the political struggle were ill-equipped to tackle a very different agenda dealing with 'resilience'? Funding was essential but far from enough to meet the challenge: building resilience. CAPHIL could take credit for proposing and nurturing a rather complicated, not to say sophisticated, answer. They dubbed it 'the whole society approach'. It had many facets. First came the many issues it would cover in order to build the self-confidence of the dispossessed and disempowered. As we have already noted, they ranged from the technical and political to the economic and personal. Second came the different levels at which the approach would operate: local, regional and national, firmly prioritising remote areas where fewer NGOs were at work and the needs and risks were most acute. Third came a whole list of people and organisations ready and able to help. Some were unusual for Christian Aid, where a good deal of mistrust, of big business for example, had to be overcome. They included: a university; an observatory in Manila run by the Jesuits; scientists and technicians; agro-businessmen training farmers, gardeners and market traders; government departments, at least one of which was headed by Ed de la Torre for a time and another by a one-time staff member of Oxfam; together with churches, present and active in every community, and social movements. If you had an issue, you had someone to turn to!

This web of joined-up goodwill was held together in part by the Disaster Risk Reduction Network (DRRNet), which Christian Aid did much to create. It remained an active friend but never became a voting member, a thoughtful move that said something about its approach to 'partnership', which a UN official once described as 'humble', not seeking a high profile but working quietly in the background. CAPHIL said it nourished and nurtured others, encouraging them to work together.

DRRNet, determined to bring policymakers face to face with affected communities, thought carefully about how best to get things done by, among other things, understanding and walking the corridors of power and engaging with government officials. One notable success came in 2010, admittedly when the political scene was calmer and more progressive. In September 2009, when Typhoon Ketsana flooded Metro Manila, 747 people died and the shanty towns of the poor went under water. If anything good could be said to come out of such misery, it wonderfully concentrated minds and offered an opportunity for progress. DRRNet provided a strong and widely representative political platform. Pressure mounted on government and was not completely resisted. The following year, in 2010, Congress passed legislation[11] that turned attention away from emergency aid towards prevention and the protection and empowerment of local communities, in line with what was increasingly being referred to as 'localisation'.[12]

When politics turned nasty again in 2016, DRRNet found it difficult to keep going and lost its sense of direction; but if in 2013, when Typhoon Haiyan struck, Christian Aid in the Philippines appeared to dramatically change course, it was not by abandoning efforts to tackle the causes of injustice in depth and strengthen its victims. Rather it was that, for the time being at least, injustice took on a rather different face.

Generosity

When energy levels flagged at times, for understandable reasons, the well-known hospitality of people who live on little or nothing showed remarkable resilience. We had spent the day in a remote Filipino village in northern Luzon finding respite from the sound of guns during the night before. It could easily have been one of those villages visited more than once by Margaret O'Grady, Christian Aid's Project Officer in the region from 1980 to 1997, where, asked about the poorest, the villagers explained that when no smoke came out of a roof at midday the family were not eating their main meal because they couldn't afford the food or the firewood or both.

As we prepared to leave, our hosts insisted on providing us with a meal. We waited for a good hour as they searched for food and cooked it. I then ate and enjoyed frogs' legs for the first time (rather like chicken, I thought) and tried to hide an Englishman's relief when they apologised for not being able to find a decent dog to make a traditional festive stew. Writing about the incident gave pause for reflection where a story about a relatively unimportant difference can foster in the hearer an unhelpful sense of alienation or, as some would call it, 'otherness'.

15
Sierra Leone

Whenever a Pandora's box is opened, whether by accident or design, out comes nothing but evil and misery, leaving only hope trapped inside. But when a very different kind of box is opened, now familiar to many remote communities in Sierra Leone, it seems to bring nothing but good. It can stand up to 2 feet tall, made from sturdy metal rather than myth, with a strong padlock on its lid. Women take care of the key.

They haven't had the key to much else. In the highly conservative areas of Sierra Leone, according to the men, 'women are not in the front, they should always be in the kitchen'. Girls would drop out of school, be subjected to Female Genital Mutilation (FGM) and forced into early marriage. All household chores, from cleaning to cooking and the care of children, were theirs. Gender-based violence was severe and prevalent. If women did escape the kitchen, it was to sell crops from the farm at the side of the road, or work on the land for a pittance. They had virtually no say in family or community affairs. 'When the lion roars, women are silent.'

Village Savings and Loans Associations (VSLAs) were a catalyst for change. By 2023 there were twenty of them in Pujehun, one of Sierra Leone's poorest regional government districts where Christian Aid was working with local civil society organisations. Women in remote villages saved what little money they could in the metal box. Then they took out small loans, sometimes in desperation to pay for food but often to invest in small business ventures such as selling palm oil, making soap, dying cloth, even raising goats on community farms. Any surplus earnings went to repay the loan and in time made bigger ones available.[1]

In the 2020s the boxes began to give way to mobile phones and 'Orange' banking. The big commercial banks were far away. It took precious time for the women to go there. On arrival the banks could well be closed. Interest on deposits was low and interest on loans was high. The Orange Mobile Company in Sierra Leone collaborated with Christian Aid through its subsidiary, Orange Money, on a community-friendly venture which opened forty access points for small cash deposits and withdrawals nearer to home. Using mobile phones, VSLAs could now keep their records more easily than making endless entries by hand into notebooks; and the women could make business transactions and keep an eye on their personal accounts as they saved and borrowed and paid their way.

All of this should be celebrated but not romanticised. It did not solve everything! VSLAs, however, did yield huge benefits beyond the financial. The game changer was the growing confidence of the women over time. Yes, they now had some money for food and school fees, but they also had an increasing degree of self-reliance and, what Christian Aid was looking for, empowerment. In 2022 this was demonstrated dramatically when women representing VSLAs, who had benefited from the Kailahun Women in Governance Network (KWIGN) managed by Social Enterprise Development (SEND), turned up to a high-level meeting about funding with World Vision and the Foreign, Commonwealth and Development Office, all dressed up in glass slippers, traditional robes and carrying handbags!

Instead of hiding their money from their husbands, they openly flaunted this traditional sign of their strength and independence. Women out and about with handbags (maybe with a mobile and not too much cash inside) were walking a good deal taller than women who knew their place in the kitchen.

On the domestic front relationships improved. There was less violence, even though domestic violence remains a massive issue in the country. In public affairs women increasingly made their presence felt. They stood for election to village councils,[2] and won. The lionesses were beginning to roar. Mary Sellu was the first woman to be elected to the council in a conservative and predominately Muslim district with its outdated ideas as to where women did and did not belong. Later on, in 2018, women like Rebecca Yei Kamara, Emilia Lolloh Tongi and Bernadette Wuyatta Songa were elected to Sierra Leone's national parliament and subsequently attended the International Congress of Parliamentary Women's

Caucuses in Dublin. Alice Foyah had been re-elected as MP for Kailahun District in 2012 where KWIGN had issued a manifesto highlighting their political priorities and mobilising women to vote. The Gender Equality and Women's Empowerment Act of 2023 decreed, not altogether successfully, that a minimum of 30% of MPs should be women.[3]

Once installed as local and district councillors and national MPs, women began to influence the agenda. Issues like maternal and child health care, sanitation and clean water supplies were prioritised, along with access to markets and improved roads to get there. Government services were either non-existent or in disarray. After the civil war Sierra Leone had the highest child and maternal death rates in the world. Government spending was insufficiently transparent, corruption was rife and money unaccounted for. Planning for the country's economic development and improving the lives of all its people was far from evident. Taxes, which could have helped turn things around, were not properly collected, not least from big business.

Mark Vyner, Christian Aid's Africa divisional manager from 2011 to 2018, recalled in an email note a visit by James Cleverly, a businessman and later a UK government minister with family roots in Sierra Leone who, after hearing about work on tax justice, quipped that as a businessman he did not believe in tax. Vyner showed him a dirt track just outside Freetown which passed as a main road as just one example of 'what you get when there's no tax take'.[4]

Governance

These comparatively recent events in the 2020s reflected what had been Christian Aid's overriding concern going back to the 1980s and shared by the UK government's Department for International Development: to achieve good governance in Sierra Leone. It involved a myriad of players in complex networks, from NGOs like Christian Aid to CSOs implementing programmes, to VSLAs and pioneering women.

To take a few examples, in 2006, following earlier conversations, the Methodist Church in Sierra Leone and the Network Movement for Justice and Development set up Partners Initiative for Conflict Transformation (PICOT) supported by Christian Aid. They worked together for democracy and accountable governance right down to the grass roots. Gbuagahun (meaning 'shedding old attitudes and behaviour'), 2009–11, was one of its projects, sponsored by Christian Aid's In Their Lifetime (ITL) programme (see below) and working for reform with the chiefdoms. In 2011 it presented a policy involving universal suffrage in all paramount chief elections, which the cabinet fed into a wider review of the constitution beginning in 2013.

Enhancing the Interaction between Citizens and the State in Sierra Leone (ENCISS) was a large-scale, presidential award-winning (in 2013) programme running from 2010 to 2015, funded by DFID and managed by Christian Aid, aimed at improving people's access to information and their participation in decision-making. Between October 2010 and September 2011, 243 grants totalling £3.8m were made to CSOs to make sure villagers were well able to communicate their concerns. Training included song and dance, drama and storytelling, all part of a public education campaign in 2014. Its innovative Short Message Service (SMS) Voices project with its community reporters used the web and mobile technology to connect citizens and district councillors. It proved to be a powerful tool for exchanging information during the Ebola outbreak. After 2020, when DFID was absorbed into the FCO, the funding dried up.

Power to Women (2015–17) built on an earlier Christian Aid and DFID-funded programme in Kailahun District aimed at increasing the number of women councillors.

Strengthening Accountability and Building Inclusion (SABI), again funded by DFID (2016–20), was a large consortium of NGOs and CSOs, led by Christian Aid, working for accountable governance. Better working relationships were built between local people and the authorities. Volunteers were trained to use smartphones for gathering information about the quality and availability of health and other government services. The information was fed back to communities where levels of literacy were low, by way of handmade 'infographics' or black and white pictures and diagrams – for example, of a small building marked 'health clinic' with a big 'X' barring the door – to raise awareness and stimulate action.

ITL was an appeal to better-off individuals in the UK for sustained support for innovative and potentially risky programmes. Women's

Economic Empowerment and Leadership (WEEL) was one of the key projects, originally running from 2022 to 2024. It was specifically focused on using mobile technology to strengthen VSLAs: out of the metal box and into the Orange bank. In Pujehun, one group of women held a small ceremony with singing and dancing to 'transition' the box and celebrate all it had meant to them. Then they gave it away for personal use.

Nearly twenty years before, between 2006 and 2011, Christian Aid established and nurtured the Budget Advocacy Network (BAN), which then became an independent organisation while remaining a close ally, looking for clarity about government revenues and how they were spent.

All of these and more were of one mind as to what kind of government was urgently needed in Sierra Leone.[5]

Lion Mountains

Centuries ago, tribes from the interior settled in virgin forest protected by high mountains and the sea. Portuguese sailors, led by the explorer Pedro de Sintra, landed there in the fifteenth century and called it 'Lion Mountains', or Sierra Leone. Muslim traders brought Islam, which became the religion of the majority, and Westerners, including traders, colonisers and missionaries, brought Christianity. It was not long (in the 1670s) before the traders took an interest not only in ivory but in human beings, and began transporting captives to Europe, America and the Caribbean. In 1787 the British set up a naval base in what became known as Freetown. The transatlantic slave trade was abolished in 1807 but continued illegally for many years. British ships intercepted the slave ships and rescued their captives, creating for them a settlement known as the 'Province of Freedom'. After slavery was abolished in 1833, 'liberated Africans' were also sent to Sierra Leone from Nova Scotia along with Maroons, formerly enslaved people from Jamaica, many of them Christians. Between 1807 and 1864 the British navy brought more than 50,000 Africans into Freetown. A life of 'freedom' was not what it sounded like, since a life of coerced labour awaited many.

In 1808 the colony became a British Crown Colony, gaining independence in 1961 and Republic status in 1971. In 1827 the Church

Missionary Society (CMS) established Fourah Bay College, the first higher education college south of the Sahara. Many educated Sierra Leoneans went on to enjoy highly successful careers as traders, doctors and lawyers (sometimes referred to as West Africa's elite) at home and abroad, Britain included.[6]

For the majority, however, their prospects were far from good, only made worse by a cruel civil war (1991–2002), followed in 2014 by one of the worst outbreaks of Ebola in living memory and, after that, the Covid-19 pandemic of 2020.

The government had plenty of headaches, not the least of which was the sheer diversity of its citizens. Indigenous peoples, traders, European settlers, freed slaves, townspeople and rural people, Christians and Muslims (who had an unusually interesting interfaith relationship, often attending one another's places of worship) – all had to learn to live together. It was not helped by the stark contrast between the ways of ancient authoritarian chiefdoms in the rural areas and the aspiring democratic ways of the city, two jurisdictions somehow needing to be made one.

Earlier days

Christian Aid refers to establishing itself in Sierra Leone in 1988, but it was at work in the country, at arm's length, well before that. One of its strongest allies was the Methodist Church in Sierra Leone, a leading member of the United Christian Council in Freetown, later to become the Council of Churches in Sierra Leone. From 1978 to1980, funded by the Overseas Development Administration UK (ODA), Christian Aid supported the publication of reading materials and subsequently, with Evangelische Zentralstelle für Entwicklungshilfe of Germany (EZE), books in the vernacular rather than English, Sierra Leone's official language, offering useful information on health, nutrition and farming in the hope of advancing literacy and bringing about changes in an unhealthy way of life.[7] A VSO placement, also supported by Christian Aid, worked on small-scale community projects.

Two interesting letters from the Christian Aid archives reflect relationships between Christian Aid and the churches, both written in 1982. One had to do with familiar issues around churches and what Christian Aid was prepared to fund and what it was not. The Revd Evan Johnson, a minister in Freetown, wrote to Sally Meachim at Christian Aid in London wondering whether Christian Aid might help to build a new church hall and vicarage. Turning down the request, Meachim pointed out that Christian Aid did not fund 'building projects involving a big outlay of capital' (she probably had 'church' building projects in mind but did not say so); rather, it was far more interested in funding the United Christian Council's Commission on Churches in Development projects on health and agriculture in the rural areas, and the efforts of the Methodists in Njaluahun community to get village families to dig latrines!

A second letter was written by Sarah Hughes to say how much Christian Aid's staff and supporters had enjoyed the month-long visit to the UK of the Revd Christian Peacock of the Methodist Church in Freetown, touring parishes and schools and supporter groups. Peacock was one of the first visitors under the newly established Exchange Programme. Cordial as the letter was, behind it were several murmurings from area staff due to play host to the visitor and ferry him round. They warmly welcomed him but challenged HQ colleagues as to what exactly was the purpose of the visit and why it had been scheduled during the busy period leading up to Christian Aid Week.

Once Christian Aid was firmly established in Freetown in 1988 under the leadership of Jeremy Craft and then Mercy Melaku,[8] it set about creating and strengthening a whole network of NGOs, CSOs, including those already mentioned, together with faith-based organisations like the Methodist Church and the now Council of Churches, all involved in the struggle for good governance. Between them they implemented huge programmes like SABI and ENCISS and cooperated on a range of issues mainly, but not exclusively, focused on health. They worked together in seven remote rural districts, later narrowed to four against the background of cuts in UK government funding.

Conflict

Humanitarian aid came to the fore during and after the vicious civil war of 1991–2002. Coping with the aftermath was one reason for opening the country office. Children had gone missing, many forced by rebels to commit atrocities. Their schools had been destroyed and their teachers killed. By the turn of the millennium, half of Sierra Leone's population of 4.5 million was either displaced or had left the country. In 1999 two planeloads of plastic sheets, high-energy biscuits, blankets and medicines worth £360,000 were flown in by Christian Aid and ACT and distributed by the Methodists and the Council of Churches. They were used to help feed 40,000 people stranded in the national stadium and others camped out in churches and schools.[9] At the same time Christian Aid did its best to uphold its commitment to work with local people and respect their knowledge and skills as to their needs and how best they could be met.

The horrors of war cried out for conflict resolution. During the spring of 2000 the churches trained 150 community leaders in human rights, paid for by the Diana, Princess of Wales Memorial Fund. They encouraged reconciliation, including the forgiveness of returning boy soldiers. Given the high levels of illiteracy, training included drama, acting out the killings, the devastation of a village, what it was like to return and mourn the dead, the fear that the rebels might come back, and the good effects of reintegration. The drama would end with soldiers on all sides disarming.[10]

Unrelated to the civil war but often violent were the stand-offs between farmers and cattle herders accused of allowing their cows to roam on to farmlands and eat the crops of rice and vegetables. From 2006 to 2009 the EU funded and Christian Aid managed efforts to work with traditional leaders in seventy-eight communities to ease tensions. Eventually new byelaws were drawn up in 2019 allowing herders to graze their animals from February to June, while reserving the land for farmers from May to January to sow and harvest their crops.

Producing palm oil, widely used in the food and cosmetics industries, also provoked conflict, this time not between local people but between them and multinationals like SOCFIN, a Luxembourg-based palm oil producer. Local chiefs in Malen in Pujehun District and the Sierra Leone government leased thousands of hectares of land to the company over the heads of small farmers in return for jobs and compensation. The plantation created less than 1,200 full-time jobs; 2,500 became casual labourers earning on average less than half Sierra Leone's minimum wage. Partly due to the lack of a land register and to uncertainty as to who owned what, farmers did not receive their due. What they did get was heavily taxed at up to 50%. Many were ruined and, unable to feed themselves, left the area.[11]

Others, notably from Green Scenery and the Malen Affected Land Owners and Users Association, were arrested and jailed for exposing the scandal, and sued for defamation. Peaceful protests were met with violence from the police and the army. Two villagers were killed in 2019. In 2022, ownership of land was clarified and SOCFIN had to renegotiate.[12]

Health

Christian Aid had become all too familiar with HIV/AIDS in many countries, at times handling huge, multi-million-dollar programmes.[13] Gillian Paterson, a member of staff for some years, wrote extensively about it, particularly in relation to women.[14] In Sierra Leone from 2006 to 2009, Christian Aid and members of its network, notably the Network of HIV Positives in Sierra Leone (NETHIPS, an umbrella organisation for people living with AIDS), implemented an EU-funded programme reaching out to 75,000 people, including 1,500 actually living with AIDS. Youths were taught about prevention, and communities were urged to fight against stigma and discrimination. The programme was extended to 2011 with the support of Comic Relief and Irish Aid.

Some of the issues raised in the battle with HIV/AIDS, in the hope of stopping the scourge spreading, were also highly relevant when it came to Ebola and, after that, the Covid-19 pandemic. From 2014 to 2016 Sierra Leone suffered one of the worst outbreaks of Ebola in living memory. In the rural areas little was done to stop it spreading; traditional practices, like washing the dead before burial, rubbing corpses with oil, hugging and kissing dead bodies and dressing them in fine clothes, only spread it further. Some 3,600 died, 221 health workers included. According to the World Health Organisation (WHO), 365 died after catching the disease at a single funeral. When the outbreak finally came to an end, Christian Aid and many CSOs had to more or less start all over again.

When help arrived from outside the villages, it was at times insensitive, such as using black ambulances which only spoke of death (eventually repainted white), and distrusted. It could also be ill-informed. For example, aid packages contained no pepper. No one in Sierra Leone cooks without it, so girls were sent to market to buy it and brought the disease back home. When DFID flew in consultants and opened much-needed Ebola treatment centres, the locals failed to turn up. According to Jeanne Kamara, Christian Aid's country manager in Sierra Leone, there was 'a big trust deficit'. The way in had to be through trusted local leaders and committees who, once informed and trained, were far better placed to advise others on how to protect themselves and limit contagion.

Faith leaders

In Christian Aid reports on the Ebola and Covid-19 crises, there are a number of appreciative references to the part played by faith leaders, Christian and Muslim.[15] Some faith-based organisations in Sierra Leone, as elsewhere, were judged to be badly run with little or no ability to contribute meaningfully – so much so that even the World Council of Churches and ACT, so committed to working with ecumenical partners, were driven to look elsewhere. Religious leaders in Sierra Leone, however, once better informed, scored highly and received a few accolades for once, including from Christian Aid!

Outside officials, trying to contain the virus with draconian measures like quarantine and lockdowns, running counter to traditional culture and values, were met with hostility, conspiracy theories and outright denial. Faith leaders, embedded in the community, understood the sensitivities. Christian and Muslim worked together. They were trusted by almost everyone. They backed up the medical advice using selected texts from the Qur'an and the Bible. They ensured burials were dignified and safe. They advised on how people could protect themselves by adopting simple habits like washing their hands and not visiting family or the sick, or joining large congregations, however much it went against the cultural grain. As when facing the scars of war and HIV/AIDS, they discouraged stigma in favour of acceptance. Overall, they were judged to have played 'a transformational role'.[16]

Healing

In late 2023, Paul Grime travelled to Sierra Leone as part of a group of Christian Aid supporters from across the UK actively involved in ITL. They went to see the village women with their savings clubs and metal boxes. He was evidently moved by what had come out of them and wrote the following meditative poem, not about 'outcomes' as we often think of them, but about the healing of a marriage.[17]

Moving lion mountains

he is storm she is cotton tree   there are disputes   there are choices
sometimes he slaps her

you touch one   you touch us all   it multiplies   ask the one who is
crying in the middle of the night

don't touch me   lef mi bodi!

he is capsicum she is cassava   she cannot count money   her business
makes a loss

we are your mouth   we are your money   he says

we are more frequent users of money   she doesn't say

he is badger she is bird   it's hard   she leaves   she returns   again   he
is touched   he chooses

there's training   they become a family he for she   it multiplies

women bring it home   men throw it away   he says

they are rain they are sun   now they work side by side   closing
the gaps

now they fall in love with their lives day by day   waiting to see how it goes

storms are over they are very happy about it   now there is peace at home

you help one woman   you help the community   it multiplies

they are guava they are goat   she learns a lot   a lot   she doesn't need much

a box   we save money in the box

money earned   loans lent   lessons learned   money spent   cash in cash out

it's community   women and men   a spill effect   it multiplies

that's how we go about it

money makes confidence   nicer clothes   vibrant vibrant

they are village they are union   women lead   now we speak with one voice as all women

all women   not divided by religion or politics or status   men give space

amplifying voices   it multiplies   it changes lives   a lot   a lot

Leh AI Go!

16

Pie charts and all that

From its earliest days Christian Aid's annual reports and accounts and its more popular reviews of the year have consistently itemised its expenditure under three headings with only minor variations: Fundraising, Charitable Activities, and Management and Administration.

Fundraising

At the start, Christian Aid Week and Christian Aid, born out of the BCC's Inter-Church Aid and Refugee department, were virtually one and the same.[1] CAW was all there was of Christian Aid and its major, if not only, source of income apart from emergency appeals for refugees. As the charity grew, so did the need for more and more funds, and with it increasingly sophisticated and successful methods of raising them. It always relied heavily on volunteers alongside dedicated fundraising and communications teams, mostly in London.

Apart from the CAW house-to-house collections and all that went with them, from attention-grabbing stunts to TV adverts,[2] how was the money raised? Emergency appeals were often but by no means always issued jointly with the Disasters Emergency Committee.[3] Funding longer-term projects was the responsibility of the international department applying to governments and other institutional donors and corporates like AquAid and the Co-operative Bank.

At a more personal level, appeals were made through the letterbox to existing supporters and, it was always hoped, to potential new ones. They were encouraged not only to give one-off donations but to sign up to direct debits and Gift Aid: GIVE, even if you're not yet ready to ACT and PRAY. Cold calling was briefly considered and dropped. A large number of supporters and staff objected to it. It was resumed however in 2025! Child sponsorship was always opposed, but more personal links between donors and the organisations they were supporting, such as the 'Celebrate a Life' scheme of 2008, were explored, allowing them to understand just how their money was making a difference. The offer of the free services of a solicitor in one month of the year (Will Aid) provided an incentive to make a will and leave money to Christian Aid and other charities while going about it.[4]

A brave experiment called ITL was created in 2009 and relaunched in 2021. It invited adventurous types, probably with more money than most, to contribute £15,000 over three to five years to build up a fund of £5m by 2026. It would be used to invest in innovative, even risky, attempts to tackle some intractable problems in development, with a strong emphasis on learning-as-you-go from what did and didn't work. From a growing number of experiments, tested for a year and then supported over a longer period with sums of up to £400,000, women in Nicaragua successfully set up a business growing and selling hibiscus flowers; in Colombia a bold attempt was made to create humanitarian spaces in cities where women and children especially could feel safe and lead a more normal way of life; and in Ethiopia improved ways of responding to health emergencies have been tested and refined.[5]

Profile was important. Few were likely to give to a charity they'd never heard of. They were more likely to if Christian Aid could catch the attention of journalists and broadcasters by way of well-researched and well-timed reports on issues such as child labour dropping into the public domain at the start of CAW.[6]

Photographic exhibitions and films involving well-known names such as David Bailey, Sebastião Salgado, Mike Goldwater, Don McCullin, Tim Hetherington and the British war artist John Keane, who made two visits to Gaza in 2022 supported by Christian Aid, added to Christian Aid's profile. So did sending Bianca Jagger to India for World Aids Day in 2002, as did setting out its stall at the Chelsea Flower Show for a number of years, and winning a medal at Hampton Court for a display of a Sudanese garden planted with drought-resistant plants.

Not everyone would agree that all publicity, including bad publicity, is good publicity but some of Christian Aid's staff apparently did. In 1999 media experts like Martin Cottingham, under the creative eye of Kate Phillips, worked on yet another billboard poster for Christian Aid Week. It depicted all the G7 leaders at a summit meeting with their trousers down, revealing boxer shorts in their national colours. It was related to their repeated failure to act on debt issues. The headline was 'All mouth' – and, presumably, no trousers! The advert was banned by the Advertising Standards Authority as likely to cause offence, just as its perpetrators rather expected. It never appeared but the loud criticism and public debate that followed achieved their aim at minimal cost, namely to get Christian Aid talked about in that one week in the year when it was as vital as ever to be seen and heard. Three days after the G7 summit Gordon Brown, then Chancellor of the Exchequer, cancelled 100 of the UK's bilateral debts. The year before, in 1998, a TV advert directed by Anthony Minghella received similar treatment, banned but screened in cinemas across the country and causing a stir.[7]

There could be internal debates as well as public ones. For some, fundraising appeals and the visuals that went with them were not easily reconciled with hard-hitting campaigning or cool-headed educational materials. The fundraisers wanted to melt hearts and demonstrate the urgent needs of the poor while showing them respect and avoiding any suspicion of 'poverty-porn'. Campaigners wanted to cry out not for money but for justice, and to win status and respect for marginalised people who were often shown little if any respect at all. Some insisted that these tensions never really existed and that provocative campaigns often boosted income. If there were differences they were between colleagues who in their different ways were nevertheless on the same side.

A great deal of hard work by all sorts of fundraisers was rewarded when Christian Aid's income from all quarters exceeded £100m for the first time in the early 2010s, fulfilling one Director's (Daleep Mukarji) dream of topping £100m. In the early days Christian Aid's financial support came mainly from the voluntary sector. As time went on it became more mixed and headed the other way, notably after the creation of DFID in 1997, followed by substantial government support. In more recent times government support has decreased and voluntary income has come to predominate once again.

Charitable activities

The second of the three recurring headings in Christian Aid's accounts more or less speaks for itself. It is mainly about delivering humanitarian aid and longer-term development projects, as described in many chapters of this book,[8] with some additional references to 'support costs'. It came to include education (see Chapter 11), campaigning (see Chapter 3) and communications.

Communications involved dealing with the press, radio and television, and with supporters. Here the issue of respect became relevant once again. A 'transactional relationship' is an unfamiliar term to most but adds up to taking money from the public and leaving it at that. It overlooks the possibility that members of the public might be interested in the people they are asked to help and are well aware that helping them through Christian Aid is not going to be all plain sailing. They would like to know about what happens after a donation is sent; about the problems as well as the achievements. They need to be taken seriously. Newsy and honest follow-ups rather than bland thank-you letters became important.

Management and administration

Overheads

The third heading referring to management and administration is where the argument about overheads kicks in and where the 'pie chart watchers', as I think of them, are on the alert. Pie charts (see Appendix, p. 217) are intended to sum up financial matters clearly and at a glance. The slices or segments of the pie indicate how the money was spent, with so-called overheads showing up as the smallest at around 2% or less. At times reference to them is omitted altogether: not so misleading as at first it might appear.

The overheads of charities have long been a bone of contention. Donors, large and small, have been anxious to make sure that as much of their money as possible was spent on what Christian Aid existed to do, namely feed the hungry and strengthen the powerless. Some demanded that all of it should go straight to where it belonged, as if money could jump out of their pockets straight into the pockets of the poor with no charge for delivery services.

Donors got particularly upset in 2013 when the *Daily Telegraph* and *Daily Mail* published details of salaries paid to fourteen of the UK's aid charities; Loretta Minghella, Christian Aid's CEO from 2010 to 2017, salary of £126,206 was among them. Letters poured into Christian Aid's HQ, rarely expressing support. Some expressed sorrow, even anger, that their hard-won takings from CAW collections seemed dwarfed by these figures. The most extreme suggested that staff should accept a minimum salary or even expenses only. Not a few wondered why, as a Christian charity clothed therefore in the mantle of sacrificial service, Christian Aid could not find anyone from among the churches willing and able to do the CEO's job for half the amount.

Those responsible for fixing salary levels, caught between a highly competitive market, the rising demands of the job and the escalating 'professionalism' of charity workers including highly sought-after and highly paid fundraisers, did their best to explain and defend their actions. Carolyn Gray, chair of Christian Aid's finance committee (2007–15), cited the CEO's growing responsibilities and how her salary had been 'benchmarked' against NGOs and church-based organisations of similar size and complexity. Rowan Williams, Chair of the Board, referred to some of Paul's letters to the Romans, Corinthians and Ephesians in the New Testament and turned away from arguments about sacrifice to arguments about fairness and the right to fair compensation for a hard day's work.

Coming at things from a different perspective, the Charity Commission had more than once warned charities that too much cutting back on overheads could put at risk their ability to manage and spend their money well.[9] In 2013, however, William Shawcross, chair of the CC, told the *Daily Telegraph* that 'disproportionate salaries risk bringing organisations and the wider charity world into disrepute'.[10]

What then might 'overheads' or 'management and administration' refer to? The list of candidates is long.

Buying and maintaining equipment like computers is one of them. Paying for the long-forgotten typing pool or the tea trolley and its modern equivalents is another. Paying the electricity and cleaning bills is another. Working away in a rather unglamorous but absolutely essential finance department, keeping a close eye on the accounts and budgeting for the future is yet another; and buildings don't keep standing up if they're not taken care of. It all costs money.

Governance

Charities like Christian Aid have to be well governed – another substantial overhead. For Christian Aid that meant in the early days a fully funded committee of volunteers and then a board, representative of its stakeholders, well briefed, meeting on a regular basis, trusted above all with Christian Aid's money, ensuring compliance with financial regulations and the law, and seeing that Christian Aid is heading in the right direction with the right strategies and policies in place. Again, it all costs money.

Some of those policies were unheard of in the 1960s and 1970s and only came to prominence in later years. RISK was one of them, and for understandable reasons. It is mentioned along with a risk register in a single short paragraph in the annual report of 2001/02, as in the two following years. By 2021/22 it took more than six pages, with risks on every side from partnerships that could go wrong, to staff in danger of their lives, to reputational damage and loss of identity, to what amounted to legal warfare ('lawfare') and cyber-attacks causing its work to grind to a halt. As if exhausted, the long list ends with the reassurance that Christian Aid's 'risk appetite' remains, which presumably means it well knew it was in a risky business and that taking risks in the name of people wholly at risk remained an essential part of its calling. In the 2023/24 report, however, came the remark (p. 47) about how understanding risk increasingly 'underpinned' Christian Aid's decision-making.[11]

Safeguarding

Safeguarding, which became a matter of widening public concern, is another policy that belongs to more recent times in Christian Aid's story. It is mainly, but not exclusively, to do with keeping people – mostly women and children – safe from sexual exploitation. It hit the headlines when in February 2018 Oxfam staff in Haiti were accused of sexual misconduct following the earthquake of 2010, and Christian Aid had to tighten its policies and make sure that all was well in its own ranks. The CEO, as chief safeguarding officer, reported regularly to the board on any incidents and how they were dealt with.[12]

Roger Riddell, when in charge of Christian Aid's international work, expressed concern about the growing dangers faced by staff when travelling or working in war-torn countries, and argued strongly for another kind of 'safeguarding'. He organised training for them and remembers an afternoon with the army in a muddy field, throwing himself to the ground as he was shot at, before experiencing at first hand the terror and violence of a mock but realistic armed vehicle kidnap. Security systems for travel began to be set up. I myself never felt at serious risk, due to the care of my hosts and travelling companions, but like many others I heard the guns and fled from advancing armed 'rebels' on more than one occasion. For others the danger was far more real. Kate Phillips was one of them, ambushed at night at gunpoint in the wilds of Somalia in an incident reminiscent of that mocked-up kidnapping. Health workers were murdered in Afghanistan. In 2022, UK staff were trapped in Gaza for three days when hostilities flared up between Israel and Hamas. In 2024 there was a fatal attack on a partner in Burkina Faso.[13]

The line between 'governance' and 'management', where the board approves the policies and strategies and leaves the CEO and colleagues to carry them out within an agreed budget, has never been easy to draw or hold. Responsibility for Christian Aid's relations with governments, particularly the UK government, while of huge concern to the board, usually fell to the Director or CEO. They could be challenging but very constructive, as when Clare Short was the cabinet minister in charge of the newly created Department for International Development under Tony Blair. They were tense when Margaret Thatcher was Prime Minister and apartheid, among other contentious issues, was high on the agenda. As funding grew, Christian Aid needed to guard against what Jenny Borden called becoming 'contractors' to government by adopting its agenda rather than pursuing Christian Aid's own. Relations became highly critical under later Conservative governments, especially when DFID was absorbed into the Foreign and Commonwealth Office and the aid budget was cut from 0.7 to 0.5% in 2021, a good deal of it spent in the UK on housing refugees and overseas by the military with little obvious links to poverty. Critics described it as an act of political vandalism. It was certainly a time for Christian Aid to speak truth to a power close to home! For the aid community worse was to come when in 2025 the budget was cut even further by the Labour government and the money diverted to defence.

The legal structure of Christian Aid can be seen as mainly a matter for the board. At first Christian Aid was a department of the BCC. It became an independent charity when the BCC gave way to CTBI in 1990, later becoming technically 'corporate' rather than 'incorporate' in 2004.

Christian Aid's internal structure had to be approved by the board but was a management responsibility with a long story to tell about 'restructuring'. It was often precipitated by the harsh realities of falls in income due to a declining supporter base, to donations diverted to high-profile emergency appeals, to changes in government policies, or in 2022 to Covid-19, all of them 'spun' as opportunities to refocus and do better, including closing twelve country programmes and regional offices in the UK in 2019–20. Repeated restructuring, sometimes referred to as 'organisational design', might also have something to do perhaps with the need of successive directors and CEOs, including me, to make their mark.

In the beginning it was hardly a case of 'restructuring' since there was hardly any structure at all, only people with jobs. Famines in Ethiopia in the 1970s stretched Christian Aid's administrative capacity to the limit. The report of an Aid Advisory Committee in June 1975, chaired by Sir George Sinclair, recommended a reform of Christian Aid's management systems. After this, for many years four regional committees, involving staff, board members and advisers, covered Asia and the Pacific, Africa, Latin America and the Caribbean, and the Middle East, deciding how to spend money, only a few grants being left to the board.

When Charles Elliott left in 1984, the board decided that the management structure was unsatisfactory. It proceeded to set up what became known as the Appleby Committee, comprising once again board members, staff and advisers, with Mary Appleby at the helm.[14] The outcome was a matrix management system inside which staff looked, as it were, two ways: 'vertically' towards their line manager, maybe the head of a country programme, and 'horizontally' to a senior staff member responsible for a cross-cutting discipline such as fundraising, education or campaigning.

The 'Good Climb' (note the 'spin') followed under my watch, given a name that I lived to regret, not least when a disaffected member of staff in front of the rest accused me of marching my troops to the top of the hill and marching them down again. It involved some painful redundancies. It replaced the matrix in 1994 with fully resourced task teams, including the necessary expertise to do a clearly defined job. In the case of a country team, for example, it included development specialists but also a fundraiser charged with raising that team's funds, a campaigner on its behalf and an educationalist.

Life-changing restructuring was to follow. Devolution or decentralisation to in-country offices had no real beginning since Christian Aid (strictly speaking, 'Inter-Church Aid and Refugee Service' at the time) had a staff presence in Palestine in 1948. The pace of change quickened when, immediately after the Rwandan genocide, in 1995, Jenny Borden opened an office in Rwanda, where Christian Aid had been working since 1963, and in Burundi, because few organisations had been left standing and humanitarian aid was uncoordinated and in chaos. By 2002 there were nineteen offices in eighteen countries. The financial crises of 2008 and 2012, when Christian Aid left twelve countries almost entirely, led to considerable downsizing, as did Covid-19 and the demise of DFID, but by 2024 there were twenty-five offices in twenty countries. The traditional way of working from London and engaging with partners by way of correspondence and visits was shifting.

One driver of change, almost forced upon Christian Aid, was when ODA (Overseas Development Administration) and DFID gradually refused to talk to Christian Aid about funding programmes in their London and Glasgow offices in preference to their overseas, regional ones. Christian Aid had to follow. Another was when enquiries into the running of the Nairobi office in 2004 revealed serious flaws and sharpened questions about decentralising management and what was involved, especially as operating on a basis of trust and solidarity was eroded as Christian Aid grew and an increasing range of professional standards, from quality control and safeguarding to financial accountability, was introduced or imposed.

Any cost–benefit analysis had to admit that decentralising, however necessary, was not cheap. There were additional overheads to be paid for as well as new management skills to be learned, both in London and overseas. On the other hand, there was the promise of increased funds, better relations, coordination and networking on the ground, and improvements in the assessment and accompaniment of programmes. In London came the prospect of fewer staff, smaller premises and lower costs.

More fundamentally, devolution and decentralisation were part of that long-term vision of 'localisation' whereby serious attempts were made not only to hand over resources to the South but, along with them, the authority to make their own decisions about how best to use the money and accept the responsibilities and accountability that go with it. Some board members and staff adjusted to it more readily than others.[15]

Restructuring also costs money!

Human resources (HR)

HR was another area where the board made sure that adequate policies were in place and management implemented them. The HR team responsible certainly felt the pressure when staff were being made redundant or asked to reapply for their jobs. Salaries were frozen in 2009. Fair pay was an ongoing issue long after the 'scandal' of 2013. Under the leadership of Amanda Khozi Mukwashi, Christian Aid's CEO from 2018 to 2021, reflecting what was happening in society at large, serious attention was paid to racism and gender issues, the pay gaps relating to both, and to diversity and equality.

Lawfare

Being taken to court is hardly going to get a mention on any pie chart but it has lurked within 'Management and Administration' and those overheads that cost Christian Aid so much money. Of huge interest to the board, it has nevertheless placed great pressure on directors and CEOs. Two cases more or less bookend Christian Aid's story. The first centred on a Mr Smithers and a mistake. In 1974, after staff visits to Lazaret Camp in Niger followed by horrifying reports that supplies of milk powder had run out and children were dying, Christian Aid made an emergency grant which, due to an administrative failure, was never sent from London. The Bishop of Niger was informed about it but failed to report its non-arrival. Smithers was Deputy Director of Christian Aid at the time and brought considerable expertise to its work. Appalled by what had happened, and judging it had led to even more children dying, he resigned; but as he was regarded as a valuable colleague, his resignation was not accepted by the Director, Alan Booth. Smithers carried on but did resign, however, two years later. After this came unceasing attacks on Christian Aid's reputation and criticisms of its staff, followed by Christian Aid's attempts to defend itself,[16] absorbing what Booth's successor, Kenneth Slack, called immense amounts of time and energy. The matter dragged on when Slack, under pressure in a BBC radio interview, described Smithers' behaviour as 'insensitive, arrogant, ill-informed and impetuous'. Smithers sued for libel against Slack and the BBC. It led to an official apology from Christian Aid in the High Court, which Smithers accepted, together with an agreement to pay his costs and expenses. The settlement owed a lot to the mediation and generosity of Geoffrey Smith, Christian Aid's treasurer for a number of years.

In 2017 came 'lawfare'. David Abrams, as Executive Director of the New York-based Zionist Advocacy Center, accused Christian Aid, which he named a 'virulently anti-Israel NGO', of fraudulently obtaining money from USAID and using it to fund, directly or indirectly, Jihad al-Binaa (a Hezbollah-linked development organisation) to run training courses in Lebanon for people with disabilities under the aegis of what was then one of Christian Aid's partners, namely the Lebanese Union for People with Physical Disabilities. Exhaustive enquiries followed, involving endless requests by USAID to Christian Aid for information, after which the US government authorities declined to get further involved. Abrams then served a summons on Christian Aid in a New York court in November 2020, which was dismissed. His appeal was also dismissed but TZAC was given a period of ninety days to appeal against that decision. The case came to an end, along with the whole saga, on 14 September 2022. Christian Aid had fought its corner and won. Others had fought and lost.

Winning the case might well be regarded as a relief and a success, which for Patrick Watt as CEO and others it certainly was, but with serious qualifications. It had the potential, whatever the outcome, to damage Christian Aid's reputation. It added to tensions between Christian Aid and sections of the Jewish community. Despite its absolute commitment to continue, it made Christian Aid and others very wary when working in Palestine, as was intended. One commentator described its 'chilling effect' on the NGO sector. It could make solidarity extremely costly from a financial point of view. Despite winning, Christian Aid came away with legal fees amounting to £700,000, added to which was the equally serious cost in terms of anxiety, energy and time, sapping attention away from all the constructive things that there were to do.[17]

Overheads again

Returning to the issue of overheads and how to be straight with donors in the face of demands to cut them to the bone, the truth is that most, if not all, of those mentioned apply in one form or another not just to what people think of as Christian Aid's headquarters but also to its field offices and all the organisations it regards as partners, from national Councils of Churches to national NGOs and local community organisations. All have to be 'governed' in some shape or form, whether by committees or boards. Most have premises to look after, ramshackle or splendid, owned, rented or borrowed. All have to keep accounts and answer for them, sometimes heavily weighed down by donor demands. All have to look after their staff, manage and pay them. More and more of them as time goes on will have to pay their mobile phone bills and hire computers – even the remotest. Some fundraise for themselves, others are increasingly encouraged to do so. It all costs money!

Overheads are not actually 'over-heads' but run right through, down to the ground. Once recognised, pie charts that reduce 'Management and Administration' to a tiny percentage or pie slice of expenditure, or in some cases make no reference to it whatsoever, can be misleading. In reality, aid and development cost a great deal more than pie charts often imply, though if 'support costs' are also mentioned that may be less so. Where overheads are not referred to, it can be an acknowledgement that it is almost impossible to separate them out or it can reflect the fact that they run through every aspect of the enterprise and not lumping them all together properly represents that reality; but once again it can be misleading if nothing makes clear just how much it costs to deliver the goods.

Probably the best response to those who think overheads should more or less disappear is to break them down and itemise them under expenditure while Christian Aid explains rather than minimises them and makes every effort to keep the bills as low as possible, both for good housekeeping and 'green' reasons as in the case of cutting travel expenses, especially by air, amounting to thousands of pounds every year.

Annual reports and accounts along with pie charts do not make the most interesting of reads, important sources of information as they are. They do, however, chart something of Christian Aid's history in their own way. Those three lines of expenditure – charitable, fundraising and administration – testify to a remarkable degree of continuity alongside astonishing change from, for example, small to large, 'amateur ecclesiastics', as Smithers called them, running the show in the 1970s to experts and professionals as time went on, from informal to institutional, charitable to business-like, centralised to devolved, risk-taking to highly risk-aware (but not averse?), and opening envelopes by hand to outsourcing the mechanics of fundraising to a commercial enterprise.

Sometimes supporters criticise Christian Aid in amusing as well as worrying ways. A local CAW organiser, entirely missing the irony, wrote in to insist that all TV adverts, expensive as they were, should emphasise the high proportion of Christian Aid's income actually devoted to its aims. An elderly collector in Canterbury asked why so much money was being spent on people who, in the photographs, looked so well! Another wanted to know why Christian Aid was always sending money to Africa when 'surely its government could help a bit', and was astonished to learn 'it' was over fifty different countries. One collector found himself with a lot of explaining to do when questioned about money going to coffee producers in Nicaragua when they were wearing jewellery, and to farmers in Kenya when their low-tech mobile phones for weather monitoring were assumed to be fancy smart ones! None of which detracts from the duty of charities to use public money carefully and well; and pie chart watchers are right to hold Christian Aid to account.

17
Sudan and South Sudan

Two young boys, Dak and Pouk, run off in the sunshine to hide in the long grass outside their village. An idyllic picture of childhood or a horror story of hide and seek – and kill? One of them didn't make it.

Oil

Oil began to flow in Sudan in 1979. There was plenty of it. The following years brought major finds across almost a third of the country, mainly in the often-contested central regions between North and South in the Muglad and Melut basins in the shadows of the Nuba mountains. By 1997 oil companies from Canada, China, Malaysia and Sweden, as well as Sudan itself, were involved. Roads, pipelines to the sea, oil terminals and later refineries were built and in 2006 Sudan became a member of the Organization of the Petroleum Exporting Countries (OPEC).

Here was the potential for vast national wealth and, almost inevitably in this war-torn country, yet another cause of conflict. Chevron USA, the earliest of the oil explorers, abruptly shut down all activities in 1984 when its main base near Bentiu was attacked. Security became a serious issue. Besides being caught in the crossfire as different factions struggled for territory and control, there were disputes over oil revenues – only partly resolved in 2005 by the newly formed National Petroleum Commission's efforts to ensure equal shares of oil revenues between Khartoum and Juba – and catastrophic abuses of human rights.

By the turn of the century between 60,000 and 200,000 people had been displaced to clear the way for oil industry infrastructure and help crush the opposition, chiefly the Sudan People's Liberation Movement (SPLM), led by John Garang until 2005 when he died in a helicopter crash, and its army (SPLA), which at times attacked the oil fields as legitimate targets.

In the northern area of Ruweng from April to July 1999, over half the population was displaced as a result of savage government attacks. The oil companies claimed they found 'an empty landscape' so were inconveniencing and harming no one, but it was empty not because it was uninhabited but because its inhabitants had been driven out so that the oil giants with their drills, pumps and access roads could move in unhindered.

In 2002 the Sudan government attacked a World Food Programme distribution depot as it pursued its scorched-earth policies in the southern Rubkona County with its large reserves of oil, clearing out the SPLM 'rebels' and the civilians who allegedly supported them.

This was where Dak and Pouk, 8-year-old cousins, lived and played together in a small village close to the Nile. This was where they were attacked by government forces, first with bombs and then, almost unbelievably, by gunships and locally recruited horsemen and foot soldiers shooting them down. They ran for their lives to hide in grassy swamps where the horses could get into difficulties and could not come; but the gunships could, killing Pouk and many others. The soldiers burned down the village and left. The survivors fled to a relatively safe place 'between the streams', as they described it, and later moved on to areas where they built their fragile tukuls (grass shelters). Hungry and afraid, they were cared for by already desperately poor people who shared the little they had.

In April 2002 Christian Aid and DCA, at the forefront of NGO campaigning, published the report 'Hiding between the Streams: The war on civilians in the oil regimes of Southern Sudan', written up by Nils Carstensen. Insisting that protection for civilians should be part of humanitarian aid, it followed Christian Aid's 2001 report, 'The Scorched Earth: Oil and war in Sudan', which was in turn followed by 'Oil and Sudan' (Christian Aid, 2011) with its indictment of the oil companies' complicity in all that had happened.

As usual these reports and the terrible stories they told were evidence-based. On 29 March 2000, for example, as reported in 'Hiding between the Streams', a small assessment team from Christian Aid and DCA, helped by Operation Mercy (SSOM), flew into Wicok and the next day travelled south for six hours over seven streams to Chotchar and walked from there for two hours to Tuoc and for another two hours to Pam. On the way there and back they talked to recently displaced families about the attacks on them, their children and their homes, and listed their needs from mosquito nets to seeds and fishing hooks.

The team's reports and publications were highly praised. Their well-informed advocacy had some effect. On one occasion in 2021 they were invited to present their findings (over the phone!) to the board members of Lundin Oil, and in September 2023 two of its former executives stood trial in Sweden for war crimes. Needless to say, the oil did not stay underground.

Aid and development

During the civil war in the late 1990s a plane took off from Nairobi, where Christian Aid's staff were based at the time, heading for Juba, later to become the capital of South Sudan, surrounded as it was by rebel forces. The plane was carrying emergency supplies to starving people in a besieged city. The landing was not straightforward. It reminded me of a flight I once made into Kabul on my way to Herat in Afghanistan where the plane had to spiral down and down in order to avoid the mountains. In Juba it was the same manoeuvre, but the spiralling down was not to avoid the mountains but the missiles that would destroy the plane if it strayed outside a very limited area. The flight was one of many, sometimes with Christian Aid staff on board, including Sarah Hughes and Robert Hayward.

The need for humanitarian aid has loomed large in Christian Aid's involvement in Sudan and South Sudan caused by endless conflict and by climate change as, for example, devastating floods ruined crops and led to serious loss of livestock when streams turned to torrents. Emergency appeals by Christian Aid and the DEC[1] were all too familiar. One, in October 2015, referred to South Sudan's worst food crisis with 30% of the population hungry and in need of food aid. By 2023 the statistics were much worse: three-quarters of the population of South Sudan, including half a million refugees fleeing from the fighting in the North, had little or nothing to eat. But the stories of war go back way before that.

Boats have long been an essential means of transport, especially in the Upper Nile region where for eight months of the year the land is flooded. Many boats were destroyed in the war and were difficult to replace where wood was scarce and expensive. In the 1970s the Intermediate Technology Development Group, supported by Christian Aid, used their skills and imagination to design a cheaper replacement made of locally available concrete, or more accurately ferrocement. By 1978 seven concrete boats were completed. One of them, loaded with 15 tons of food, was able to reach a remote area where a whole community was suffering from starvation. Many more boats were built and remain in use.

Years later, in 2024, the Scottish government made a grant out of its relatively small Humanitarian Emergency Fund of £250,000 divided between Christian Aid and Oxfam. Christian Aid used its share to reach 4,000 people in the overcrowded and desperate conditions of the Wedweil Refugee Camp in Northern Bahr el-Ghazal, on the borders between North and South Sudan, providing shelters, food, clean water, health care for all, and gifts of cash to 400 women.

Given the persistence of conflict since well before the 1970s, and the continuous cries for help, there seemed little room for development programmes. Under financial pressure at the time, Christian Aid closed its office in Khartoum in 2013 after working closely since 2005 with the Sudan Council of Churches and having supported work in the country since the 1970s. It left only the office in Juba, opened in 2007, where Christian Aid's equally close ally, the New Sudan Council of Churches (NSCC), also had its base. Some cross-border work between North and South was maintained until 2019.

Despite the difficulties, not all was lost. Ecumenical roundtables between funding agencies, churches and other organisations were held in the 1990s to plan work on health care, education and agriculture as well as emergency relief, while in the South the NSCC worked hard with Christian Aid on food security and other issues.

From 2018 to 2021 Christian Aid was part of a UK government programme working where few others were, with communities in the Aweil North and Jur River regions, to tackle malnutrition and not just by providing aid. It touched the lives of nearly 70,000 women and 37,000 children. In Christian Aid's report on the programme, we meet a number of interesting characters.

Mayer is one of many fishermen who has learned how to improve his skills and now has a smoker to preserve his catch. Instead of being short of food he can sell his fish at the market and afford to buy better meals for himself and his family. Elizabeth is part of a village savings and loans scheme which has helped her set up a teashop and earn money. Adut, a farmer, has trained in agricultural techniques aimed at improving his crops both in quality and quantity. Some of his seeds are from the local seed bank, where they are stored from one season to the next: maize, sorghum, cowpeas and groundnuts. Aker is a schoolboy who makes brushes out of grasses and belongs to a hygiene club sweeping the village clean – and the school floor! The community, led by Richard, has built a health centre largely from their own funds with a bit of help from their friends. It is one of the places where Abney, a traditional birth attendant, is likely to be found encouraging mothers to play safe by giving birth at the local clinic and then to breastfeed their babies.

What has happened in Aweil is one of many good stories to tell, but they remained overshadowed by the cruelties and immediacies of war. On 12 May 2024 the British *Observer* newspaper (p. 42) drew attention to a Human Rights Watch investigation and its report describing parents being killed in front of their children, communities set ablaze, up to 9 million displaced from their homes and 25 million in need of humanitarian assistance. It was not a description of the war in Gaza, grabbing the headlines at the time, but of the largely forgotten war in Sudan and the ruthless attacks of the Rapid Support Forces in their fight with the Sudan government. Piled on top of endless misery elsewhere, *The Observer* described the misery of Sudan as the world's worst humanitarian emergency – calling for yet another appeal.

As had been said repeatedly by Christian Aid and the NGO world at large, the only answer to the poverty and suffering was and remains peace, hence their efforts to help and try to bring it about.

Building peace

Deborah Doherty from Christian Aid Ireland, visiting Yei in December 2000, had a sharp reminder of what conflict in South Sudan was all about. The small market town had been bombed by Sudan government forces the day before. Twenty were killed and fifty-four injured. Survivors were digging makeshift bomb shelters. Local de-mining teams from Operation Save Innocent Lives (OSIL), set up by ex-soldiers and supported by Christian Aid, were beginning the painstaking work of clearing the town and the fields surrounding it of unexploded ordnance.

Ever since independence in 1956 and the civil war of 1955–72, efforts were made to put an end to this kind of suffering and bloodshed. A peace agreement between North and South was signed in Addis Ababa. During the war between the Sudan government and the SPLA, the Machakos Protocol was signed in 2002 accepting the right of the South to self-determination. A Comprehensive Peace Agreement followed in 2005 ceding autonomy to the South for six years, to be followed by a referendum which led to South Sudan becoming an independent republic in 2011. Heavy fighting over oil and disputes about revenues were partly resolved in 2005. After the signing of the Agreement, Christian Aid organised a joint meeting of partners from North and South. The atmosphere was uneasy, with leading delegates suspicious of the food and declining to shake hands for fear of HIV/AIDS.

A deal was struck in Darfur in 2006, bringing to an end what had often been described as 'the world's most tragic conflict' – presumably at the time! Civil war broke out again in 2016 in South Sudan after an escalation of violence in 2013. It lasted until 2020, when a peace agreement was brokered by the Community of Sant'Egidio, a lay-led Catholic organisation based in Rome. A new constitution was signed by the President, an ethnic Dinka, and the Vice-President, an ethnic Nuer. Some opposition groups refused to sign.

Following the outbreak of violence in 2013, South Sudan church leaders met and agreed an Action Plan for Peace (APP), which came into play in 2015, was renewed in 2017 and drew support from the UK government. It focused in a number of ways on the peacebuilding potential of dialogue. In 2018–21, for example, many dialogues involving thousands of people in remote areas were facilitated by the churches, including many following video screenings about peacebuilding, mounted on the back of motorbikes (Cineboda). As a result of cooperation between Lambeth Palace and the Vatican, in April 2019 South Sudan's political leaders were invited to meet with church leaders for a retreat in Domus

Sanctae Marthae in the Vatican. Probably its most memorable moment, catching the public eye, was when the Pope kissed the feet of all the leaders in an act of humility that demonstrated how much humility was needed in the search for peace. Christian Aid's adviser on South Sudan, Natalia Chan, present at the retreat, did a great deal of work behind the scenes both then and in support of all the plans for peace (APP).

Rowan Williams visited Sudan in 2014. The 'ecumenical peace pilgrimage' to South Sudan by Pope Francis, Justin Welby, Archbishop of Canterbury, and Iain Greenshields, Moderator of the Church of Scotland, in 2023[2] was actively supported by Christian Aid and CAFOD, with James Wani, Christian Aid's country manager, meeting the pilgrims in Juba. The visit brought the hope that peacebuilding could now build further on progress made, even though the agreement of 2020 remained largely unimplemented.

That new hope hadn't reckoned with yet another outbreak of civil war in 2023, this time in the North with heavy consequences for the South as thousands fled for safety to transit centres such as Renk, designed to look after 2,000 people but now trying to cope with up to 5,000. There, Christian Aid, working with Lutheran World Federation, gave out 'dignity' kits to 800 women and gifts of £82 each to female heads of households to buy food. Martha, 40 years old, was one of them, fleeing from Khartoum where she'd lived all her life: because of that she was treated as a returnee, not a refugee, and got less support from the UN.

Going local

How did Christian Aid help to build peace as one of its oft-stated aims? Apart from advocacy and campaigning, perhaps it contributed most effectively at the local level.

It is understandable when war is mentioned in Sudan or anywhere else that the image created is of fighting between well-armed government forces, legitimate or not, and their equally well-armed enemies like the SPLA and later the Rapid Support Forces. But the reality is almost always more complicated.

One obvious difference between North and South was not apparently a significant source of tension. The North was Muslim country, though the Coptic Church had been there for centuries. Christian missionaries began to make converts in the South in the nineteenth century, creating a largely Christian population of Anglicans, Roman Catholics and Presbyterians. But if Christians were attacked it was not so much because they were Christians as because of their ethnic identity. For centuries many ethnic groups and their animals had wandered the shores of the Nile (Nilotic people), interacting with one another and often raiding each other's communities for cattle. That traditional, nomadic, pastoral, though often not peaceful way of life had now been broken apart and they found little that bound their diverse communities together as a nation. Somehow they had to learn to co-exist under an unfamiliar overarching governing regime, no longer as free to go their own ways.

So peacebuilding for Christian Aid often meant going local. In 2018 it commissioned a report by Chris Milner and Natalia Chan: 'In It for the Long Haul? Lessons on peacebuilding in South Sudan'.[3] It recognised that conflict was 'multi-level' and insisted that peacebuilding must be 'multi-level' too, and that building better relations between ethnic groups and even within them, notably, for example, between men and often abused and marginalised women, could lay foundations for a broader, national peace. It provided some very practical guidance for would-be peacebuilders.

In practice that meant Christian Aid, along with others, funding and accompanying the work of organisations like the New Sudan Council of Churches. Founded in 1989 under the inspirational leadership of the Catholic Bishop Paride Taban, it had close ties with the SPLA for which, rightly or wrongly given the circumstances, it was severely criticised.[4] It was superseded in 2013, after independence, by the South Sudan Council of Churches (SSCC).

One of its best-known achievements was facilitating an end to the conflict between Nuer groups in 1999 following their reconciliation with the SPLA in 1994. In 1997 it set out its People to People Peace Process,[5] since when it has constantly brought together ethnic groups into safe spaces where village and church leaders, women and young people can share their experiences, hopes and fears, learn to empathise and counter hate speech (a major contributor to genocide in Myanmar and Rwanda), begin to build trust and weave together a more diverse and peaceful community.

A striking example of this kind of approach was the Twic Olympics, founded in 2000 on Christmas Eve. The brains behind them were Acuil's, a 7-foot, highly successful basketball player. Visiting his old trainer in the deep South he watched as two scratch teams of refugees, well used to fighting each other, laughed and joked as they played volleyball together in the street. 'I could do that,' he said to himself. Back in Twic, a remote area in the notoriously conflictual border country between North and South, he worked for Sudan Production Aid (SUPRAID), a local organisation trying to mediate between Dinkas and Nuers. In the Twic Olympics, Acuil pitted teams of mainly youths from six payams or districts against each other. Football, running, volleyball and, somewhat ironically, tug of war were all on the programme along with educational workshops on the side. In 2002 the prize for the winning team was a mechanical flour-grinding mill.

If swords can be turned into ploughshares, war can apparently be turned into friendly rivalry. As one participant put it, 'The Twic Olympics challenges everyone who thinks nothing good can happen in Sudan.' Christian Aid was privileged to help fund the Games!

The Twic Olympics continued for year after year as did the fighting, still raging in 2025 and always threatening to destroy what so many tried patiently to build.

18
Untold stories

April fool

On 1 April 1993 a fax was sent to Christian Aid's area staff in the name of Tim Moulds, their manager, informing them that negotiations between the Fairtrade Foundation and a well-known tobacco company to endorse a tobacco product were at an advanced stage. The company had paid a cash-strapped Foundation for a full assessment, which had made clear that the product met all its criteria. Partners in Zimbabwe and Kenya had been consulted and were supportive of the idea since it would provide a fair return for tobacco farmers and pickers. Expensive legal action and reputational damage to the Foundation might follow if it now refused to award its well-known kitemark according to the rules. A decision had to be made in two weeks' time; meanwhile the Foundation and Christian Aid were looking for advice.

Should the mark be awarded? If so, should Christian Aid cut its ties with the Foundation? If however there were no objections, should Christian Aid stock the product and area staff be asked to sell it?

Fifty per cent of staff twigged it. The rest were split equally between support and opposition. One wrote to Tim at length about a relative who had recently died from lung cancer due to smoking, warning that if expected to sell cigarettes he would be forced to resign – which was why Tim found it hard to see the joke!
(Paul Brannen)

Marmalade

Christian Aid with other UK NGOs took a strong if measured stance on the pursuit of retaliatory military action in Iraq and Afghanistan following the 9/11 terrorist attacks on the USA. In November 2001

Roger Riddell from Christian Aid, along with Julian Filochowski (CAFOD) and Mike Aaronson (Save the Children), were invited to have breakfast with Tony Blair. In an anteroom beforehand they were berated by one of Blair's political aides and told there was incontrovertible evidence that Iraq had weapons of mass destruction and that they were ignorant and should keep quiet. Riddell forgot what was said at the private breakfast (with printed menu) that followed, but remembered that Blair was friendly and that he ate vast quantities of marmalade.
(Roger Riddell)

Greenbelt

Since 1974 the Greenbelt festival has been a place where music, art, justice and faith (mainly Christian) have met, along with hundreds, not to say thousands, of people who, according to one enthusiast, 'dance and debate, pray and party'.

But it has always been on the move, and in more than one way. It started out on a pig farm in Suffolk, followed by a castle in Bedfordshire, Knebworth Park in Hertfordshire, the grounds of Castle Ashby and then Deene Park, both in Northamptonshire, a racecourse in Cheltenham, and back to Northamptonshire to Boughton House, driven out sometimes and on by financial crises, rising and falling numbers (20,000 a year in the early 1980s, declining in the 1990s).

A different kind of journey saw Greenbelt continually broadening out, Cliff Richard, Bob Geldof, U2 and Ed Sheeran all included. It belonged very much in the evangelical Christian tradition. It didn't grow out of it. A reporter, Jessica Reed, an atheist, sent to investigate by *The Guardian* in 2009, admitted to initially mellowing to what she called 'post-evangelism' but felt 'evangelism' still 'lurked', and left. True or not, Greenbelt opened up to worldwide issues of race, trade and climate justice, championing the causes of Palestine and Nicaragua along the way, and providing a safe place for gay and lesbian people. It was one of the catalysts of J2000. It began to engage with other faiths.

Christian Aid, seen as in a more 'liberal' Christian tradition, also broadened out to become a major supporter and funder for over thirty years from 1993. In 2024 Christian Aid declared a 'No Fly Zone' where festivalgoers heard 'face to face' about the struggles and achievements of its friends around the world by way of 'the strongest broadband connection you'll find in a field'!

Meanwhile, year by year, hundreds of volunteers and thousands of festivalgoers, young and not-so-young, still get ready to 'be on the move' on foot or by train, car and bike, as the August bank holiday comes round again.

The old banger

Ken Forrest, musician, artist and one-time head of Christian Aid's area staff, arrived in El Salvador to be met by a priest and taken to the Archbishop's office. A conversation followed about the state of the country and the armed gangs who, unlike the Archbishop, weren't bothered about the poor. After that he vividly remembers being driven around the outskirts of San Salvador by the Archbishop in his clapped-out Austin Princess, pointing out the simple houses being built for the homeless. Weeks later, in March 1980, Archbishop Oscar Romero was assassinated.
(Ken Forrest)

Birds

We rode (only a little) on camels, ate camel meat, drank their milk and slept under the stars on their skins. This was camel country after all. Deep into the Horn of Africa we were suddenly blinded by the sun, reflected off the solar panels standing proud in the sand. The panels fuelled the pumps that drew up the water from the deep for the gardens, and for camels and cattle and, separately, people to drink. As we talked, a local shouted, 'sh*t' (or the Somali equivalent), for once used as a noun as well as an expletive. Yet another bird had perched and fouled yet another solar panel. Stones thrown to shoo them away often hit the panels and missed the birds. The precious glass could be cracked while the birds kept on coming.
(Michael Taylor)

Undercover

In 1995, in the classified section of the magazine *Exchange & Mart*, Christian Aid found a sordidly suggestive advertisement for holidays in the Philippines, placed by a tour operator called Paradise Express, and ordered a copy of its brochure. It featured a holiday in a red-light area described as a 'Sin City'. In a phone call to the travel agent, a 48-year-old Eastbourne man named Michael Clarke suggested he was prepared to set up tourists with underage girls. Christian Aid reported its findings to the police who advised they could not take action without concrete evidence of wrongdoing.

Christian Aid took its report to ITN who decided to investigate. It asked Christian Aid for support and assigned its reporter Alan Holloway to the task. Holloway booked a holiday for himself and Martin Cottingham of Christian Aid through Paradise Express. They travelled together to the Philippines posing as tourists to expose Clarke, in the Philippines at the time, through hidden camera filming.

Holloway's report was broadcast by *News at Ten* over two nights at the beginning of Christian Aid Week 1995. The 'concrete evidence' boosted the campaign for legislation which, by 2003, allowed the government to prosecute in the UK abusers who had offended while travelling abroad. Clarke was sentenced in October 1996 by a court in the Philippines to sixteen years in prison, where he died.
(Martin Cottingham)

Friendship

In 1998 Christian Aid sent round details of On the Line, a project inspired by Jon Snow of *Channel 4 News*. He was fascinated by the link between communities all round the world living on the meridian line at almost exactly the same time of day and night, and wanted them to discover more about their 'neighbours'.

In 1989 the Middle School in Burley-in-Wharfedale, a village not far from Leeds, tucked into the Yorkshire Dales, started collecting newspapers for recycling and raising money for charity. Over ten years, donations to Christian Aid funded well-digging in the Dogon region of Mali, West Africa. Zakari Saye, a schoolboy who later qualified as a doctor, sent drawings of his village, Tereli, and of the wells. Christian Aid passed them on to Mary Wood, a Christian Aid Week organiser, and the school in Burley. The pupils sent back their own drawings, Zakari replied and they all became pen pals. Tereli was on the line!

Many links were set up. Jean Robinson of Christian Aid suggested that Burley–Tereli should be one of them. By 2001 an agreement was signed between the chief of Tereli and the chair of Burley's community council. Exchange visits were made, friendships became strong, money was raised, calendars were produced annually, full of news and pictures, and recycling paper in England turned to planting mango trees in Mali as the climate crisis deepened. The Burley–Tereli Friendship Trust was still going strong in 2025.[1]

On the boat

When Israel invaded Lebanon in the summer of 1982, the Middle East Council of Churches (MECC) appealed to Christian Aid for volunteer doctors and nurses. Twenty-two were recruited. Accompanied by Kate Phillips (going as a journalist), they could not enter by air as the Beirut airport was closed, so went by boat from Larnaca. On board an elegantly dressed resident of East Beirut, returning from an opera festival in Italy, asked who they were and why on earth they would want to go to Beirut at such a dangerous time. They explained about the conditions, not least in refugee camps like Sabra and Shatila, to which he replied, 'You are going to heal the wounds of the Palestinians and we will go in to kill them.'
(Kate Phillips)

Dressing up

In 1995 Christian Aid campaigned against government cuts to overseas aid under the slogan, 'Aid Cuts Cost Lives'. At a photo shoot outside the Treasury, an 'executioner' with the face of the Chancellor was to 'behead' one of Christian Aid's partners. Persuaded to play the part, I was sent to change in the men's toilets in the Red Lion pub opposite. To pull on thigh-high boots I had to lie on the floor outside the cubicles, whereupon

four early morning drinkers stepped over me without a word as if a man dressing up as an executioner in the toilets was entirely normal.
(Jack Arthey)

A dream job

Twenty years to date but seems like yesterday. Travelling across Kenya, Uganda and Tanzania. No money for flights. By road in a 4x4 land cruiser. Tough gender dynamics. Post-election violence. Lean staff, doubling up on jobs. Poor communities taking the lead. Accompanying partners with dignity and respect. Climbing Mount Kenya for Christian Aid Week. Dreaming of a new dawn where dreams are valid. Inspired by a belief in life before death. Disrupting the status quo. Giving life to millions with multiple vulnerabilities.

I love Christian Aid forever!
(Jane Machira)

Krishnamall

She was a woman; he was a man. She was from Tamil Nadu; he was from Galilee. She was married; he was single. She was a Hindu; he was a Jew. She was followed by thousands; for him the crowds melted away. She won many awards as a social activist; he was mocked. She died in old age; he was executed aged 30.

And yet they were alike. Krishnamall was born into poverty. With her husband, she spent her highly active but frugal life in the Gandhian tradition empowering the landless and persuading landowners to hand over to them at least 6% of their land. She protested about the big commercial prawn farms along the coast, turning fertile soil into salty deserts. He came, he said, to lift up the poor in his own land, to bring them good news and confront the powerful who kept them down.

When I met her with what appeared to be little more than the clothes on her back, some pots and pans and a mat, travelling light with apparently nowhere permanent to lay her head, I thought of him.
(Michael Taylor)

Magnificat

My soul magnifies the Lord
and my spirit rejoices in God my Saviour,
for he has looked with favour on the lowliness of his servant.
Surely, from now on all generations will call me blessed;
for the Mighty One has done great things for me,
and holy is his name.
His mercy is for those who fear him
from generation to generation.
He has shown strength with his arm;
he has scattered the proud in the thoughts of their hearts.
He has put down the powerful from their thrones,
and lifted up the lowly;
he has filled the hungry with good things,
and sent the rich away empty.
He has helped his servant Israel,
in remembrance of his mercy,
according to the promise he made to our ancestors,
to Abraham and to his descendants for ever.

Luke 1:46–55, New Revised Standard Version (Anglicized Edition)

19
Hope and realism

In 2025 Christian Aid prepared to move out of its spacious offices in Lower Marsh, London, to smaller ones, for several reasons.[1] For one thing the offices were expensive to run as the pennies needed watching even more closely than ever; on top of which, Covid-19 had made working from home the preference of many, leaving rows of empty desks.

Two other considerations were of more significance in the long run. One was a great deal of heart-searching among NGOs, including Christian Aid. The other, closely related, was the consequence of devolutionary policies pursued by Christian Aid almost from the beginning, putting responsibility and resources, including money and staff, in the right place. Neither of them had much to do with whether there was still work to be done: there certainly was!

Almost every issue faced by Christian Aid over eighty years had not gone away. Unfair trade, debt, tax, war, refugees, racism, migration, gender violence, human rights, health and education, deforestation, land rights, all of them aggravating poverty and shot through with injustice, stubbornly stood their ground.[2] Climate change only made matters worse.

Hope

Clearly there had been progress, often at the hands of medical research, science and technology; and, of course, a huge amount had been achieved by Christian Aid and the NGO community. Almost every issue listed above could be revisited to prove it: fairly traded goods like tea and coffee, debts cancelled, increased tax revenues, better social services, rehabilitation, more productive agriculture, peacemaking, trees planted, homes and families protected, fewer living in poverty,[3] people made stronger, to name but a few. And that's where the much-needed hope and encouragement is to be found.

Christian Aid, and it is not alone, has not always found traditional Christian talk of hope all that helpful. The prospect of life after death, compensating for 'the evils of this present time', may be attractive to some but can sound hollow to many. Believing in 'life before death' sounds better, with its emphasis on the here and now; but as an expression of hope it cannot be stretched too far, as if this world can all be made new, which it can't. Even Christianity acknowledges that we may see signs of the kingdom but that that kingdom will not come here in all its fullness.

Another understanding of hope, which Christian Aid celebrated in 2025 as 'the unstoppable power', may make more sense, especially when we 'come up close' to unending situations that appear to be frankly 'hopeless' until we find they are not. They are never completely closed or without possibilities. However limited at first they may seem, there is always a door to be cracked open and cracks tend to widen. Once that is realised then hope creeps in, and the women and men Christians think of as 'made in the image of God' prove that it is true. They are not only of equal importance and deserve respect, but, like God, are well capable of remaking their worlds out of their creativity, ingenuity, generosity, loyalty, perseverance, skill and love.[4]

In an interview, Roger Riddell, a former head of policy at Christian Aid, spoke of visiting the slums, or barriadas, of Lima, Peru, spreading across the hillsides as more and more people flooded in from the surrounding country, building 'homes' with plastic bags. This was not the end of the road, however, as the slum dwellers became upwardly mobile, finding creative ways to make a living, such as copying designs and sewing high-end fashionable clothes on old machines and sending them off to California. They called the barriadas 'Slums of Hope', which were gradually accepted as working-class suburbs as the city prospered prior to the economic crisis and austerities of the 1980s.[5]

A bleak picture

Overall, however, despite some encouraging statistics, the outlook remains bleak.

The sermon preached at Christian Aid's fiftieth Anniversary service, with its sombre reminders, could still be preached on its eightieth. Rowan Williams's remarks on its seventieth about facing the same issues in 2015 as in 1945 ring true, as do John Sentamu's observations in 2022 on how the war in Ukraine echoed Christian Aid's founding work in 1945. Many Christian Aid veterans in interviews express doubts: 'It's all very depressing,' said more than one. Patrick Watt, writing in 2022, is at times no more cheerful.[6] And 2025, with its vicious wars and accelerating climate change, did little to cheer things up, quite the opposite in fact.

Christian teaching tries to explain why this is so, often in the unhelpful language of 'original sin' (born bad) and disobedience. It is unhelpful because the reality is that as human beings we are not so much diehard sinners as vulnerable human beings, insecure on every side. The condition is existential (having to do with the nature of our very existence) so that, being vulnerable, we tend to act in ways that protect ourselves, whether as individuals or communities or nations, at the expense of others, causing chaos and misery. Christian realism fully acknowledges that bad things are not going to go away. The poor, regrettably, will always be with you.

Questions

The questions for Christian Aid, then, are not about whether there is still work to do, or about whether it is worth doing, but *what* that work now is and *how* best it can be done. The questions have not suddenly appeared out of the blue. I raised some of them in a lecture in 1997 called 'Past Their Sell-by Date? NGOs and their future in development'.[7] Jenny Pearce wrote about them in 2000.[8] Sarah Hughes, representing Christian Aid, was involved in a study of the future of NGOs organised by the START network in 2013. Oxfam issued a discussion paper headed 'Fit for the Future' in 2015. The issues were examined again in 'International NGOs and the Long Humanitarian Century: Legacy, legitimacy and leading into the future' in 2022,[9] and in that same year they were explicitly addressed in relation to Christian Aid by Patrick Watt in 'Challenges and Choices'.

It is a cliché to say we live in a changing world. It is nevertheless true that eighty years after 1945 the world is a very different place, cursed in 2025 by wars in Ukraine, Sudan, Palestine, Lebanon, Syria and elsewhere in the Middle East, rather than relieved by the end of a war in 1945, to mention nothing else. BRICS, the economic and political alliance between Brazil, Russia, India, China and South Africa, points to another highly significant change in the landscape of power and leadership, challenging the dominance of the West. India, Brazil and South Africa are three examples of the growing capacity of countries in the 'South' to deal for themselves with issues previously dealt with by northern international NGOs, together with a wariness of the influence of these outsiders as they challenge their 'legitimacy' (who for example do they represent?) and, as in India with its tightening restrictions, attempt to shut them out. In the West, NGOs have long been criticised as nothing but 'business', or as 'ineffective', or even for making 'matters worse', and more recently as 'colonial' and 'racist'. In the South civil society has also grown stronger, finding its voice and in many cases the ability to cut out the NGOs as middlemen when looking for funds. Meanwhile the UK government has not been alone in reducing support for international development as 0.7% of GDP became 0.3% and even less,[10] while USAID all but came to an end and aid money was spent on war.

Devolution

Without evaluating these changes, they point to a changing and probably diminished role for the likes of Christian Aid. At worst it could even be out of business, not because poverty is over (it won't be) but because Christian Aid's usefulness is over. Patrick Watt comments that for INGOs the challenge is how to ride waves rather than how to create them.[11] That is not entirely true. Take as one example the long-term policy alluded to earlier. Today it is referred to as 'devolution' or 'localisation',[12] but the seeds were sown way back. 'Partnership', its close associate, committed Christian Aid from the beginning to a cooperative and not an operational way of working. That was worked out, with the WCC, in roundtable discussions where efforts were made at mutuality, with considerable difficulty due to the realities of power, where all were givers and receivers and all were party to the decision-making. The same trend was evident as Christian Aid established country offices, not to have more control but to support local organisations, bringing decision-making, authority and responsibility even nearer to the ground and away from London where the office began gradually emptying out. 'Localisation' (driven by the South and not just an initiative of the North) was where needs were uncovered and responded to rather than assumed; where resources were more readily handed over to communities and their organisations (as the WCC's Resource Sharing programme had long wished for) out of respect for them as agents rather than victims, recognising their knowledge and skills; and where Christian Aid stepped back, ready with advice and support and to foster useful contacts and networks when asked. One of localisation's most radical expressions was putting cash directly into the hands of those who needed it and were thought to know best how to use it.

Visually for me this overarching story 'looks' like 'white' supremacy, however benign, turning into a 'rainbow' of inclusion. Its setting is an even bigger story, striding the stage of history, which in so many ways has shaped its own: of imperialism and its consequences and a growing degree of self-awareness.

None of this avoided sensitive issues around trust and accountability, but in pursuing devolution over many years Christian Aid could claim to be somewhat ahead of the curve (or the wave) in understanding where the key to unlocking inequality and injustice was to be found. It is likely to remain a highly significant criterion of its work in the future and fits well with the emerging so-called 'internationalist' model, where Christian Aid is no longer centralised in London and ACT Alliance is another possible example.

Health checks

In finding a way through a complex and demanding, not to say unsettling scenario, on its way to tomorrow, what other criteria might Christian Aid consider? Looking back over its history a number of 'continuums' might prove worth considering such as:

Advocacy .... Aid and development
Big .... Small
Consistent .... Contextual
Faith-based .... Secular

Free money	Institutional funding
Innovative	Traditional
Knowing	Listening
Lay	Professional
Poorest	Poor
Remote	Accessible
Risk-taking	Risk-averse
Top-down	Collaborative
Valiant	Discreet[13]
Voluntary	Bureaucratic

The board was pretty clear where it stood on two of them when in its Annual Report of 1979 it insisted that government or institutional funding was not to exceed 10% of income and that 'it is essential that we maintain the ethos of a voluntary body'!

Not all the pros belong to one end of a spectrum with all the cons at the other, and decisions about them cannot be completely black or white; but continuums like these can provide a health check as to whether Christian Aid, amid all the pressures and adjustments it faces, remains true to itself rather than losing its way.

Christian identity

One other obvious health check has to do with the churches and Christian faith and practice.

Christian Aid has little choice over whether or not to continue to be the agency of forty-one churches in the UK. That would be for the churches to decide, should the issue ever be on their agenda; nevertheless, despite decline in several of them, Christian Aid might well think it foolish not to go on serving, nourishing and inspiring such rich and faithful resources, especially where a concern for the poor is so central to their gospel calling. It might be equally foolish to underestimate the contribution of churches, national ecumenical councils and faith leaders in general across the continents.[14]

As to its faith, Christian Aid's story may well have shown the wisdom of not creating for itself theologies of this and that, instead of drawing on the experience and varied insights of the Christian tradition, as it reflects on what it is doing and plans to do next. Besides its insights into human nature referred to above where, if either of its two sides – dark and bright – is neglected, things will go wrong, that tradition has much to say about power, whether for good or evil; the need for empathy and understanding; the healing that can come with forgiveness, acceptance and inclusion; the need to stand up to tyrants; the cost of sacrificial love, without which little is redeemed; the neighbours and ourselves; and much else. These ideas, woven into Bible stories and tradition, ancient and modern, coming from near and far, are to be engaged with, not idolised. They have not always been honoured when it comes to Christian practice and they have at times been misleading, notably about the dignity of women, sexuality and what has turned out to be our abuse of the planet.

* * *

Christian Aid has had its ups and downs, its friendships and fallings-out. It has made its mistakes and been open to criticism. It, along with others, has not made poverty history and sadly never will. Despite good intentions, it remains a human organisation with all the strengths and frailties that implies. Some have spoken of a 'golden age' and others of when the shine rubbed off. Overall it seems fair to say that its interesting and inspiring story is more than able to speak for itself, since a woman went to war against poverty in 1945.

Meanwhile, as it goes on its way, it has a gritty song to sing, about a reversal of fortunes where the poor are lifted high; it has a gospel to embody, about bringing good news to the poor; and a lodestar to follow: a rough and ready Galilean with a sharp tongue, a warm heart and nowhere to lay his head, heaven-bent on justice.

Appendix

Pie charts

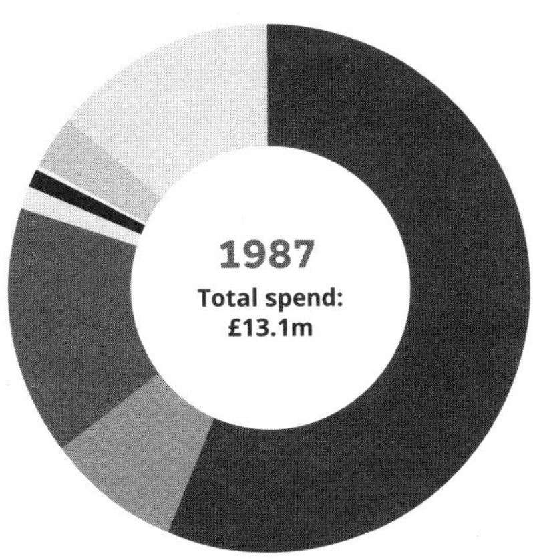

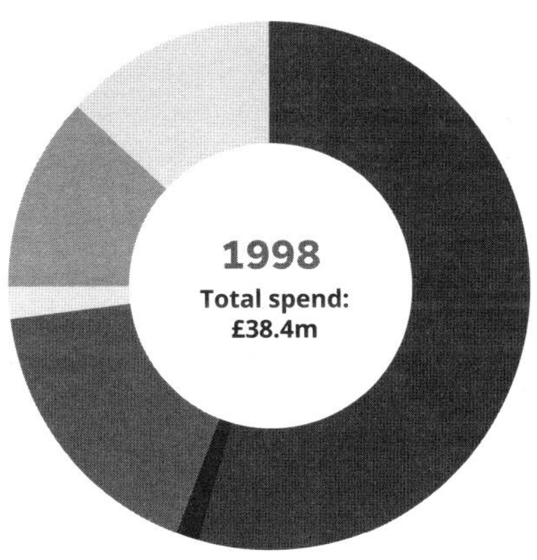

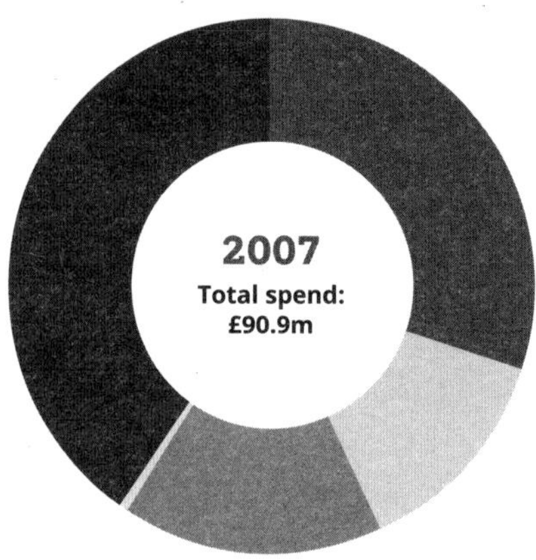

Emergencies £27.8m
Campaigning and education £12.1m
Fundraising £14.4m
Governance £0.6m
Development £36m

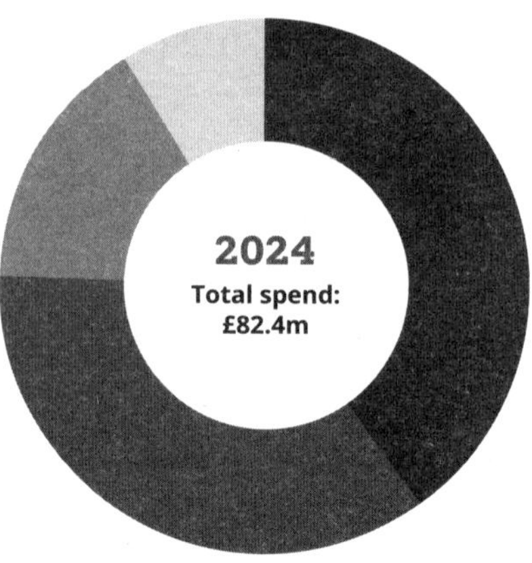

Development £33.0m
Emergencies £29.4m
Fundraising £12.8m
Campaigning, advocacy and education £7.2m

Timeline

1917	Balfour Declaration
1939–45	Second World War
1942	British Council of Churches (BCC) established
	Beveridge Report
1944	Bretton Woods Agreement
1945	Birth of the United Nations (UN)
	Christian Reconstruction in Europe (CRE)
	Over 50% of global population living in poverty
1947	India gained independence
1948	Israel gained independence
	CRE expanded to the Middle East
	Burma gained independence
1949	CRE renamed Inter-Church Aid and Refugee Service (ICARS), absorbed into the BCC
1952–68	Janet Lacey first Director of ICARS/BCC
1956	Hungarian Uprising
1957	First Christian Aid Week
1958	Voluntary Service Overseas established
1959–60	World Refugee Year
1960	Freedom from Hunger campaign
1963	Launch of Disasters Emergency Committee (DEC)
1964	ICARS/BCC renamed Christian Aid
1964–71	Ronald Goodchild Chair of the Board
1965	60% of global population living in poverty
1966	First DEC appeal
1967–70	Biafra war
1968	Haslemere Declaration
	Christmas Appeal featuring Dame Judi Dench in the Holy Land
1968–70	Alan Brash Director

1969	First edition of *Christian Aid News* published
1970	UK Overseas Development Administration established
	Launch of World Development Movement, renamed Global Justice Now in 2015
1970–75	Alan Booth Director
1971–78	David Edwards Chair of the Board
1972	Total income £2,885,296, Christian Aid Week £1,611,802
1973	Launch of *New Internationalist*
1973	First Christian Aid Edinburgh book sale
1975	Total income £4,206,935, Christian Aid Week £2,474,837
1975–82	Kenneth Slack Director
1978	Christian Aid London offices move from Eaton Gate to Ferndale Road, Brixton
1978–83	Diana Reader Harris Chair of the Board
1979–90	Margaret Thatcher Prime Minister
1980	BBC's *Panorama* programme 'The Politics of Compassion'
1982	Israel invades Lebanon, massacres in Sabra and Shatila refugee camps
1982–84	Charles Elliott Director
1983–90	Brian Young Chair of the Board
1983–85	Ethiopian famine
1984–85	Martin Bax Acting Director
1985–97	Michael Taylor Director
1986	Total income £17,167,216, Christian Aid Week £5,684,929
1987	First Palestinian Intifada
	BCC and Christian Aid issue 'To Strengthen the Poor'
	Christian Aid moves London office to Lower Marsh
1988	Chico Mendes assassinated
1988–89	212 staff members (no overseas staff)
1989	Burma renamed Myanmar by military government
	Launch of Southern African Coalition
1990	Nelson Mandela released from prison
1990–97	John Major Prime Minister
1990–97	Marion Fraser Chair of the Board
1991–2002	Sierra Leone civil war

1991	Founding of The Burma Campaign (UK)
	Christian Aid's first TV advert
	Apartheid legislation repealed
	Record number of 400,000 collectors for Christian Aid Week
1992	Founding of Fairtrade Foundation
1994	Rwandan genocide
	'Official' Apartheid ends in South Africa
1994–95	Christian Aid opens first field offices (in Rwanda and Burundi)
1995	Yitzhak Rabin assassinated
	General Agreement on Tariffs and Trade becomes the World Trade Organisation
1995–96	Total income £39,545,000, Christian Aid Week £8,899,000
	273 staff members in 1995, 259 in 1996, working in more than 60 countries
1997	Jubilee 2000 debt campaign launched
	UK Department for International Development (DFID) established
	first Dalit President of India
1997–2007	Tony Blair Prime Minister
1997–2008	John Gladwin Chair of the Board
1998–2010	Daleep Mukarji Director
1999	40% of global population living in poverty
2000	Second Intifada
	Founding of Trade Justice Movement
2001	9/11
2003	Founding of UK Tax Justice Network
2004	Boxing Day tsunami
2005	Launch of Make Poverty History campaign
2005–2006	Total income £90,500,000, Christian Aid Week £14,600,000
2007	Armed takeover of Gaza by Hamas
2007	Cut the Carbon march
2007–10	Gordon Brown Prime Minister

2008–12	Anne Owers Chair of the Board
2010	Haiti earthquake
2010–16	David Cameron Prime Minister
2010–17	Loretta Minghella CEO
2011	South Sudan gains independence
2012–13	Kumar Jacob Acting Chair of the Board
2013–21	Rowan Williams Chair of the Board
2013–25	UK hits the UN target of spending 0.7% of Gross National Income (GNI) on aid, cut to 0.5% in 2021, and then 0.3% in 2025
2014	Ebola outbreak in Sierra Leone
2015–16	Total income £107,000,000, Christian Aid Week £11,300,000 958 staff members (556 in Britian, Ireland, and Spain, 402 overseas), working in 39 countries
2016–19	Theresa May Prime Minister
2016–21	Aung San Suu Kyi State Counsellor of Myanmar
2017	Zionist Advocacy Center vs Christian Aid
2018–21	Amanda Khozi Mukwashi CEO
2019–22	Boris Johnson Prime Minister
2020	Christian Aid withdraws from 12 countries (Angola, Bolivia, Brazil, Dominican Republic, Egypt, El Salvador, Ghana, Guatemala, Nepal, the Philippines, South Africa and Zambia) and closes many UK regional offices DFID merged with the Foreign and Commonwealth Office, renamed the Foreign, Commonwealth and Development Office Covid-19 pandemic
2021	Taliban take power in Afghanistan
2022	Russia invades Ukraine
2021–23	John Sentamu Chair of the Board
2022–24	Rishi Sunak Prime Minister
2022–	Patrick Watt CEO
2023	Renewed conflict in Sudan Hamas attacks Israel

2023–24	Total income £83,300,000, Christian Aid Week £5,300,000 700 staff members (307 in Britain, 250 in Africa, 103 in Asia and the Middle East, 33 in Latin America and the Caribbean and 5 in Ireland), active in 25 countries
2024–	Sarah Mullally Chair of the Board
2024–	Keir Starmer Prime Minister
2025	USA imposes 90-day freeze on all foreign development assistance (USAID) UK aid cut from 0.5% to 0.3% GNI 8.5–10% of global population living in poverty
2025	Christian Aid moves office from Lower Marsh 400 staff members, the majority international

Notes

Introduction

1 Nathan Hill, *Wellness* (Picador, 2023), p. 514.
2 'All Shall be Included in the Feast of Life', a statement prepared by Christian Aid for its fiftieth anniversary in 1995.
3 Christian Aid published several books of songs itself, for example: Margaret Hamilton, *Sing Freedom* (Christian Aid with Novello, 1993); Garth Hewitt, *The Feast of Life* (Christian Aid, 1998); Ken Forrest, *Common Ground* (Christian Aid with Stainer and Bell, 1982).

1 How it all began

1 Janet Lacey, *A Cup of Water* (Hodder and Stoughton, 1970).
2 Lacey, *A Cup of Water*.
3 See archived note by Jack Arthey, 'From the archives – why did Christian Aid push for the creation of the Disaster Emergencies Committee (DEC)?', January 2021.
4 Typically 30% of it within six months, and all of it within two to three years (see DEC Manual): https://www.dec.org.uk/what-we-do-with-your-money (accessed 16 May 2025).
5 By the 2020s it was set to be entirely so.
6 Lacey, *A Cup of Water*, p. 164.
7 See the extended account in Maggie Black, *A Cause for our Time* (Oxfam, 1992), pp. 117ff.
8 See Christian Aid's film *Brian in Biafra* (2020).
9 For a fuller account, see Max Peberdy, *Tigray: Ethiopia's untold story* (REST UK Support Committee, 1985).
10 For a detailed study of the 1984 famine, see Ondine Barrow's thesis, 'Charity, Relief and Development: Christian Aid in Ethiopia 1960s–1990s' (SOAS, 1998).
11 By 2002 there were nineteen overseas offices in eighteen countries; by 2025 the numbers were almost identical.
12 At that time working for Concern Worldwide, and from 2001 to 2020 for Christian Aid in charge of humanitarian aid.
13 The trauma of war had given rise to an increase in premature births.
14 See Chapter 16.

2 Afghanistan

1 See 'Tim's Legacy for Life', *Christian Aid News*, April/June 1994, and the Supplement to the *London Gazette*, July 1993.

2 The Taliban are an ultra-conservative political and religious movement that emerged in the mid-1990s after the withdrawal of Soviet troops.

3 Referred to as 'minority' groups though large, including Hazaras, Tajiks, Uzbeks and Pashtuns.

4 See Michael Paratharayil, Ramani Leathard and Engineer Fazl Rabi, 'Hope Breeds Life', Evaluation Report, Christian Aid Afghanistan Appeal (2001–06) (Christian Aid, 2006).

5 Christian Aid, Annual Report Afghanistan, 2001–02.

6 See Christian Aid's written evidence submitted to Parliament in October 2021, catalogued as AFG0018.

7 See Paratharayil, Leathard and Rabi, 'Hope Breeds Life'.

8 See, for example, 'Building Resilience in Fragile States, Herat Province, Afghanistan', internal document (Christian Aid, 2011–16).

9 It was renamed the International Assistance Mission (IAM) in 1978 and was still at work in the 2020s.

10 Other major partners at this time included the Coordination of Humanitarian Assistance, Ansari Rehabilitation Association for Afghanistan, Agency for Rehabilitation and Energy Conservation, and the Agency Coordinating Body for Afghan Relief and Development.

11 See, for example, 'Afghanistan Country Programme Strategy Plan Refresh' (Christian Aid, 2022).

12 See 'Building Resilience'.

13 See Christian Aid, Annual Report on Afghanistan Programme, 2023–24.

14 See 'Building Resilience'.

15 See Christian Aid, Annual Report on Afghanistan, 2023–24. Cf. attempts, funded by Christian Aid, to modernise the traditional silk industry in 2012, the work of RAADA, and the Zaan Herat Silk Production Co., which CAID helped to set up in 2016.

16 See Silk and Saffron Project, 'Silk and Saffron: Lifelines for women in Afghanistan', In Their Lifetime series (Christian Aid, April 2024).

3 On the campaign trail

1 See, for example, the conclusion of 'The New Global Debt Crisis' (Christian Aid and Jubilee Debt Campaign, 2019) on 'the need for a prophetic voice'.

2 See Matthew Anderson, 'Charity, Activism and Social Justice: Revisiting Christian

Aid's role in public campaigns for fair trade, 1968–1973', *Contemporary European History* 28 (2019).

3 See 'No Small Change' (Christian Aid, 2007).

4 See Susan George, *How the Other Half Dies: The real reason for world hunger* (Penguin, 1976).

5 Following the multi-agency IF campaign claiming there would be food for everyone, legislation was introduced in the Finance Act 2015, section 122(1), (4), (5) and (6), giving the Treasury power to make regulations to require multinational enterprises to provide HMRC with a country-by-country report.

6 Sue Richardson, a staff member at the time, commented on a 'brave' decision 'when most of us wanted a softer target after years of work on debt and trade'.

7 Visited over time by several Directors, CEOs and senior staff.

8 John Mitchell headed up the World Development Movement before joining the WB staff in the early 2000s.

9 An initiative proposed by the WB and the IMF in 1996; in 1997 the total external debt in developing countries was over $2bn, 11% of which was owed by the HIPC group (cf. House of Commons Research Paper 98/81, August 1998).

10 Pettifor wrote a full and interesting account of 16 May 1998 in 'The Economic Bondage of Debt – and the Birth of a New Movement', *New Left Review* 1(230), July/August 1998.

11 See Kirsty McNeill, 'A Great Generation: Make Poverty History ten years on', Global Dashboard, July 2015.

12 Another clever poster got Christian Aid into trouble not with the Charity Commission but with the British Red Cross. It featured an actual photo of a health worker in Bangladesh on her bike with a shoulder bag displaying a big red cross under the slogan, 'Keep the health service going' – a sly reference to its being under threat in the UK. The Deputy Director of the British Red Cross rang me in a fury threatening legal action. Too readily I sent out the troops to paint the red crosses green!

4 Brazil

1 Regressive and more progressive policies have been pursued under military dictatorships between 1964 and 1985, and by governments led by Fernando Collor de Mello (1990–92), Fernando Cardoso (1995–2003), Luiz Inácio Lula de Silva (2003–11), Dilma Rousseff (2011–16), Jair Bolsonaro (2019–23), followed by Lula de Silva again. See 'The Real Brazil: The inequality behind the statistics' (Brazilian Centre for Analysis and Planning, supported by Christian Aid, 2012).

2 See the Power to the People project mid-term review (Christian Aid, May 2011).

3 See Chapter 16.

4 According to the Comissão Pró-Índio (São Paulo-Indigenous Commission), which lobbied for change.

5 Christian identity, faith and theology

1 See *The Times* survey of Anglican clergy, 30 August 2023.
2 John A. T. Robinson, *Honest to God* (SCM Press, 1963).
3 'All shall be included in the feast of life', a 50th Birthday Statement adopted by the board of Christian Aid, June 1995.
4 Janet Lacey, *A Cup of Water* (Hodder and Stoughton, 1970), p. 186.
5 See Sathnam Sanghera, *Empireworld* (Penguin, 2025). See Chapter 4 on 'White Saviours'.
6 Charles Elliott, *Comfortable Compassion?* (Hodder and Stoughton, 1987).
7 Elliott, *Comfortable Compassion?*, pp. 156–78.
8 See, for example, Christian Aid, 'What We Believe' (2010).
9 Previously referred to in Paula Clifford, *All Creation Groaning* (Christian Aid, 2007).
10 Cf. 'Putting God to Rights: A theological reflection on human rights' (Christian Aid, 2016), Susan Durber's extensive discussion about the tension between human rights and Christian faith.
11 Catherine Loy, *Development Beyond the Secular* (SCM Press, 2017).
12 Rowan Williams, 'The Holy Spirit in the Bible' in Jane Williams (ed.), *The Holy Spirit in the World Today* (Alpha International, 2011), pp. 64–71; and *Tokens of Trust: An introduction to Christian belief* (Canterbury Press, 2007), p. 50.
13 See, for example, Paula Clifford, 'Theology and International Development' (Christian Aid, 2010), p. 5.
14 See, for example, Susan Durber, 'Of the Same Flesh: Exploring a theology of gender' (Christian Aid, 2014).
15 See, for example, Christian Aid papers on climate change, gender, etc. and their more conversational style.
16 Durber, 'Of the Same Flesh' and 'Putting God to Rights'.
17 Cf., for example, 'Christian Aid and the Prophetic Voice' (Christian Aid, 2020).

7 Christian Aid Week … the little red envelope

1 See Christian Aid archives, SOAS Box CA Aid/I/2 (Christian Aid Week Papers 1956–57).
2 See Michael Taylor, 'The Week that Turned into a Battleground for Truth', *Christian Aid News*, July–September 1991.
3 See Stephanie Denning (independent consultant), 'Christian Aid Week Literature Review', internal document (2018).
4 Denning, 'Christian Aid Week Literature Review'.
5 See Chapter 9.
6 Denning, 'Christian Aid Week Literature Review'.

7 Report, 'Christian Aid Week Reimagined: Vision and roadmap', Aha Consulting, internal document (March 2023).

8 Haiti

1 Import tariffs on rice and sugar went from 50% down to 3%, on chicken from 40% to 5% and wheat from 50% to 0%; see Claire McGuigan, 'Agricultural Liberalisation in Haiti' (Christian Aid, 2006).

2 The factory was reopened in 2000, subsidised by the government in an attempt to compete.

3 See McGuigan, 'Agricultural Liberalisation in Haiti'.

4 See material written for Christian Aid Week in 2018.

5 A pattern repeated in Sierra Leone.

6 See Chapter 9 and the WCC's 'Project List'.

7 See Christian Aid archives, SOAS Box CA/CA3/03 (Haiti, 1964–79); and Helen Spraos, interview (2024).

8 See Chapter 6, for example. See also 'Christian Aid Week 13–19 May 2018' (April 2018): https://ctbiarchive.org/christian-aid-week-13-19-may-2018/ (accessed 18 August 2025).

9 Helen Spraos was in charge for ten years until 2007, when she was succeeded by Prospery Raymond until 2020.

10 Haiti was not the only country from which from time to time Christian Aid had virtually to withdraw under financial pressures demanding tough decisions. An office however remained open.

11 GARR found it difficult to recruit and train human rights monitors from local people, who had little time or energy to spare.

12 'Christian Aid Encourages Haitian and Dominican Border Communities to Promote Mutual Cooperation'; see 'Christian Aid in Haiti' online: https://www.christianaid.org.uk/our-work/where-we-work/haiti (accessed 19 May 2025).

13 Regarded by Christian Aid as one of its 'flagship' programmes, to which many references can be found online.

14 Helen Spraos of Christian Aid initiated it and Prospery Raymond, her successor, was still on its board in 2024.

15 Prospery Raymond interview.

16 A review of SCLR in 2022 was highly positive. Cf. Jessica Doley and Duquesne Prophète, 'SCLR Learning Analysis – Haiti' (Christian Aid, 2022).

17 They were not the only ones by far to dance despite the circumstances; for example, the street dancers, acrobats, jugglers and stilt walkers of Caja Lúdica, Guatemala, working against widespread gang violence.

18 See 'Haiti: Unconditional Cash Transfers', Christian Aid, 2012.

19 A useful correspondence between the two of us followed; one of his letters, apparently typed on foolscap by himself, was posted from the Royal Yacht *Britannia*, moored at Cowes!
20 Helen Spraos interview.
21 See a detailed account in Tara Korti, Marc Pascal Desmornes and Anupama Ranawana, 'Addressing Impunity for Gender-based Violence among Displaced Communities in Haiti: Community perspectives on barriers to accountability and justice' (Christian Aid, 2023).
22 For example, Gwoup Fanm Franchiz, a grass-roots women's organisation in the KORAL network, working in Southern Haiti.
23 The year 2007 only marked the bicentenary of the abolition of the transatlantic slave trade. Slavery itself was not abolished until 1835–38 and black leaders in Haiti, where it was abolished some thirty years earlier, later reinstated it.
24 These were run by the Association for the Promotion of Family Integrated Health, a partner of Christian Aid founded in 1998; see also 'Homeless in Haiti' (Christian Aid, 2018).
25 See the description of the *Freedom!* sculpture on the National Museums Liverpool website.

9 Partnership ... you'll never walk alone

1 See Dinis Salomão Sengulane and Jaime Pedro Gonçalves, 'A Calling for Peace: Christian leaders and the quest for reconciliation in Mozambique', *ACCORD* 3 (January 1998).
2 See Derek Knight's vivid account of the atrocities in *Mozambique Caught in the Trap* (Christian Aid, 1988).
3 Bond is a network for UK organisations working in international development, formed in 1993 with forty-one members and growing to over 400.
4 In 2023/2024 Christian Aid funded 410 projects in twenty-five countries and worked with 260 implementing partners, 33% of which were faith-based.
5 See 'Standing Together', Christian Aid's Global Strategy 2019–2026: 'Christian Aid works with people and partners of all faiths and none', p. x: www.global-strategy-web.pdf (accessed 19 May 2025).
6 Janet Lacey, *A Cup of Water* (Hodder and Stoughton, 1970), p. 29.
7 'Partnership for Change' was adopted as its strategy in 2012, giving way in 2019 to 'Standing Together', with references to the 'Power of Partnership'.
8 See 'Christian Aid Partnership Policy: Towards mutual partnership', undated but the result of discussions in 2021.
9 See Chapter 5.
10 See note 5.

11 Christian Aid Partnership Policy and Approach (Christian Aid, 2021), p. 4.
12 The WCC's *Baptism, Eucharist and Ministry (BEM)* (WCC, 1982) was perhaps its greatest achievement.
13 See Michael Taylor, *Christ and Capital: A family debate* (World Council of Churches, 2015), ch. 7.
14 Christian Aid was involved from the start of course. Christian Aid Ireland became a separate member in 2024.
15 See Chapter 7.
16 See Michael Taylor, *Not Angels but Agencies: The ecumenical response to poverty; A primer* (SCM Press, 1995), ch. 4.
17 See 'South Africa Learning Review' (Christian Aid, 2021), p. 23.

10 India

1 Cf. 'Feet on the Ground' (Christian Aid, 2021–25).
2 Under the Bharatiya Janata Party (BJP), for example, elected in 2018 and returned to power in 2024. Christian Aid supported Safai Karmachari Andolan and its campaign against manual scavenging, which brought about legal changes enforcing existing laws banning the practice (Prohibition of Manual Scavenging Act and Amendment providing Relief & Rehabilitation to Manual Scavengers, 2013).
3 The historic long march in Gandhi's time was organised by Christian Aid partner Ekta Parishad supported by annual grants of £50,000 from Christian Aid, which, according to government regulations, could not be used to fund campaigns. Christian Aid, therefore, funded its development work. See *Christian Aid News*, Autumn 2012.
4 See Nitin Tagade, Ajaya Kumar Naik and Sukhadeo Thorat, 'Wealth Ownership and Inequality in India: A socio-religious analysis', *Journal of Social Inclusion* 4(2), pp. 196–213 (Institute of Dalit Studies, 2018).
5 See 'Christian Aid in India' online.
6 Cf. 'Action Aid, 2014', 'Human Rights Watch, 2007' online; Ramani Leathard, 'Hidden Apartheid' (Christian Aid, 2001).
7 Climate Action Network South Asia, 'Low-carbon South Asia: India' (Christian Aid, 2014).
8 Minority Rights Group, 'Dalits in India', March 2024, online.
9 For example, Agrarian Development Institute for Sustenance and Improved Livelihood; Association for Rural and Urban Needy; Christian Medical Association of India; Church's Auxiliary for Social Action (CASA); Climate Action Network South Asia; Dalit Sthree Sakthi; Deccan Development Society; Jan Sahas Social Development Society; Mahatma Gandhi Seva Ashram; Partnering Hope

into Action Foundation (PHIA); Purvanchal Gramin Vikas Sansthan; South Asia Coalition on Child Servitude; Sustainable Environment and Ecological Development Society; and many others. Links with CSI and CNI were severed after failures to account for funds.

10 See Christian Aid archives, SOAS Box CA/CA1/02 (India: general correspondence 1956–66).

11 Letter in Christian Aid archives, Christian Aid/C/4; there is no record of the outcome.

12 During the crisis, Action for Food Production was set up by the National Christian Council of India, the Roman Catholic Social Institute and Oxfam to ensure cooperation at the local level and nationwide; see newsletter from John McLeod, BCC/Christian Aid, 17 March 1967.

13 See Chapter 13.

14 See, for example, Tom Palakudiyil and Mary Todd, 'Facing up to the Storm: How local communities can cope with disasters' (Christian Aid, 2003).

15 See Chapter 16.

16 *Christian Aid News*, July/September 1981.

17 By Agrarian Development Institute for Sustenance and Improved Livelihood.

18 See Chapter 11, for example.

19 See archive CA3/A/PAC 74.

20 See 'Celebrating Inclusion – PACS India final report' (Christian Aid, 2016).

21 See Chapter 11.

22 Renu Thomas and John Stirling, 'Review of Christian Aid's Ways of Operating in India' (Christian Aid, 2024).

23 CAPL made its first 'profit' of £50,000 in 2022–23; £480,000 of its £700,000 income came from fees paid by Christian Aid.

11 Learning to care

1 Janet Morley (ed.), *Bread of Tomorrow: Praying with the world's poor* (SPCK and Christian Aid, 1992), p. 22.

2 Chine McDonald and Wendy Lloyd (eds), *Rage and Hope: 75 prayers for a better world* (SPCK, 2021).

3 See the report by Jessica Woodruffe (World Development Movement, 2000).

4 All editions are available online.

5 'How Evaluation Can Shift Perspectives and Influence Organisational Strategies', a review of a six-year-long Christian Aid Ireland programme from 2016 to 2022 (not publicly available).

6 Roger Riddell, *Does Foreign Aid Really Work?* (Oxford University Press, 2008).

7 'Learning and Leaving' (Christian Aid, 2020).
8 'Learning and Leaving'.
9 See further Chapter 19.
10 See online, 'Picture Power: Understanding impact through a community lens' (Christian Aid, 2015).
11 Riddell, *Does Foreign Aid Really Work?*
12 See Susan Durber, 'Putting God to Rights: A theological reflection on human rights (Christian Aid, 2016).
13 *The Limits to Growth* (Massachusetts Institute of Technology, 1972).
14 World Commission on Environment and Development, *Our Common Future*, The Brundtland Report (United Nations and Oxford University Press, 1987).
15 See Chapter 9.

12 Palestine

1 William Bell, 'Where is Palestine?' (Christian Aid, 2021).
2 *The Times of Israel*, 13 July 2014.
3 See 'Lifelines' (Christian Aid, 2007).
4 Martin Wroe, 'One Land Many Visions' (Christian Aid, 2017).
5 As of November 2024, 700,000 Israeli settlers lived in 350 settlements established in the West Bank, including East Jerusalem, in contravention of international law (UN Office for the Coordination of Humanitarian Affairs).
6 See James Fergusson, *In Search of the River Jordan* (Yale University Press, 2023).
7 A phrase used by Ariel Sharon when suggesting that any future negotiations should accept the settlements as given 'facts' and move on from there.
8 William Bell, 'Israel and Palestine: A question of viability' (Christian Aid, 2007).
9 For example, the Fourth Geneva Convention 1949, Hague Regulations of 1967, UN Security Council Resolutions 242 and 338 calling for withdrawal from the Occupied Territories.
10 See Katie Roxburgh, 'Christian Aid Response in Gaza and Update on our Partners', internal update (Christian Aid, 2024), and Christian Aid Ireland's programme 2016–22.
11 Christian Aid, Global Results, 2022–23.
12 See also 'Trading Away Peace' (Christian Aid and others, 2012), criticising EU trading with settlers.
13 Christian Aid, Global Results, 2022–23.
14 See 'Christian Aid claims it was subject to act of "lawfare" by pro-Israel group', *The Guardian*, 2 March 2023.
15 'One Land and Many Voices' (Christian Aid, 2017).

13 The Big Issue

1 See Christian Aid's Annual Report 2006/07, p. 2: 'We must and will increasingly frame our work in the context of climate change'; also, 'Climate Change – It's now or never' (Christian Aid, 2019).

2 See Chapter 5 and the problems associated with it.

3 A theological reflection by Bob Kikuyu on 'Loss and Damage' also focuses on relationships (Christian Aid, 2022).

4 Genesis 9:13; Leviticus 25; Amos 9:13; Psalms 24, 104, 148; Matthew 5:5; Romans 4:18 and 8:21; Revelation 21.

5 Christian Aid's 'Resilience Framework' approach (2016) referred to climate change and other issues and extended the approach of ECRP in Malawi to other country programmes; see also Chapter 14, 'The Philippines', one of the worst-hit countries, for further examples.

6 APRODEV published an extensive 'tool kit' in 2007, and Tearfund in 2021, adopted and promoted by Christian Aid and others.

7 Paul Homewood, regarded as a climate denier, has been commenting on climate change for many years. See his online blog, 'Not a Lot of People Know That.'

8 'COP28: Time to harness progress and shape an inclusive new goal on finance' (Christian Aid, 2023).

9 Christian Aid Annual Report 2021, p. 35.

10 In 2023 Christian Aid launched its flagship 'Climate Change and Sustainable Energy (CCASE)' programme in twelve countries (Africa, Asia and Latin America), costing £2.9m over three years, aiming to integrate programming and policy work with advocacy, and support women and marginalised communities affected by climate change as they raise their voices.

14 The Philippines

1 Paulo Freire, *Pedagogy of the Oppressed* (Herder and Herder, 1970).

2 See 'Christian Aid in the Philippines', an exit learning review, 2021.

3 See *No Time for Crying*, filmed in Mindanao, about active non-violent groups opposing the regime (Christian Aid, 1986).

4 See Chapter 9.

5 See 'Breaking Promises, Making Profits: Mining in the Philippines', report by Christian Aid and PIPLinks (2004).

6 Two examples of schemes circumventing middlemen, funded by Christian Aid, involved a 10-ton truck to get goods directly to market and a loan scheme enabling pedicab drivers to buy their own vehicles instead of renting them; see *Christian Aid News* 1979 and 1985.

7 For example, Karl Gaspar.
8 See Edicio de la Torre, *Touching Ground, Taking Root* (Catholic Institute for International Relations, 1986).
9 See exit learning review, 2021.
10 See Rice Watch Action Network and its Climate Resilience Field training Scheme (CRFS), covering thirty-three local government areas.
11 The Disaster Risk Reduction and Management Act, Republic Act No.10121, passed on 27 May 2010.
12 See Chapter 1.

15 Sierra Leone

1 Cf. the microfinance schemes of Bangladesh.
2 Christian Aid worked in seven and then in four of Sierra Leone's districts: Pujehun, Kailahun, Kono and Western Area.
3 See report, 'Stand Strong: Women and politics, Kailahun, Sierra Leone' (Christian Aid, 2015).
4 Mark Vyner email (2024).
5 Including ALLAT, NMID, Green Scenery, RD, CARL, RADA, SEND and the government's Ministry of Local and Rural Development.
6 Jeanne Kamara, country director of CASL 2011–22, worked for fifteen years with the British Council in UK; and of the three women MPs mentioned above, Tongi worked in international banking and Songa as a psychiatric nurse in London.
7 Cf. the roaming libraries of Peru, some in people's homes, providing books on agriculture, beekeeping, carpentry, forestry, local history, law and literature; *Christian Aid News*, October–December 1993.
8 It opened its own office in 2002; Linda Kerley was the first country manager, followed by Jeanne Kamara.
9 *Christian Aid News*, April–July 1999.
10 See Louise Orton, 'Peace of Mind', *Christian Aid News*, Spring 2000.
11 Sources of information: FIAN International and Green Scenery.
12 The Customary Land Rights Act and the National Land Commission Act, 2022, also gave women the right to own land.
13 In the Democratic Republic of Congo, for example, funded by USAID; Roger Riddell interview.
14 For example, *Love in a Time of AIDS*, WCC Risk Books (World Council of Churches, 1996); see also 'Theology and the HIV/AIDS Epidemic' (Christian Aid, 2004).
15 See the report by Andy Featherstone, 'Keeping the Faith: The role of faith leaders in the Ebola crisis' (Christian Aid, CAFOD, Tearfund and Islamic Relief, 2015).

16 Featherstone, 'Keeping the Faith'. Interfaith cooperation, including with traditional healers and priests, was not confined to Sierra Leone: Side by Side, for example, was established in 2015 as a global interfaith movement.
17 See 'Visit to ITL WEEL Project, Sierra Leone': https://www.christianaid.org.uk/appeals/philanthropy/their-lifetime/visit-itl-weel-project-sierra-leone (accessed 19 May 2025).

16 Pie charts and all that

1 See Chapter 1.
2 See Chapter 7.
3 See Chapter 1.
4 Similar schemes included Farewill and Faith Will.
5 See 'In Their Lifetime' (Christian Aid, 2021), and Impact Report (Christian Aid, 2024).
6 For example, 'The New Global Debt Crisis' (2019); 'Scorched Earth: The impact of drought in 10 world cities' (2022); see also Chapter 7.
7 'Brief Encounter – Charity embarrasses ministers on debt relief', *The Guardian*, 16 December 1999.
8 See Chapter 1 and the chapters that relate to country programmes.
9 See online Ondine Barrow's thesis, 'Charity, Relief and Development: Christian Aid in Ethiopia 1960s–1990s' (SOAS, 1998), p. 44.
10 'Charities Defend Big Money Paid to Top Executives', *Church Times*, 9 August 2013. Into the late 1990s the Director of Christian Aid was paid no more than three times that of the lowest paid member of staff; in 2013 the highest salary was no more than four times the average; in 2024 the CEO was paid £147,084, in 2023 £139,175; in 2023 the CEOs of Oxfam and Save the Children were paid £125,418 and £143,000 respectively.
11 See also the reference to 'risk appetite' in the 2021/22 Annual Report, p. 37.
12 Seventeen in 2021/22, and fifteen in 2022/23.
13 See 'Christian Aid Condemns South Sudan Aid Worker Killings, after Death of Partner Staff', press release, Christian Aid media centre, April 2018.
14 Appleby was a former Director of the National Association for Mental Health, now MIND; she was involved with the churches and Janet Lacey in Germany after the war, and was an early member of Christian Aid's board.
15 See 'Christian Aid's Overseas Presence', a paper to the board in February 1996 by Jenny Borden, and 'Devolution in the International Department of Christian Aid', a report to the board in 2024.
16 See, for example, a letter to *The Times* from Sir George Sinclair, a Conservative MP and member of Christian Aid's board, 23 January 1976.

17 See 'Christian Aid's Experience of Lawfare: Investigation by USAID & civil case in US court' (May 2023), internal document; and Lizzie Davies, 'Christian Aid Claims It Was Subject to Act of "Lawfare" by Pro-Israel Group', *The Guardian*, 2 March 2023.

17 Sudan and South Sudan

1 For example, in 1988, 1998, 2004 and 2007.
2 From 31 January to 5 February 2023, delayed from 2017.
3 Christian Aid, November 2018.
4 David Hoile, 'Christian Voice, or Mouthpiece for War Criminals?', The European Sudanese Public Affairs Council, June 2005.
5 See Hadley Jenner, '"When Truth is Denied Peace Will not Come": The People-to-People Peace Process of the New Sudan Council of Churches' (CDA Collaborative Learning Projects, 2000).

18 Untold stories

1 For further details, see Mirella Moxon and others, *A Most Unlikely Friendship* (Mirella Moxon, 2023).

19 Hope and realism

1 Kenneth Slack moved Christian Aid from scattered offices near 10 Eaton Gate to Ferndale Road, Brixton, in 1978, and from there it moved to Lower Marsh in 1987.
2 See 'Poverty Report' (Christian Aid, 2022).
3 Over 50% of the global population lived in poverty in 1945, 60% in 1965, 40% in 1999, 8.5–10% in 2025. According to the World Bank, in their 'Poverty, Prosperity and Planet Report 2024', progress has stalled and 2020–30 is likely to be a lost decade due to Covid-19, climate change, conflict and other factors.
4 In an interesting dialogue, Ed de la Torre, a friend of Christian Aid, addresses the issue of 'hope' and speaks of 'patient impatience', combining an urgent passion for change with a perspective on history which disciplines our expectations. The phrase 'patient impatience' and a discussion of its meaning can be found in Ed de la Torre, 'The Spirit of 1968', *Verbum* 59(1–2), pp. 83–103.
5 Peter Lloyd, *Slums of Hope?: Shanty Towns of the Third World* (Penguin, 1979).
6 'Challenges and Choices: Christian Aid Strategy Mid-term review' (Christian Aid, 2022).
7 University of Bradford, 1997.
8 Jenny Pearce, 'Development, NGOs and Civil Society: The debate and its future' (Development and Practice, 2000).
9 See the INGO Leadership Survey report, University of Oxford, News and Events, July 2022.

10 See Chapter 16.

11 'Challenges and Choices'.

12 See Chapter 11.

13 See Trevor Beeson, *Discretion and Valour: Religious conditions in Russia and Eastern Europe* (Fontana, 1981).

14 See Waseem Ahmad and Patrick Watt, 'The World is Becoming More Religious. That matters for development', Roots of Change series (Christian Aid, April 2024).

Subject index

ACT Alliance 50, 52, 103, 107, 111, 133, 214
Action Aid 114, 156
advertising/TV 44, 81, 83, 139, 181, 183, 193
advocacy *see campaigns*
Afghanistan xxvii, 21–31,187, 196, 203
Al-Qaeda 22–3
Angola 133–4
Anti-Apartheid Movement 47, 75
apartheid 34, 45–8, 101, 106, 108, 130, 134, 187
AquAid 102, 181
Arusha Accords 11
Association of Protestant Development Agencies in Europe/ACT Alliance EU 103

Band Aid 8, 10–11
Bangladesh 43, 57, 72–3, 104, 130, 154, 157, 162
BBC 8, 11, 44, 84, 132, 147, 191
Beveridge Report 1
Biafra 5–7, 34
board/trustees (Christian Aid's) xxv, xxvii, 51, 58, 61, 62, 65, 68, 70, 102, 186–8, 190, 215
Bolivia 40, 43, 51
Bond 102
Brazil 49–54, 106, 132, 133, 162, 164, 213
Bretton Woods 1
BRICS (Brazil, Russia, India, China, South Africa) 49, 213
British Council of Churches (BCC)/ Churches Together in Britain and Ireland (CTBI) 2, 46, 62, 68, 81, 117
British Overseas Aid Group 102
Buddhism/Buddhist 14, 57, 72, 77, 117
Burkina Faso 187
Burma/Myanmar xxv, 71–7, 201
Burundi 189

campaigns xxv, 33–48, 88, 137, 161, 183
Catholic Agency for Overseas Development (CAFOD) 17–18, 37–8, 56, 102, 127, 138, 160, 200, 204
Catholic Institute for International Relations (CIIR) 47, 102
Charity Commission 6, 33, 48, 131, 149, 185
child labour 37–8, 182
child sponsorship 132, 182
Christian Aid Ireland 61–2, 69–70, 148, 157, 198
Christian Aid News xxvi
Christian Aid Week (CAW) xv, xxvii, 2, 21, 23, 39, 45, 62, ch. 7, 95, 102, 108, 125, 128, 139, 181, 183, 206, 208
Christianity/Christians 26, 42, 56–70, 72, 87–9, 117, 149, 155, 173–4, 201, 211
churches xvii, xxviii, 2, 12, 36, 46–7, 50, 54, 56–70, 79–89, 101, 102, 106, 108–10, 126, 128, 131, 148–9, 154, 158, 175, 176, 192, 197, 199, 215
Churches Against Poverty (CAP) 102
climate change/justice/environment xvii, 8, 18, 27, 41, 44, 53–4, 66–7, 87, 92, 105, 111, 134–8, ch. 13, 166, 196, 210

Colombia 182
colonialism/colonial 59–60, 103, 134, 137, 213
Co-op bank 37–8, 102, 181
Conference of the Parties (COP) 138, 159–60
Covid 22, 74, 83, 85, 118, 124, 133, 159, 161, 174, 177–8, 188, 189, 210

debt xv–xvi, 35, 38–39, 41–45, 92, 97, 113, 130, 137, 143, 158, 183, 210
deforestation 51–2, 92, 96, 210
Democratic Republic of Congo 12, 121, 136, 162
dependency theory 137
designated/non-designated funding 50, 84, 132
development projects xxv, 2, 60, 103–5, 115, 184
Disasters Emergency Committee (DEC) xvii, 3, 102, 181, 196
disasters/preparedness 15, 17, 22, 82, 90, 92–3, 96–8, 105, 117, 125, 134, 153, 158, 165–6

Ebola 35, 105, 172, 174, 177–8
Ecuador 154
ecumenism 2, 49, 58, 77, 86, 103, 106–11, 116
education 23, 28, 35, 59, 73, 93, 99, 100, 102, 114, 126–40, 145, 164, 172, 174, 184, 188, 197, 210
El Salvador 154, 162, 205
emergencies/disasters/appeals xxv, 3–5, 10, 16, 18, 22, 24, 34, 35, 86, 97, 107, 146, 181–183, 188, 196; *see also disasters/preparedness*
Eritrea 8–9
Ethiopia 5, 8–11, 43, 83, 182, 188
European Union (EU)/Common Market 35, 37, 176
exclusion 113–15, 120–1

Fairtrade Foundation 37–8, 131, 203
France 1, 91–2, 160
Freedom from Hunger campaign 34
fundraising/funding/funders xxv, 5, 21, 33, 50, 79–89, 181–93

G8 42–4
gender-based violence (GBV) 31, 95, 105, 169
genocide 11–12, 59, 72, 107, 189, 201
Ghana 43, 133–4
Goma 11–12, 14
governance 50, 125, 146, 165, 171–3, 175, 186–7
Greenbelt 76, 204–5
Greece 23
Guatemala 133

Habitat for Humanity 14, 95
Haiti/Dominican Republic 4, 17, 90–100, 186
Haslemere Declaration 36
health/healing 179
HIV/AIDS 16, 98, 103, 125, 177–8, 199
holism 58, 118
Honduras 105, 156
hope 153–5, 210–16
human resources (HR) 190
human rights 31, 38, 61, 64, 69, 71, 75, 94, 104, 124, 137–8, 144, 145, 146, 148, 164, 176, 210
humanitarian aid xxv, 3, 4, 15, 16–17, 22, 24, 26, 31, 73–4, 115
Hungary 7–8, 16

identity (Christian Aid's) 26, 56–70, 113, 215–16
India xvi, 4, 49, 84, 107, ch. 10, 154, 157, 162, 213
Indonesia 13
InspirAction Spain 51

Intermediate Technology Development Group/Practical Action 119, 197
International Broadcasting Trust (IBT) 132
International Monetary Fund (IMF)/IMF policies 1, 35, 40, 43–4, 131, 137
Iran 23
Iraq 141, 203–4
Ireland 24, 61–2, 70, 102, 148
Islam/Muslims 22, 26, 29, 42, 57, 72, 77, 87, 103, 113, 170, 173–4, 178, 200

Jamaica 43, 103–4, 173
Jesus 14, 33, 66–7, 125, 129, 155
Jewish organisations/Jews 16, 42, 103, 141, 144, 149, 150
Jubilee 2000 (J2000) 36, 41–4, 131, 204

KAIROS document 46
Kenya 103, 135, 161, 162, 193, 203, 208

learning 126–40
Lebanon 3, 141–2, 145, 191, 207, 213
LGBTQ+ rights 49, 61
Liberation Theology 53, 63–8, 91, 144, 164
Libya 14
localisation/local organisations/devolution 4, 13, 15, 16–18, 22, 27, 71, 96, 97, 103, 106, 110, 111, 120, 134, 138, 146, 167, 189–90, 210, 213–14

Make Poverty History (MPH) xvi, 36, 134
Malawi 43, 105, 155, 158, 160
Mali 133, 207
Middle East 24, 47, 103, 188, 213
mines 21, 25, 28, 51–2, 77, 105, 115, 119, 157
missionaries 14, 26, 57–9, 62, 72, 110, 173, 201
modernisation 62, 136–8
Mozambique xxvii, 43, 51, 101
multinationals 35, 40, 131, 176

neoliberalism 137
Nepal 136
neutrality 9, 17, 106
New Economics Foundation 42
New Internationalist 37, 102, 131
non-governmental organisations (NGOs) 5, 9, 13, 16–17, 22–3, 30, 34, 38, 42, 44, 54, 59, 60–1, 96, 111, 123, 132, 134, 138, 172, 175, 192, 203, 210–16
Nicaragua 43, 63, 156, 182, 193, 204
Niger 190
Nigeria 5–6, 42

oil 6, 47, 74, 152, 194–6, 199
One World Week 131
operational/non-operational xxvii, 4, 16, 61, 73, 105, 110, 146, 163, 213
overheads 56, 119, 126, 184–6, 189, 190, 192–3
OXFAM 3, 6, 11, 18, 34, 36–7, 60, 126, 131, 132, 186, 197, 212

Pacific/islands 35, 103, 160, 188
Pakistan 22–3, 25, 117
Palestine/Gaza/Israel/Lebanon 3, 56, 102, 104, 141–50, 155, 182, 187, 189, 191–2, 198, 204, 207, 213
partnership xvii, xxvii, 50, 63, 66, 101–11, 167, 186, 213
peacebuilding xxiv, 10, 27, 28–9, 31, 69, 101, 198–200
Peru 211
Philippines 15–16, 38, 51, 92, 106, 133–4, 163–8, 206
power/empowerment 30–1, 33–4, 65–9, 92, 105, 109, 116, 120, 126, 127, 135–6, 137–8, 142, 149, 167, 170, 187, 208, 211, 216; *see also localisation/local organisations/devolution*

Programme to Combat Racism 108
prophecy/prophetic voice 33, 59, 69, 138

racism 11, 59–60, 96, 128, 160, 190
realism 68, 161, 210–16
Red Cross 3, 6, 9, 13, 17
refugees/displaced persons/migrants xxv, 1–18, 22–5, 71, 75, 82, 87, 95–6, 99, 116, 117–18, 124, 141–2, 144–6, 181, 187, 196, 202, 210
rehabilitation 15, 17, 97, 118, 210
resilience 16, 27–8, 31, 90, 134, 147, 165–6
resource sharing 66, 109, 139, 214
restructuring (internal) 188–90
risk 69, 83–4, 156, 167, 172, 182, 185–6, 193, 215
Rwanda 5, 11–13, 59, 107, 189, 201

safeguarding 186–90
sanctions 23–4, 46–7, 75
Save the Children 3, 25, 60, 126, 204
Scotland 44, 50, 52, 80–1, 159, 200
Second World War xxv, 1, 7, 57, 71
Sierra Leone 35, 120, 169–80
slavery 42–3, 45, 59, 91, 99–100, 173
solidarity xxix, 10, 36, 49, 61, 71, 106, 111, 134, 189, 192
Somalia 187
songs xxvi, 47, 127
Southern Africa Coalition 46–7
South/Southern Africa xxv, 32, 45–7, 49, 101, 106, 108, 110–11, 133–4, 161, 162, 213
Spain 51, 91
Sri Lanka 4, 14
staff/area staff xxv, 8, 24, 25, 26, 36, 42, 43, 46, 47, 61, 62, 66–9, 73, 84, 87–9, 102, 108, 109, 126, 133, 148, 163, 175, 181–93, 210
structural adjustment policies 35, 41, 43, 137
structural change/underlying causes xvi, xxv, 17, 18, 41, 60, 63, 74, 86
Sudan/South Sudan xxv, 8, 9, 58, 84, 130, 143, 194–202, 213
Suez 7
supporters/organisers/collectors xxv, 15, 24, 33–48, 50, 67, 69, 79–89, 102, 106, 108, 130–2, 133, 147, 158–60, 181, 184, 193
sustainable development/goals 96, 138
Switzerland 16

Taliban 22–30
Tanzania 43, 108, 208
tax 35, 39–41, 43, 44, 50, 54, 67, 133, 137, 153, 171, 177, 210
Tearfund 18, 56, 57, 160
theology 56–70, 153–5, 163
Tigray 8–11
trade 1, 34–6, 36–9, 44, 53, 92, 131, 153, 204, 210
trade unions 38, 44, 46, 96
tsunamis 4, 13–15, 115, 117–18
Turkey 4, 23

UK government 22, 27, 75, 121, 131, 171, 175, 187, 197, 199, 213
Ukraine 1, 16–17, 139, 212, 213
United Nations (UN) 1, 12, 24, 34, 46, 75, 90, 91, 132, 141, 142, 147, 159
USA/US government/USAID 8, 22, 26, 28, 35, 42, 63, 69, 91, 96, 149, 191, 203, 213

Voluntary Service Overseas (VSO) 2, 102, 130

Wales 50
War on Want 3, 34
Warsaw Pact 7
water 4, 15, 22, 27–9, 96, 104, 114, 115, 118, 135, 144–5, 148, 155, 156, 160, 167
Women's Institute 37

women's rights 29–31, 54, 61, 95, 114, 121–2, 125, 147, 158, 169–73; *see also power/empowerment*
World Bank (WB) 1, 34–5, 40–5, 51, 53, 92, 136–7, 152
World Council of Churches (WCC) 2, 16, 22, 25, 37, 58–9, 93, 101, 103, 106–8, 116, 117, 130, 139, 149, 164, 178, 213–14
World Development Movement (WDM)/ Global Justice Now 37, 102, 131
World Jewish Relief 16, 103
World Trade Organisation (WTO) 36, 38
World Vision 56, 63, 105, 170
worship/worship materials xxvi, 88, 128–30, 157

YMCA/YWCA 2, 147

Zambia 39, 45, 131
Zimbabwe 85, 105, 203